Charting the agenda

Educational activity after Vygotsky

Edited by Harry Daniels

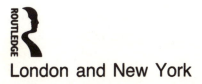

London and New York

First published in 1993 by
Routledge
11 New Fetter Lane, London EC4P 4EE

Simultaneously published in the USA and Canada by
Routledge
a division of Routledge, Chapman and Hall, Inc.
29 West 35th Street, New York, NY 10001

Phototypeset in Bembo by Intype, London
Printed and bound in Great Britain by
Mackays of Chatham PLC, Chatham, Kent

British Library Cataloguing in Publication Data

A catalogue record for this book is available
from the British Library.

Library of Congress Cataloging in Publication Data

Charting the agenda : educational activity after Vygotsky /
   edited by Harry Daniels.
   p.   cm.
Includes bibliographical references and index.
1. Educational psychology.   2. Learning, Psychology of.
3. Education–Social aspects.   4. Vygotskiĭ, L. S. (Lev
   Semenovich),
1896–1934.   I. Daniels, Harry.
LB1051.C33265   1993
370.15–dc20   92–12223
                                                          CIP

ISBN 0–415–05510–5

Charting the agenda

In formulating his theories, Vygotsky drew on a wide range of influences. His studies involved the reformulation of many ideas from various disciplines into a general theory of semiotics. In turn, his theories have been developed through the practice of the different disciplines that have interpreted his work.

Charting the Agenda provides readers in education and related fields with an insight into the cultural processes that have influenced the development of Vygotsky's work. The contributors offer their views on the practical and theoretical pedagogic developments that have taken place within their own professional and academic cultures, and also reflect on what lies ahead.

The collection acts as a forum for cross-disciplinary discussions in education. It provides lecturers, teachers and students with a general, detailed overview of important developments outside their own field to enable them to re-examine practice in their own discipline.

Harry Daniels is Senior Lecturer at the Institute of Education, London.

This book is dedicated to my long-suffering family.

Contents

List of figures   ix
List of contributors   x
Foreword   xiii
Basil Bernstein
Preface   xxiv
Harry Daniels

1 **Reading Vygotsky**   1
Tony Burgess

2 **Some implications of Vygotsky's work for special education**   30
Peter Evans

3 **The individual and the organization**   46
Harry Daniels

4 **Continuing the dialogue: Vygotsky, Bakhtin, and Lotman**   69
James V. Wertsch and Ana Luiza Bustamante Smolka

5 **Vygotsky's contribution to the development of psychology**   93
V.V. Davydov and V. P. Zinchenko

6 **Peer interaction and the development of mathematical understandings: a new framework for research and educational practice**   107
Geoffrey B. Saxe, Maryl Gearhart, Mary Note and Pamela Paduano

7 **The practice of assessment**   145
Ingrid Lunt

8 **Learning in primary schools**   171
   Andrew Pollard

9 **Learning English as an additional language in
   multilingual classrooms**   190
   Josie Levine

   Index   216

Figures

2.1 A model of school-based curriculum development in
    special education   36
6.1 Saxe's four-parameter model of emergent goals   112
6.2 The Treasure Hunt Game   132
6.3 The turn-taking structure of Treasure Hunt   133
6.4 The structure of a portfolio practice   137
8.1 The relationship between intra-individual, interpersonal
    and socio-historical factors in learning   173
8.2 A model of classroom task processes   177
8.3 Individual, context and learning: an analytic formula   184
8.4 A social-constructivist model of the teaching/learning
    process   185
8.5 A model of learning and identity   186

Contributors

Basil Bernstein is Emeritus Professor at the Institute of Education, University of London. His interests include: the sociology of education as a field for the study of the sociology of knowledge; pedagogic codes, formal and informal, their modalities and social base; and the construction of principles for description. His major publication is *Class, Codes and Control*. Vols I–V.

Tony Burgess is Reader in Education in the Department of English, Media and Drama at the Institute of Education, University of London. He has written extensively about English teaching and is co-author, with Harold Rosen, of *The Languages and Dialects of London School Children* (Ward Lock, 1981). His more recent work has included investigation of classrooms of cultural sites and his current interests are in historical and philosophical issues in English teaching.

Harry Daniels is Senior Lecturer in the Department of Educational Psychology and Special Needs at the Institute of Education, University of London. His main research interest is the relation between the social organization of schooling and pupil learning.

V. V. Davydov is Deputy Director of the Russian Academy of Education. He has been a senior member of the Academy of Pedagogical Sciences of the former Soviet Union, specifically as Director of the Institute of General and Pedagogical Psychology. He has written extensively on the role of instruction in schooling.

Peter Evans studied Experimental Psychology at the University of London and completed a PhD at the Hester Adrian Research Centre at the University of Manchester on individual differences in learning in children with mild and severe learning difficulties. He moved to the Institute of Education in London in 1976 as Tutor for the specialist diploma concerned with teaching pupils with learning difficulties. After a period co-directing a DES project on curriculum development for pupils with moderate learning difficulties, he moved to the OECD in Paris in 1989 where he directs work relating to the integration of children with disabilities and the education of children and youth at risk.

Maryl Gearhart is a project director at the Center for the Study of Evaluation, University of California, Los Angeles, where she is responsible for research on the impact of new technologies on instruction and student learning. She is currently investigating the design, implementation, and impact of methods of using portfolios to assess students' writing and mathematics.

Josie Levine is Senior Lecturer in Education at the Institute of Education, University of London, and an educational consultant. She is closely associated with the innovation and development of interactive pedagogy for multilingual, multicultural classes, and with the teaching and learning of English as an additional language through mainstream education. She is editor of *Bilingual Learners and the Mainstream Curriculum* (Falmer Press, 1990), which was written in conjunction with experienced teachers collaborating in an action research project.

Ingrid Lunt is Senior Lecturer at the University of London Institute of Education where she is course tutor responsible for the training of educational psychologists. In her work as an educational psychologist before taking up her present post, she developed strong interests in the theory and practice of psychological assessment of learning. Her publications include work in a range of areas, including the areas of developmental psychology and cognitive assessment.

Mary Note is a doctoral candidate in the Graduate School of Education, University of California, Los Angeles. Her studies focus upon applying neo-Vygotskian, motivation, and underclass theories to improving education for children of poverty.

Andrew Pollard is Professor of Education at the University of the West of England at Bristol. His main interests are in the sociology of primary education with particular reference to pupil perspectives, classroom interaction and learning. Amongst his books are *Reflective*

Teaching in the Primary School (Cassell, 1987), *The Social World of the Primary School* (Cassell, 1985) and *Learning in Primary Schools* (Cassell, 1990).

Pamela Paduano is a doctoral student in the developmental studies program in the Graduate School of Education, University of California, Los Angeles. Her interests and research have focused on two areas: peer interaction and mathematics learning; and the development of occupational interests. Her current dissertation research is on the influence of gender on occupational interests. She is also Vice-president of a career and educational consulting firm.

Geoffrey B. Saxe is a professor in the Graduate School of Education, University of California, Los Angeles, and was a Fulbright fellow at the University of Pernambuco (Recife, Brazil), and was 1992 Program Chair for the Division on Teaching and Learning of the American Educational Research Association. Saxe is author of *Culture and Cognitive Development: Studies in Mathematical Understandings* (Erlbaum & Associates, 1991) and is co-author with S. R. Guberman and M. Gearhart, of *Social Processes in Early Number Development* (Monographs of the Society of Research in Child Development, 1987).

Ana Luiza Bustamante Smolka teaches in the Faculdade de Educacao of the Universidade Estadual de Campinas in Campinas, Sao Paulo, Brazil. She has written extensively on issues of literacy, classroom interaction and the institutional constraints of schooling on development and learning. In 1990 she was a Fulbright scholar in the US.

James V. Wertsch is a professor in the Department of Psychology of the Frances L. Hiatt School of Psychology at Clark University, Massachusetts. He has written several works on the ideas of Vygotsky and the Vygotskian school of psychology in the Soviet Union and in Russia. His main interests are the relationship between language and thought and a socio-cultural approach to mediated action. His publications include *Vygotsky and the Social Formation of Mind, Culture, Communication and Cognition: Vygotskian Perspectives*, and *Voices of the Mind: A Sociocultural Approach to Mediated Action*.

V. P. Zinchenko is a member of the Department of Psychology in Moscow State University and has written extensively in the field of neo-Vygotskian psychology.

Foreword

Basil Bernstein

It may be that these comments might serve better as an afterword than a foreword.

At the beginning of the twentieth century, two grand narratives of the travails of modern society shared the analysis, diagnosis and treatments of its social and individual pathologies. In both narratives, structures of power/domination and the conflicts these engendered propelled the narratives. Both shared strategies for exposing false consciousness and revealing transparent relationships. Both pointed to the duplicity of authority and its repressive regulation. Both claimed scientific status. Marx's theory had little or no purchase on micro levels of interaction and Freud's theory had little or no purchase on discussing and explaining macro structures. Marx projected the macro on to an unmediated micro and Freud projected the micro on to an unmediated macro. Base and superstructure appeared in both theories with similar generating power. In Freud, the id could be conceived as the biological level, ego/superego as the fragile superstructure. The superstructures in both theories were, in today's talk, discursive formations, dependent and regulated by their respective base. These discourses mask reality, rendering it opaque, misrecognised, and so establishing a fragile, pathological status quo. Yet neither theory singled out language as of special theoretical concern; neither was discourse given a special status. However, there was no doubt that there was a reality to be discovered and lived.

At the close of the twentieth century, from different perspectives, language and discourse are aspects of crucial concern. Indeed, it could be said that language and discourse enjoy a hegemony in theoretical and applied fields. But the grand narratives of the beginning of this century are at a discount and are suspect in terms of the stories they tell and, more importantly, in terms of the very possibility of such stories. Holism is to be replaced by the local, by the particular, the contextually contingent. Authors are to disappear; texts are created by readers having a temporary significance as a set of differences. If you like a radical de-centering of discourse, let a thousand flowers bloom in a democracy of de-centred texts. From a complementary but more radical perspective, the challenge is to the possibility of any relation between language, truth and reality. Reality is no more and no less than a managed symbolic simulation, referable only to the procedures of its own simulation (Baudrillard). Language is a complex set of strategies to mask a fundamental emptiness (Derrida). Discourses negate the concept of a singular subject. The subject is a node, an intersection, in the criss-cross fire of discourses, a position normalised by these discourses (Foucault).

From another perspective, that of language as information systems, codes, or grammars, these have weakened discipline boundaries and opened the relations among them. The boundaries between the social and natural sciences are crossed, giving rise to the potential technologizing of everything. Realities are on supply rather than on demand. Perhaps this is the major reversal between the beginning and end of the twentieth century.

From yet another perspective, closer to the issues of this book, there is a contrary view. Here I am referring to the emergence, or rather, the re-emergence of language as the study of development *and* its pedagogic facilitation. Language here is a system of meanings, a relay for the social, a primary condition for the formation of consciousness and the levels and variety of its function. Relation to (the social) precedes relations within (the individual). This insight was, of course, Mead's, much earlier than Vygotsky, but his insight produced a very different model. The I/Me dualism of the Meadian self is a dualism endemic to European thought, perhaps even to Christianity, with its distinction between inner/outer and individual/society. The relaying, mediating role of language is shared with Durkheim.

One term is missing so far. Relaying and mediating, place the emphasis upon the construction of consciousness rather than upon consciousness as constructing, as initiating, as agency. Here we meet the age-old dualism and suspicion of language. Language as a deception, language as a means of revelation. Language as a mask of the other, language as emancipation from the other.

Language as the message of authority, language to speak one's own voice, where 'one' may include gender, race, class, region. It is here that Vygotsky's theory of development and of its facilitation becomes crucial: the pedagogizing of development. Development is maturation plus instruction. Exit Piaget; enter the pedagogue. The concept of the zone of proximal development, which is discussed in most of the papers in this book, brings the adult (and, of course, the peer group, not necessarily working together) firmly into the context of development. But what kind of adult, what kind of relationship, what kind of knowledge, what kind of context, what criteria of development?

VYGOTSKY AND PEDAGOGIC PRACTICE

I would like to consider under this heading the relation between Vygotsky's theory of the social basis of mental functions and of their development, and theories of the appropriate pedagogic practice for the realization of this development. Now in the case of Piaget, the pedagogic practice inferred, associated and legitimized by the theory was created not by Piaget but by educators. However, in the case of Vygotsky where instruction is foregrounded, where cultural formations are privileged as 'tools' rather than systems or structures internal to the individual, pedagogic practice is necessarily foregrounded. It is not incidental that Vygotsky spent some years as a teacher. It is also no accident that this theory arose in the Soviet Union. A crucial problem of theoretical Marxism is the inability of the theory to provide descriptions of micro level processes except by projecting macro level concepts on to the micro level, unmediated by intervening concepts though which the micro can be both uniquely described and related to the macro level. Marxist theory can provide the orientation and the conditions the micro language must satisfy if it is to be 'legitimate'. Thus, such a language must be materialist, not idealist, dialectic in method and its principles of development and change must resonate with Marxist principles.

Language is a crucial site for study (and, of course, there was a great tradition of that study in the Soviet Union) but a site fraught with ideological pitfalls. Further, Marxist theory, when translated into what was thought to be 'state policy', could not admit any theory of mental functions, and even more of their development, which placed these processes under the aegis of the child's own activity, independent of adult regulation, where the source of development and its facilitation were unfolding structures internal to the child. Thus, any theory of development must be primarily social and offer a pedagogic practice which places development firmly in the control of socializers. Of course, it is not possible to move from the conditions for a legitimate theory to the theory itself. But the conditions restrict, orient and ground the surveillance of the theory for illegitimate deviations.

Thus, in Vygotsky's case, we have a theory and a necessary pedagogic practice, but which? Daniels, in his introduction, brings up the fascinating point that Vygotsky's theory can provide grounds for different, if not opposing, epistemologies and pedagogies. Vygotsky's is not the only theory which creates these possibilities for educators. Ideological divisions within the field of educators acts selectively on which theories are appropriated and how a theory is used. Theories, usually not constructed by educators but recontextualized by them, ground positions of power, carry resource allocations, construct careers and so on. The point I want to pursue is rather different. How did Vygotsky see the link between the zone of proximal development and pedagogic practice? It is interesting here that Wertsch and Smolka, in their chapter, supplement Vygotsky with Bakhtin and Lotman to point to their preferred pedagogic process. It may well be that the less preferred practice could be relevant to some learning contexts but not to all. Similarly, Levine feels the need to engage with what she infers to be Vygotsky's view as to how foreign languages are to be learned because it is antipathetic to the practice to which she is committed, and for which she skilfully argues. Vygotsky seems to think that crucial to learning a foreign language is an understanding of the formal grammar and the application of its rules, rather than situating the language in contexts of relevance to the learner. It is worth while mentioning in this context the imaginative research of Vygotsky and Luria in the 1930s, where they studied the ability of groups of adults, distinguished by the presence or absence of schooling/literacy, to solve syllogisms where the contexts and relationships of the syllogisms were drawn from the local culture, contexts and relationships. Vygotsky and Luria were interested in which groups of adults would give primacy to the logical relations of the syllogism and which groups would foreground the cultural context and relationships. The translators in their introduction issue a health warning to readers in order that the 'wrong' conclusions are not drawn from this study of the capacity of peasants. Thus, the context in which Vygotsky is recontextualized shapes the reading.

It seems to me that Vygotsky saw the zone of proximal development very much in terms of the extension of cognitive functions to levels of increasing complexity and generalization. There may be grounds for believing that Vygotsky saw school subjects, such as he saw foreign language teaching, to be taught by exposing the specialized systems of formal relations which distinguished the bodies of knowledge. The term 'tool' as a metaphor clearly resonated with the theoretical orthodoxy but may well have facilitated the abstraction of the formal properties of knowledge from the contexts in which they were realised and the pedagogic relations of their transmission and acquisition. The form and the content of the pedagogic relations may well have been taken for granted as they were currently operating in Soviet schools in the middle 1930s.

SOME THEORETICAL ISSUES

I would like very briefly to consider some theoretical issues which arise out of Vygotsky's work which forms the basis and focus of the papers in the book.

The zone of proximal development raises fundamental questions as to what counts as developmental facilitation at any one level of maturation and the means of facilitation. Vygotsky appeared to have a restricted view of development, essentially cognitive and a practice which appears to privilege the acquisition of the 'tool' rather than the social context of acquisition. It is clear that once development is viewed more generously then the zone which is the space for pedagogizing becomes a site for ideological struggle, for new agendas. The metaphor of 'tool' draws attention to a device, an empowering device, but there are some reasons to consider that the tool with its internal specialized structure is abstracted from its social construction. Symbolic 'tools' are never neutral; intrinsic to their construction are social classifications, stratifications, distributions and modes of recontextualizing.

The socio-historical level of the theory is, in fact, the history of the biases of culture with respect to its production, reproduction, modes of acquisition and their social relations. In Vygotsky, this level may well have been left vague because there was a crucial key to this study of the biases of culture and their conflicts: Marxism. There is now some doubt about this key. Even in Vygotsky's time such a study would have been fraught with ideological issues.

Finally, interesting questions arise out of the use of Vygotsky and the consequences of such use for the theory. In a way we have caught up with Vygotsky. It's not so much an idea finding the time, but a time selecting its idea. Vygotsky lays out levels of analysis in which two levels are vague: the socio-historical and the social construction of the child, including the child as an agent in his/her own development. When one considers what was accomplished in this short life there are no ground for complaints. However, Vygotsky did develop a methodology in which he outlined the requirements of his theory of description. I am not sure whether what follows is a correct inference from this methodology but it seems to me that if the basic unit must be a term which condenses within it possibilities of extension to other levels, then we can ask of applications to what extent do these applications permit or facilitate such extension. We could also enquire whether the use of Vygotsky arises because the language of a pre-existing model can be, or is, translated into Vygotskian terms. And if so, what are the implications of such a translation for the Vygotskian *total* project? We could distinguish such implications for any one level and for relations between levels. In other words, does an application entail a sideways move, or a hierarchical move or both? It is clear that most but not all of the chapters in this book focus at the micro level of local practices within the school, class or peer group in an interactional setting. On the whole, the emphasis is upon pedagogic contexts in which the practice is mediated by the students rather than mediated by the demands of the teacher. Pollard sees Vygotsky as taking over from Piaget in legitimizing primary school practice, moving the practice from child-centred to the more socio-centred focus of Vygotsky.

If one looks at the language of description of applications one can ask, irrespective of the level the language addresses, whether it facilitates movement to other levels. (Here we are asking how generative the language of description is.) Is it confined to one level? Has it been constructed for only one level or one type of context? We should also perhaps distinguish between diagrams or maps which refer to processes to be described and models which generate principles for the understanding and description of processes. If we consider Vygotsky's total project, then the deepening of our understanding of any level, and especially of the relations *between levels*, may well fall foul of the boundaries between disciplines and cleavages within them. The Vygotsky project is intrinsically interdisciplinary.

On the whole, the application of Vygotsky by linguists, psychologists and sociologists has been limited to interactional contexts, often pedagogic contexts. It follows that the descriptions offered are confined to these contexts. In the case of sociology, the theories from which these descriptions are likely to be drawn are ethnomethodology or symbolic interactionism. In the case of ethnomethodology, with its focus upon how members create and negotiate social order in well-bounded contexts, the emphasis is usually restricted to what is said. Within this theory it is not possible to ask, 'How is it that it is this order which is created and not another?' Extra-contextual structures of power and their discursive regulation are necessarily excluded from the analysis. The less radical but more open approach of symbolic interactionism, focuses upon meanings, their negotiation, the construction of identities and their careers as these emerge out of face-to-face encounters in well-bounded contexts. Here there is opportunity for showing relations to external constraints and possibilities in which interactions are embedded but not necessarily determined. Yet there remains the crucial conceptual issue of explicating this interrelation. This is not solved by a set of boxes which index only the very processes to be described. Symbolic interactionism provides sensitive and insightful descriptions of interactions within the pedagogic format. The description it gives necessarily stems from its own selective focus. It tends to take for granted that it does not include in its description how the discourse itself is constituted and recontextualized. The theory focuses upon interactional formats rather than the way the *specialization of knowledge is constructed*. From the point of view of Vygotsky the '*tool*' is not subject to analysis although the articulation of the zone of proximal development may well be. This absence of focus is common to both linguistics and psychology. Once attention is given to the regulation of the structure of pedagogic discourse, the social relations of its production and the various modes of its recontextualizing as a practice, then perhaps we may be a little nearer to understanding the Vygotskian 'tool' as a social and historical construction. And such a study is more than an analysis of the curriculum.

VYGOTSKY AND PIAGET IN EDUCATION

Finally, I would like to speculate about the positioning of Vygotsky in the *educational* field. Perhaps we could refer to this as Vygotsky (E) in order to indicate this mode of appropriation. I would like to follow Pollard's point about Vygotsky as the new legitimator following Piaget (E). The present climate's emphasis upon instruction, upon basic and specialized technological skills, upon effective means of their acquisition under conditions which optimize their economy and accountability, have spectacular implications for pedagogic practice. If the above conditions of economy, accountability and effectiveness are to be satisfied, then pedagogic practices must give rise to explicit and specific criteria (or criteria thought to be clear), which lend themselves to measures of output and the evaluation of the costs of input. Such a policy leads to a change in those responsible for its implementation. Thus, we have now new forms of management and managers. There is greater de-centralization to ensure the development of a competitive market and a new means of more central control. These new forms of management and control of institutions are likely to be mirrored within institutions where departments function as markets under hierarchical central control.

In the 1960s, the context was very different, typified in the UK by the publication of the Plowden Report. The title of the report, 'Children and their primary schools', condenses the message of the whole report, as do the 36 photographs which could serve as a basis for a competition, 'Spot the teacher'. If one looks at the dominant theories of this time in linguistics and cognitive development, one finds that these were Chomsky's and Piaget's. Central to both of these theories are the concepts of competence, both linguistic and cognitive. Both theories democratized competence. All children, irrespective of culture, necessarily acquire these crucial competencies. There can be no deficits. Acquisition is creative. Consider the concept, accommodation, in Piaget, and the inferring, creating and de-coding of new sentences in Chomsky. In both theories, the source of the competence lies in the way mind is constructed. Both theories require an adult caretaker but not a *particular* caretaker. Both theories are culture-free with respect to the caretaker. Thus both theories place creativity, linguistic and cognitive development *outside* of culture and, therefore, outside of power and discursive regulation. Adult socializers wait upon internally propelled maturation and become providers of appropriate contexts in which competences can be actualized.

These theories, with others, served as powerful legitimators of, and inductors into, liberal progressive pedagogy. This had its origin, in the UK, in the activities of the New Education Fellowship in the 1920s and 1930s and was initially institutionalized in sectors of the public school system. In state primary schools during the 1960s and 1970s, the story was probably very different from the theory. But the theory was dominant, if not hegemonic, in colleges and university departments of education which contained primary departments. The fit between Piaget (E) and the ideological emphasis in primary education, with respect to the definition of the child as a pedagogic subject, the model of the pedagogic context, its interactive format, legitimate texts and their modes of creation and evaluation, was mutually reinforcing. The architecture of the new schools, with their weak boundaries and transparencies, resonated with the new model. Of importance, the 1960s were a period of expansion of all resources in education partly as a response to population pressure and state welfare policy. Thus, the concept of competence legitimated and constructed the de-contextualized but active, creative child, abstracted from gender, class, race, region – apparently the imaginative author of his or her texts under the aegis of internal motivation and peer group activities.

This model could be relayed only if institutions had autonomy over their practices, over their resources and *appointments* and were legitimized by advisory groups either to or in the government.

Today the move is away from competence and the abstracted child, to performance and the graded child. Autonomy of educational institutions is severely constrained; educators and researchers operate within equally constrained briefs. New and different criteria operate in the selection of staff, especially senior staff. As policy changes, so do the legitimators and so do the players in the new game of implementation. In this context Piaget (E) has little place. There is now both a legitimation vacuum and a crisis for *different groups*, seeking an alternative practice.

The move away from Piaget (E) may well have origins other than the change in state policy. Such a move may well find support from teachers. Since the 1960s, there has been a change in the social composition of the school class which is now more racially and ethnically mixed. Teachers are now much more aware of cultural differences and are more concerned to find ways of making these differences productive. Children now are contextualized and this shifts attention to theories of child development which contextualize such development and offer a language of description which speaks to the contexts of today's classrooms.

Finally we should consider those teachers and educators who are aware of the workings of institutionalized disadvantage (social class, race, gender) and are concerned to create a liberating pedagogic space within the normalizing structure of the classroom. Those who drew upon various forms of Neo-Marxism coupled with discourse theories which were compatible, now have to re-think their position in the new political and intellectual climate. Here there is both a vacuum and a legitimation crisis. Vygotsky is attractive for a number of different but related reasons.

The perspective is socio-centric; it points to the reflexive construction of meaning in development; it can be read as promising a pedagogic space where teachers and acquirers are players in a re-vitalised pedagogic scene with apparently negotiated scripts and readings. Of great importance is the linkage to macro structures and their discourses. The Vygotskian perspective, with a little nudge, can also be related to postmodern positions. The ambiguity which is read into Vygotsky's (and Bakhtin's) ideological position allows for recontextualizing according to a range of contemporary relevances.

Thus, it is possible to see that Vygotsky is attractive to different groups for different reasons. These speculations propel one to consider, if only briefly, why the educational field (and perhaps that of social work) is so prone to importing exemplary figures around which interested groups position. Behaviourist approaches to learning do not seem to be imbued with such sacredness. But, I suppose, neither does any technology. Yet Skinner certainly had a concept of a new social order.

There always have been priests and prophets in education but perhaps today we have new priests serving a new temple. These priests are guardians, not of culture (high or popular), but of effective transmission and organization. They tend towards technologies, for ends are not problematic for such priests. They control the import of such technologies which carry a dubious sacredness. Prophets, as of old, proclaim a new order. However, like priests in education, they rarely create the means of entry into the new order. Theories are imported, charisma is transferred and means and ends are joined in sacredness. Some prophets turn out to be pied pipers and some priests to render the word sterile.

I must return after these swings and roundabouts to this book. What is presented here is a new direction in which Vygotsky is central. Vygotsky is central for a number of reasons. His perspective can be linked with others because of his orientation and total project. Vygotsky here is more of a catalyst than a provider of a worked-out theory, which it is obviously not, nor has it ever pretended to be. In his short life, Vygotsky used broad brush strokes to outline new images. Of importance, Vygotsky can speak directly to teachers and ground development and give confidence to their own intuitions. Perhaps a major contribution will be in providing a new orientation for research. Unlike Piaget (E), who necessarily isolated the study of child development and those who studied it, Vygotsky (E) points towards more integrated research and teaching. His theoretical perspective also makes demands for a new methodology, for the development of languages of description which will facilitate a *multi-level* understanding of pedagogic discourse, the varieties of its practice and contexts of its realization and production. Today, as many chapters in this book show, Vygotsky (E) can provide the grounds of critique and, in terms of the title of this book, provide the means of charting the new agenda without determining its outcomes.

I first came across Vygotsky in the late 1950s through a translation by Luria of a section of *Thought and Speech* published in *Psychiatry* 2 in 1939. It is difficult to convey the sense of excitement, of thrill, of revelation that this paper aroused. Literally, a new universe opened.

Preface

Harry Daniels

INTRODUCTION

One of the outstanding features of Vygotsky's contribution to twentieth-century intellectual development was the range of influences on which he drew when formulating his theories. His studies involved the reformulation of a great number of ideas from different intellectual disciplines into a general theory of semiotics. Equally outstanding is the extent to which his work has influenced the development of the disciplines themselves. It is, of course, entirely predictable, from a Vygotskian point of view that the different disciplines would have interpreted his work in different ways and would have been concerned to develop different facets of the theory. In his terms, his theory has been mediated by the practice of the different disciplines. The intention of this book is to introduce a wide range of readers from different disciplines to the different interpretations and developments of Vygotskian theory that have taken place within different disciplines.

PATTERNS OF SIGNIFICATION

Vygotsky's notion of the cultural sign was essentially as an instrument of signification. He argued that different cultures created different patterns of signification which act as differential organizers within cultures. That is not to say that he was developing a theory of total cultural determination with no place for the individual subject to act. Bruner (1984) suggested that Vygotsky had to hide his views on the position of the individual within a culture for political reasons. If Bruner's suggestion is followed we are left with an image of an individual aware of a position, his own, which in turn denies him the possibility of describing his own views on how individuals are positioned in society. The irony of this situation is that it has spawned a controversy with a history of its own. The debate as to the form of political philosophy, particularly with respect to the determination of individual thought, that lies behind Vygotsky's writing is, at times, vitriolic. There are those, such as Yaroshevsky (1989), who wish to exhume the body of Vygotsky's early writing in order to construct a modern Marxist psychology, and those, such as Kozulin (1990), who wish to purge his identity of all Marxist influence. Much of this controversy centres on the question of mediation. Was Vygotsky proposing a theory in which activity mediated the social/individual relation or was a broader semiotic view intended? The range of answers that have been produced to this question arguably reveal the cultural positioning of their proponents. It is, perhaps, appropriate to understand Soviet activity theory as being as much a product of a culturally and historically mediated process of selective combination, interpretation and assimilation of writing, development and empirical evidence as the semiotic interpretations arising within literary theory. Within both of these broad groupings, the activity-based and the semiotic, there are disagreements as to the specific influences that have resulted in specific interpretations. Yaroshevsky (1989), for example, derides what he sees as an insufficiently materialist view presented by some of his Russian colleagues.

> It is wrong to assert, however, that his 'idea of the semiotic or symbolic nature of the higher psychical functions and consciousness was very closely connected with the theory and practice of Russian Symbolism' (V. P. Zinchenkov, V.V. Davydov, Preface to J. Wertsch, *Vygotsky. Social Formation of Mind*, Cambridge, Massachusetts, London, 1985, p. vii). This view ignores the consistently materialist nature of Vygotsky's theory of the higher psychical functions, in which the concept of the word or sign was treated on the analogy of the Marxist explanation of the role of labour instruments in the construction of human activity, and not at all in the style of Russian Symbolism.
>
> (Yaroshevsky 1989: 70)

In a recent extended discussion of the practical implications of some of these issues, Davydov (1988a, b, c) suggests that the way forward is to develop a less partisan account which acknowledges the advances made on a variety of fronts.

PEDAGOGIC DIMENSIONS

The question as to the nature of the 'real' theory of knowledge and the theory of pedagogy which inheres in a truly late twentieth-century neo-Vygotskian approach is also a source of controversy. Two important dimensions of difference in the set of practices which claim a Vygotskian base are with respect to control over pupil behaviour and control over the creation of knowledge within pedagogic practices. Consider for example the case of pedagogy in which the teacher defines the sequencing, pacing and criteria of evaluation. In this case a 'Vygotskian' argument could be used to support a cultural, historical view of knowledge. The teacher is charged with the responsibility of transmitting the cultural and historical legacy of a society to the individual child. Alternatively consider the 'Vygotskian' argument that knowledge is social and is created in interaction. The teacher is then charged with the responsibility of organizing appropriate forms of educational activity in which social knowledge will be created and subsequently assimilated by the individual. The emphasis on transmission of that which is drawn from culture and history may subvert what is seen by many as the original requirement for responsive instructional dialogues (see Palinscar *et al.* 1991; Reid and Addison Stone 1991, for reviews). Conversely the emphasis on interpersonal interpretation and interaction as a setting for the facilitation of developmental processes may remove the instructional invective from many Western 'Vygotskian' pedagogies (see Davydov 1988a, b, c). Different *epistemologies* and *pedagogies* arise from the same theoretical base.

CHARTING THE AGENDA

It is with these thoughts in mind that this book has been compiled. The authors offer the readership their views on the theoretical and practical pedagogic developments that have taken place within their own professional and academic cultures and also reflect on what lies ahead. They write in different styles and with different voices. This is a deliberate and consciously planned strategy.

Tony Burgess writes from the perspective of the teaching of English and proceeds to unravel his views on the reading of Vygotsky. His is an essentially methodological account which leans on the work of Davydov and Radzikhovskii to penetrate the dialogue between Marxist and pragmatic positions – a dialogue which until very recently has been conducted through the filter of Soviet isolation. The chapter by Peter Evans looks elsewhere for its inspiration. Rather than looking to literary theory, politics and general theories of semiotics, he considers the possibilities for those enmeshed in the metaphors of cognitive, developmental and behavioural psychology. The struggle that psychology as a discipline has with the concept 'social' underpins much of the analysis of his chapter and that of my own. Where the former looks to developments from psychology, the latter looks to developments drawn from sociology.

James Wertsch and Ana Smolka also explore the social/individual relation but this time via the perspectives drawn from Lotman and Bakhtin. Here the concept of dialogue is adopted and refined.

Davydov and Zinchenko point, with some humour, to the ironies in aspects of theoretical development in the West when discussing Vygotsky's contribution to Soviet psychology. They also tread on the sensitive ground of the relationship between activity theory in the Soviet Union and the Soviet literature which has influenced Wertsch and Smolka and Burgess. They identify fractures in the development of the theory and allude to the practical consequences for pedagogic practice.

Geoffrey B. Saxe, Maryl Gearhart, Mary Note and Pamela Paduano describe the practical investigation of a view of the role of peer interaction with particular reference to mathematics education. They clarify their theoretical position on a much abused topic. Peer interaction, perhaps more than any other pedagogic device which seeks a Vygotskian base, has been subjected to a very wide range of interpretations and applications. Saxe *et al.* bring a clear theoretical perspective to bear on an exciting practical initiative. The notion of emergent goals is developed to provide a unit of analysis of relations between peer interactions and the cognitive development it is designed to influence.

Ingrid Lunt develops a case for Vygotsky's influence on the

figure of psychological assessment practices. She considers the language of assessment from the perspective offered by developments of assessment practice which embody the concept of the 'zone of proximal development'. The notion of mediation shows only limited signs of penetration into orthodox practice. It is to the introduction of this concept into the theoretical discourse of assessment that this chapter is addressed.

Andrew Pollard also appeals for changes in theory and practice in his consideration of learning in primary schools. He presents a sociological view of the almost subliminal process of the incorporation of theory into primary practice. His plea is for a broader Vygotskian view of learning in theory and for its introduction into the education of young children. This chapter provides a view which has been developed from a perspective that has always rested, somewhat uncomfortably, on the cusp between sociology and psychology. The perspective is that of symbolic interactionism which has itself struggled with tensions between interactionism and dialectical analysis. Pollard develops a model of the relationship between intra-individual, interpersonal and sociohistorical factors in learning and reflects on its potential to guide research and practice.

Josie Levine provides a challenge to the received view of the relationship between scientific and everyday concepts in the context of additional language learning. The debates in the theory of second language acquisition are reflected against a reinterpretation of Vygotsky's writing to provide what is ultimately a cultural analysis of a particular form of educational practice.

At the time of writing the Soviet Union is breaking up into smaller political units. It remains to be seen whether any overarching system of organization will emerge. We can only speculate as to whether the demise or disappearance of central authority will find its educational and psychological analogues. Following Vygotsky, this new set of social circumstances will mediate the development of the new understandings to arise. Certainly one would expect a new responsive/dialogic interpretation of Vygotsky to be a consequence of these changes. It may be the case that the old Soviet interpretation of his work carries with it too much of the semiotic baggage of the old order to allow for anything but the search for a new source of psychological imagination (Daniels and Lunt, in preparation).

In the case of this volume the agenda is to establish and celebrate the variety of responses to Vygotsky's writing and to identify directions for the future in a range of social contexts.

REFERENCES

Bruner, J. (1984) 'The Zone of Proximal Development: the hidden agenda', in B. Rogoff and J. Wertsch (eds) *Children Learning in the Zone of Proximal Development*, San Francisco, Jossey-Bass.

Daniels, H. and Lunt, I. (in preparation) 'The theoretical basis of primary school teaching: Some comparisons'.

Davydov, V.V. (1988a) 'Problems of developmental teaching: the experience of theoretical and experimental psychological research', *Soviet Education* 30 (8), 1–97.

Davydov, V.V. (1988b) 'Problems of developmental teaching: the experience of theoretical and experimental psychological research', *Soviet Education* 30 (9), 1–81.

Davydov, V.V. (1988c) 'Problems of developmental teaching: the experience of theoretical and experimental psychological research', *Soviet Education* 30 (10), 1–77.

Kozulin, A. (1990) *Vygotsky's Psychology: A Biography of Ideas*, London, Wheatsheaf.

Palinscar, A. M., David, Y. M., Winn, J. A. and Stevens, D. D. (1991) 'Examining the context of strategy instruction', *Remedial and Special Education* 12 (3), 43–53.

Reid, D. K. and Addison Stone, C. (1991) 'Why is cognitive instruction effective? Underlying learning mechanisms', *Remedial and Special Education* 12 (3), 8–19.

Yaroshevsky, M. (1989) *Lev Vygotsky*, Moscow, Progress Publishers.

Chapter 1

Reading Vygotsky

Tony Burgess

FORM AND ANALYSIS IN VYGOTSKIAN THOUGHT

I work in English teaching rather than psychology. I want to concentrate on what, it seems to me, might be a promising, mutual topic: reading Vygotsky. Unusual in many ways, Vygotsky is also unusual in this. We read him. For many psychologists, the shell suffices. It is enough to grasp abstractly the framework of theoretical programme, research design, experimentation and empirical work. With Vygotsky, text and argumentation matter. Also, for historical reasons, interpretation matters in a quite distinctive way.

To read Vygotsky is to work one's way among competing analyses. One sets out in a familiar landscape, but then the known comes into focus against arguments having larger implications. Beyond, lie the huge horizons of the theory of human development and human history. The thought is dialectical. The interest seems to lie as much with indicating a form of analysis as with constructing a comprehensive picture of the behaviour being studied. Particular analyses are transcended in general arguments. Fundamentally, the argument is methodological.

One grows used to a recurrent form. An everyday concept appears: words, inner speech, concepts, play, writing, learning, development. The invitation is to think. There are no introductory words, no preliminary skirmishes. The question is, 'How should the problem be posed?' The enemies become familiar: the Buhlers, Piaget, Sterne, Koffka, Wertheimer and the Gestalt psychologists, Watson, Associationist psychology, Behaviourism.

Out of the antitheses, there comes a movement in time as well as in logic, as the thread is carried forward from the problem incorrectly posed to its correct formulation. The formulation determines what solution can emerge. In the end, the undertaking has been concerned to reveal how most adequately the problem should be studied as much as it has been directed towards establishing findings. In turn, the form of analysis has mediated larger concerns with studying human psychology.

In Vygotskian analysis, one comes to recognize a kind of movement: from past to future, from fragments to unity, towards a formulation which permits thinking to confront what needs to be explained where this is concealed in studies which are in the Vygotskian view mistaken or incomplete. The offer is to reformulate, not simply to add to or supplement other accounts. There has been much commentary in recent years which has taken forward understanding of the bases of Vygotskian thinking. In what follows I want to approach interpretation as an issue.

OVERLAPPING PROJECTS IN POST-WAR ENGLISH TEACHING

Vygotskian psychology has interested English teachers for many years. This hardly needs saying to English teachers. But it is an interest which has arisen and been maintained within a specific stretch of post-war British educational history, and I want to recall how this has come to be so. Vygotsky's stress on language in thinking emerged as a powerful influence on English teaching in the 1960s. The sources of this impact were complex. In James Britton, there was an unrivalled interpreter (Britton 1970). Teachers had a ready ear for a psychology which provided an alternative either to measuring and identifying abilities or to behavioural accounts of learning. English teaching was organizing itself on a national basis, and a number of researches sponsored by the Schools Council were initiated into different aspects of the subject. Vygotsky's work became available at a key point in curriculum development.

The psychology was formative in many of English teaching's subsequent themes. In contemporary English classrooms, collaborative learning, the exploration of ideas through informal talk, writing as a process, language across the curriculum: all have their source in insights gathered from his psychology. Vygotskian approaches, it followed, underpinned many of the messages of the Bullock Report (1975). It is not too strong to say that the version of the subject in its contemporary form which is most widely and most commonly held among English teachers is very largely owed to a reading of Vygotsky's work.

Vygotsky, then, has mattered to English teachers. Practices in classrooms have been grounded in his thought. For nearly thirty years, the Vygotskian emphases on the development of word meaning, inner speech, language's contribution to mind have provided work in English classrooms with continuity and rationale.

Meanwhile, against the background of this continuity, the subject has been opened up in other ways. There have been new influences which also have had intricate patterns of development. One such set of influences, emerging in the 1970s, has been that of sociolinguistics, resulting in attention to language variety, bilingualism, dialects and standards. Another, more recently, has been the perspectives made available through cultural studies, feminist and anti-racist work and literary theory. Work from these several quarters has multiplied the perspectives available in English teaching, while the emphasis on language and learning, deriving from the 1960s, has been held constant, together with the importance accorded to Vygotskian thought.

It would be wrong to suppose that this diversification of theory has been conjured into harmony by the framework for English within the national curriculum. At best, it has been schematized. The reality of English teaching now is a loose federation of overlapping projects in language and learning, in sociolinguistics and in different forms of cultural critique.

The point I want to make is this. In this more diverse theoretical context, what is actually being understood within the Vygotskian rationale becomes something to be negotiated. New questions being asked about English teaching influence the formulation of Vygotskian thought. It becomes possible to perceive from different angles the Vygotskian project and to turn it to face in different ways. How Vygotsky should be read, then, becomes a central issue in the continuity and change of English teaching. For if one feature of the history which I have been outlining has been the continuing influence of Vygotskian thought, another has been the emergence of different interpretations of the thought itself.

TWO INTERPRETATIONS OF VYGOTSKY

It is possible to perceive two readings of Vygotsky which now exist alongside each other within English teaching. In one reading, Vygotsky is approached from a tradition of thought about the role of symbol in human affairs. In the other, Vygotsky is read within a stress on the politics of culture. Grounds for both readings exist, it seems to me. But there are questions in this which go beyond whether one or another reading is to be preferred. I want to come back to these, after distinguishing more fully among the interpretations of Vygotskian thought, now current.

I shall need to be more specific if I am to illustrate the difference between two readings and to justify my sense of contrast. But I am pointing towards tendencies which are implicit in references made to Vygotsky and in the ways in which his thought is invoked. I am not reporting explicit accounts. If I am therefore a bit general in my comments, I hope that enough will emerge to indicate a comparison and to convey a sense of the traditions within which these tendencies might be anchored.

In the first reading, it is the relevance of Vygotskian thought to the individual child which is given most attention. Readers of this persuasion are interested in learning, development and the role of language in thinking. They are drawn to the account of the symbol and symbolizing because this fits well with a stress on creativity and the child's active contribution to her learning.

These readers do not neglect the social, contrary to what opponents sometimes say. But they tend to treat social considerations in general and beneficent terms. They stress interaction rather than society. They emphasize the constructed nature of institutions rather than institutional constraints or the contestable quality of common sense. They regard both culture and history as important, but they keep both mainly in the background of their interpretations and they tend to illustrate culture without reference to power or conflict. Their interest is in processes and practices, the agency of human actors and the ethical dimensions of learning and education. The points which are underlined are that learning is interactional and that culture is socially constructed.

The reading draws strength from the rediscovery of Kantian thought towards the end of the last century and from new work in this tradition which was made available in the post-war years.

An element in this was the general influence of Piagetian developmental psychology. More specifically, the post-war impetus to neo-Kantian thought came with the publication of the writings of Susanne Langer in the 1940s and 1950s (Langer 1960, 1967). Langer's emphasis was on the symbol as a 'new key' in philosophy and on a theory of art within a majestic, synthesizing account of human mind. Langer paid tribute to Ernst Cassirer. The line goes back to nineteenth-century idealist thought about language, through Cassirer's work in Germany in the 1920s (Cassirer 1955), and was also a substantial part of the inheritance of Vygotsky.

In post-war English teaching, the symbol has provided the impetus for several themes. Let me highlight just two. English teachers (and others) have been interested in the connections (and differences) between artistic and discursive symbolizing (Britton 1970: 97–124). And at the heart of contemporary English teaching has lain an account of learning which stresses the categories placed on experience by human mind in contrast to an empiricist (or behaviourist) approach (Bullock Report 1975: paras 47–50). This is one reading of Vygotsky, then. It inherits the emphases on the human subject, on ethical freedom and on the human origin of ideas about reality which are characteristic of Kantian thought.

Meanwhile, the second reading has as its central influence the cultural politics of the Italian Marxist and political activist, Antonio Gramsci (see Hoare and Nowell-Smith 1971). This version, then, has inherited Marx's transcendence of German idealism. It begins in a materialist version of history and consciousness. To this extent, the two readings are in conflict. But accommodations are possible and have been made. To continue historically, these perspectives have entered English teaching in a way which is no less complex (and accidental) than that of Cassirer's neo-Kantianism. The immediate sources have been Raymond Williams's work in cultural materialism and the work of Stuart Hall and his colleagues at the Birmingham Centre for Contemporary Cultural Studies (Williams 1977; Hall *et al.* 1980). But the line, in this interpretation, goes back further: to arguments with the theorists of the Second International.

Gramsci's account of hegemony comes from outside the academy. A full understanding would refer to its place in European and not just intellectual history. This would trace the development of politically and culturally oriented strategies in early twentieth-century struggle, in contrast to revisionism and to economist determinism, tendencies which came to predominate in Western Marxism after the death of Marx. But this is beyond my scope. It is enough to note that in this reading, Vygotsky's thought is related to cultural and political struggle. In cultural analysis, interests in ideology and in methods of analysis have been explored most fully. But a reading of Vygotsky as a psychologist which starts from here focuses on the politics of development. It stresses resistance and deconstruction as well as internalization and individual construction.

Let me try to set out this alternative reading in parallel with the earlier approach. Here the beginning is made from ideology and culture rather than from the child. Readers of this sort stress the political nature of culture and they are interested in the ways in which this political nature is often disguised. They attend to social mechanisms which manipulate consent. They insert qualifications about power and control and capitalism into the predominantly benevolent view of culture which tends to prevail within a Kantian account. Within Marxist arguments, they insist on the significance of the political and cultural level as a site for achieving change, against economistic or deterministic social analyses.

In this interpretation, then, there is a more developed concept of the social. These readers recognize conflict. They relate developments in culture to the gaps in interest between dominant and subordinate classes, fragments, groupings in society. They interpret culture through a Gramscian version of hegemony. They are interested in power, and especially the power to maintain some meanings as the dominant 'common sense' to the exclusion or subordination of others. They stress ideology and the ideological nature of signifying systems. In contrast to Kantian readers, they tend to be less interested by the aspects of Vygotskian theory concerned with learning than by the account of semiotic mediation. The point which is underlined is the need for a politics of culture and critique.

It may seem that my appropriate course would be to adjudicate between these two readings. Instead, I shall want to argue for retaining both and for an account of interpretation in psychology which permits different readings. Let me note, though, that there seem grounds for either interpretation. Vygotsky's social psychology has in its account of the word a Kantian inflection, derived from his reading of the German humanist scholar Von

Humboldt and of the American linguist Edward Sapir. There is no doubt either that Vygotsky's was an attempt to construct a Marxist psychology in the years following the Bolshevik revolution in 1917, even if there is some dispute about his transcendence of idealist thought and Western psychology. So there are grounds for a Kantian reading just as there are grounds for approaching Vygotsky from a contemporary Marxism.

Let me note also that it might be argued that both risk only a partial representation. A Kantian reading may miss aspects of the social and Marxist nature of Vygotsky's thought. Alongside, there is a somewhat more complex point to be made about a Gramscian reading. Gramscian Marxism is not Vygotsky's Marxism. Nor is a politics of culture the same as a Marxist psychology. Both readings might be thought, in different ways, incomplete, and both might be reinforced by taking into account Vygotsky's more specifically methodological concerns. These are points which I want to pick up later. A background to them which I now want to explore is this. We do not just derive our readings of psychological texts. We construct them.

READING IN HISTORY

Two alternative readings of Vygotsky exist in English teaching at present, not one correct and one incorrect. I can justify the statement – and make sense of English teaching – if I go behind correctness and confront the further issue of reading and interpretation. I want to do this in two ways. First, I shall outline my version of reading. Then, in the sections which follow, I shall carry the argument forward into Vygotskian interpretation itself. I cannot attempt a full discussion of all the aspects. But I can point to some considerations which arise from becoming conscious that we 'read' psychology and that reading literature and reading psychology are not without their parallels.

In a word, reading is historical. Accepting this, however, is only the beginning. For it will then become apparent that 'reading psychology' is more complex than I have so far implied. There can be readings of readings as well as just readings. And interpretations of interpretations can be resistant and critical of interpretations which are themselves resistant and critical. And so on. None of this will matter if we are prepared to live with argument and awareness rather than certainties. Nor are the possibilities of meaning infinite. We live in time and history. Text and interpretation do not proliferate in some semantic stratosphere, separate from social purposes and traditions.

But the idea of fidelity of interpretation should be reconsidered. Fidelity by whom, for whom, when, for what? There can be more than one kind. We read with different purposes. We read from different intellectual histories. We read, mindful of ways in which psychologies normally are or sometimes can be read. In educational settings, readings are constructed by readers, against the background of discursive traditions in the subject, wider educational interests and even more general philosophical, ethical and political considerations.

I can put together these complications in the following way. Reading psychological texts is not just a matter of deriving meanings; it is active and constructive and purposive. Nor is reading a transparent, natural process. Social, generic and ideological considerations enter into reading psychologies. The aim of faithful interpretation, then, is not for an absolute to be fixed timelessly and for ever. We should think, rather, of contingent sets of meanings, proposed by readers aware of their interpretation's contingency, in the spirit of negotiation and renegotiation, conscious of social traditions, institutions, ideologies, debates and circumstances in which meanings are produced.

I want to give attention to the power of the reader in shaping meaning, in this version of reading which I am sketching. It will clarify what I am saying if I pick up some ideas from other places which have influenced my views. A move in literary theory recently has been to shift attention from text to reader (Iser 1974; Holub 1984). In some versions of literature, the nature of text is regarded as the sole consideration. Other theorists have wanted to place equal emphasis on ways in which readers construct meanings. Texts contain gaps and silences which readers interpret and fill. It follows that the possibility of different readings is intrinsic to literary study, not an unfortunate circumstance to be transcended. This is one line of argument, worth considering in psychology as well, which lies behind the view of reading which I am taking here.

I also want to move beyond a correspondence (copy) view of science. The sources for this view are legion. But it is worth mentioning two very different philosophers who both make arguments about the contingency of scientific theory. The American pragmatist philosopher, Richard Rorty, attacks in his work the idea of 'final vocabularies' (Rorty 1989). Drawing on philosophy of science, his argument is that the most that can be hoped for is 'description and re-description'. I have reservations about some aspects of his argument. But I do not need to follow it in all its 'anti-realist' implications to find helpful the idea of theories as 'vocabularies' or to extrapolate to an idea of interpretation as 'describing' and 're-describing' theories in new and different ways.

I also want to recognize that readings are social and have ideological dimensions. To set alongside Rorty, the French poststructuralist philosopher, Foucault, has also been among those who have raised awareness of the historicity of theory (Foucault 1970, 1972). But Foucault adds a distinctive, ideological emphasis. In Foucault's work, there are accounts of discourse, regulation and power. I have again reservations – this time, about the nihilist aspects of Foucault's thought. Setting those to one side, Foucault's work offers a way of conceptualizing interpretation as a cultural and social practice and not just as the individual derivation of meaning. Drawing on a perception of the historical nature of the social sciences, reading can be seen as itself discursive, political and historical and related to interpretative discourses and to power.

In different ways, these sources in literary theory and philosophy each support an approach to reading and interpretation which recognizes that they are historical and contingent. I can sum this up by juxtaposing the complementary views of text and of interpretation which they imply. Psychological texts contain choices made by writers of psychology within the options and problems of a specific history. Interpretation of these texts is shaped by assumptions in the discourses and history which we, as readers, bring.

We will want to interpret the interpretations. This implies keeping meanings going, exploring them, not wanting always to rub out alternatives. It also implies a continuing attempt to analyse and describe. That said, there is no contradiction in arguing that in English teaching both Kantian and Gramscian interpretations should thrive. They illuminate different aspects of Vygotskian thought. Their active presence keeps alive different resources of past traditions. Both English teaching and Vygotskian thought will benefit from retaining the two interpretations: the focus on children and on their creative, active learning and the focus on the politics of culture and on ideological struggles pursued within language and literacy.

Readings themselves develop. Another consequence of this view is to recognize that interpretation is not a summary but a continuing process. Interpretations change. Interpretations of interpretations change. Vygotskian thought takes on one meaning when contrasted with the old educational psychology of measurement and control. It can be made to seem quite different if contrasted with a narrow, mechanical view of language learning. Versions and readings can be given new accents as they are related and contrasted in different ways.

Here, some contemporary feminist and anti-racist work has been of the first importance in breathing new life into old readings. This work has pointed to the different and specific meanings which can be excluded both in traditional classrooms and in universalizing theories in psychology and in all forms of social science theory. This holds implications which challenge both the dominant interpretations to which I have referred.

In feminist analysis, a social account of difference is the crucial point. Both lines of Vygotskian interpretation have often left implicit their accounts of gender, race and social class, and both can be seen as needing to rethink universalist assumptions. If in the one, Kantian, version there is a temptation towards representing all children through the shadowy, universal child, there are also risks in the other, Gramscian, version. Here, women, girls, race, the multiple social histories and experience which are present in society may be incorporated into an undifferentiated account of hegemony and cultural transmission.

My colleague, Jane Miller, has written a critique of the reluctance to admit that women possess independent histories in the work of Raymond Williams (Miller 1990). But the critique has many implications outside the work of just this thinker. In Miller's work, current versions of interpretations are being challenged and extended. She gives a new mobility to old readings, not by trying to think up new ones, but by calling attention, through feminist critique, to histories in them which have been suppressed. This emphasis on the history in the reading is, I hope, close to the version of reading psychology to which I am pointing. It is an emphasis with particular relevance to interpreting Vygotsky.

READING VYGOTSKY FROM WITHIN WESTERN PSYCHOLOGY

There has been nothing implied about interpretation so far which is unique to reading Vygotsky. But the historical circumstances of Vygotskian thought give particular relevance to matters we might barely trouble to notice in reading other psychologists. Basic assumptions are uncertain. Equally, Western approaches to reading Vygotsky have arisen within a specific, post-war history. It may seem bad taste to say so, but it is hardly possible to omit referring either to the Cold War or to Western understanding of Marxist thought if interpretations of Vygotsky are to be interpreted. There are also issues about the purpose and nature of psychology.

I can sum up the features of this history in the following way. Vygotskian thought has had to win its place. Advocates and interpreters have had to argue a case within a climate of psychological and cultural opinion which was mostly unaware of its existence and also dubious of the project of a Marxist psychology. It is reasonable to make the point that such doubts derived not only from hostility to the Stalinization of Soviet psychology but also from impatience with Marxist thought itself. Where Marxism has been seen principally as a state religion, it has mostly been interpreted as a political rhetoric, not as a line of intellectual descent nor as an intellectual project with explanatory potential.

To this cultural version of Marxism, it was perhaps rather too easy to attach a Western reading of Soviet psychology. Criticism of Pavlovian psychology, and its state support, could get turned into the 'form of psychology which communist regimes produce' and not much was known about alternatives. It is not surprising if some may have then looked to discover butterflies broken on the wheel of the state (one version of Vygotsky), or searched for instances of democratic mind shining in the dull body of communist reflexology (another). Political choices are surely always present in psychology. But there was some element of myth in the gap between West and East in post-war years.

Vygotskian interpretation has been inserted into this post-war history as a discourse of change. Characteristic patterns of advocacy, critique, opposition and synthesis arise from this. Advocates have sought to follow (and to contribute to) the slow *rapprochement* between West and East, together with de-Stalinization in the Soviet Union, which has been the uncertain history of these years.

They have had to re-make a climate of opinion. More recent versions teach Marxism to Western psychologists and begin from collaboration between Western and Soviet scholars. Earlier versions found other strategies. The historical nature of this process should, I believe, be made explicit. On the whole, traditions in psychology militate against this. But that way confusions lie. I can illustrate the point by commenting on an essay of the American psychologist, Jerome Bruner.

Bruner's influence has been among the first in introducing Vygotskian psychology in the West and in setting a context in which Vygotsky may be read. In *Actual Minds, Possible Worlds* (Bruner 1986) he has an essay of considerable delicacy and charm, recalling early encounters with Vygotskian perspectives. In it, he recounts a first reading of *Thought and Language* (Vygotsky 1986), newly in translation.

> I read the translation-in-progress with meticulous care, and with growing astonishment. For Vygotsky was plainly a genius. Yet it was an elusive form of genius. In contrast to, say, Piaget, there was nothing massive or glacial about the flow of his thought or about its development. Rather, it was like the later Wittgenstein: at times aphoristic, often sketchy, vivid in its illuminations.
>
> (Bruner 1986: 72)

Bruner here supplies one metaphor for reading Vygotsky. Mind meets mind. Bruner has already explained that he had been asked to write an introduction to this first translation of Vygotsky's work. Not surprisingly, he attends to and tries to describe the quality of Vygotskian thought. In the course of his reminiscence, he constructs, generically, one set of assumptions about reading psychology and then offers a way of interpreting Vygotskian thought.

Despite the autobiographical note, Bruner takes reading out of history. Reader and writer are depicted in Bruner's text as in touch, as minds, across the years. As we read Bruner reading, we take on the problem of reading as that of responding directly to the quality and centre of Vygotskian thought. We grasp, within a prose which is itself vivid, the vividness and elusiveness of Vygotskian style. There is more. We have here not just minds in contact, but a tribal meeting of psychologists. We understand, as readers, that like calls to like. Setting questions of genius to one side, this is a case of two scientists encountering each other, independently, on the grounds of science. They are in touch through a common awareness of interior mysteries, which will be contrasted, on the one hand with the mere trappings of nationalisms and political identity, and on the other with the non-essential residues of alien words adopted to disguise from political censors the thought itself.

Psychologists have lighter moments. We hear earlier of an informal party, one would not have wanted to have missed, which followed an International Congress of Psychology in Montreal in 1954. Here, Bruner first encountered talk of Vygotsky. In an essentially parallel metaphor to the one I have already noted, science finds its way past the pomp of nationalism. This party, we are told, followed 'a classically Russian reception, replete with vodka and caviare'. Vaulting beyond, in the caviare-free and no doubt abstemious environment of Wilder Penfield's flat, the men of psychology discuss 'the role of language in development and of "the zone of proximal development" and (of all things) a second signal system attributed to Pavlov' (p 71). Officialdom lumbers afterwards. The quick of ideas transcends the efforts to detain them.

Liberating ideas also transcend, in Bruner's representation, outworn formulations and temporary disguises. There can be no doubt that these include for Bruner not only Pavlovian reflexology but also Marxism. So, as Bruner comes to describe in this essay what is remarkable about Vygotskian psychology, a subtle transformation takes place. Marxism disappears. The talk now turns to 'prosthetic devices of the culture'. Vygotsky's version of tools and signs is related to Bacon but not to Engels. We hear about 'props' and 'instruments' and a Vygotskian view of consciousness, which is related to 'what today we call metacognition' but not to anything within Soviet debate. Bruner's stress falls on 'how we learn from others', on the culture's 'rich file of concepts', on 'social transaction' rather than 'solo performance' and, above all, on 'scaffolding' and the 'zone of proximal development'.

Bruner's psychology has lit memorably teachers' understanding of children. But his reading of Vygotsky naturalizes a version of transcendent science as a way of dealing with Cold War divisions and distils concepts out of their Marxist framework and into a North American pragmatism as a way of resolving difficulties with Marxism. There are several issues here. But our focus is not an account of psychological discourse. The points cannot be made without arousing some expectations of an argument about textuality which might be independently pursued. But the issue is this as a strategy for reading Vygotsky.

One of the interests of Vygotskian psychology is the impossibility of maintaining an ahistorical strategy of this kind. The issue can sometimes be blurred precisely because of the special circumstances of Vygotskian work. It is just possible to hedge bets by listing these circumstances as reasons which make such a reading especially difficult but not impossible. The texts are themselves uncertain. There are questions of translation. There are ambiguities about what was written for publication and about what form of publication was intended and with what purposes. There are gaps between the texts themselves which need to be crossed and gaps between texts, research programme, Vygotsky's own work and that of his collaborators.

All these points and others can be adduced as representing merely difficulties. The temptation is to resolve them through attending to the disciples and the insiders. But the issue should be pushed further. There is no scholarly discourse or privileged inside knowledge which will make good all these uncertainties. We are confronted with the impossibility of taking Western circumstances for granted. What follows is the necessity of attention to text as historical construction and of reflection on the interpretative discourses by which the Vygotskian texts have come to be surrounded. Bruner's insider analysis is an example of one sort of genre at the interpreter's disposal. But it naturalizes a reading which is in fact highly specific. There are other moves which can be made.

VYGOTSKY: LIFE AND SHADOW

Vygotsky made his transition from literature in 1924. He was 28 years old. In a story which is by now almost too well known, from the accounts by Luria (1979), Wertsch (1985a, 1985b), Kozulin (1986) and others, he exploded rather than sidled into psychology with his lecture to the Second All-Russian Conference on Psychoneurology in Leningrad. Within the next two years, he had published his earlier work from the Gomel years in *The Psychology of Art* (1925, 1971) and 'Pedagogical Psychology' (1926). He had also completed two programmatic articles on the charged topic of consciousness and a grand theoretical argument, written, much of it, in hospital: 'The Historical Meaning of the Crisis in Psychology' (completed 1926, but not published until 1982).

Kozulin tells us that from 1926 to 1930, 'The focus of Vygotsky's research programme . . . happened to be the experimental study of the mechanism of transformation of natural psychological functions into the higher functions of logical memory, selective attention, decision making, and comprehension of language' (Kozulin 1986). The first part of *Mind in Society* (Vygotsky 1978), drawn from manuscripts written in 1930 and 1931, contains some indication of this programme. This was written before *Thought and Language* (Vygotsky 1986), although translations have appeared in the West in the reverse order.

There followed work on literacy with Luria in Uzbekistan in 1930 (Luria 1976) and the founding of the laboratory of Khark'ov. Drawing on conversations with Vygotsky's daughter, Gita L'vovna, Wertsch, whose work has transformed our knowledge in recent years, records that 'During Vygotsky's last few years of life, he lectured and wrote at an almost frenetic pace' (Wertsch 1985a). *Thought and Language* (1934/1986), Vygotsky's best-known work in this country, was completed in these circumstances.

Vygotsky died of tuberculosis in 1934. Much of his work remains unpublished or untranslated in the West, despite the magnificent efforts of American and Soviet scholars. There is no full-scale biography. Excellent within their scope, the available commentaries and introductions still contain gaps in their details and reminiscences of Vygotsky's life. To write about Vygotsky is still to write about a figure half in shadow.

WESTERN INTERPRETATIONS – PHASE 2

It is the links between psycho-physiological and socio-semiotic levels of explanation which have come to dominate recent discussion of Vygotsky. The emergence of this theme as central is hardly surprising. Vygotsky's Marxism and key Soviet versions of traditions within Soviet psychology turn on its interpretation. If we understand the attention being paid to it as occurring, historically, within a process of *rapprochement* between Soviet and Anglo-American thought, the stakes become clearer. Construction of an adequate Western social psychology and, correspondingly, reconstruction within Soviet psychology of the Vygotskian tradition, have been all there to play for.

A commentator who writes from outside this convergence between American and Soviet psychology brings the assumptions provocatively into relief: the American historian, David Joravsky (Joravsky 1987). Joravsky's line will not win many bouquets in Vygotskian circles. Nor do I agree with it. But he has a point, and his work is interesting for this reason. Joravsky is resistant to claims for a Marxist science of mind and refuses the distinction between Vygotskian and Western psychology. But his is not a naïve reading. He sees Vygotsky as implicated in the paradoxical development of Soviet psychology in a way which has more in common with other psychologists of his generation than is usually thought and something in common with many psychologists' relations with governments in the twentieth century. He begins in this way:

> In ideological declarations Soviet psychology is both Marxist and Pavlovian, and largely indifferent to the illogic of the combination. In concrete research and teaching Soviet psychology is neither Marxist nor Pavlovian, and never has been. The most important Soviet psychologists have formed a school of cognitive studies very like Piaget's, though few of them have been willing to acknowledge the affinity.
>
> (Joravsky 1987: 189)

Joravsky's reading is not unsympathetic to Vygotsky. But it is unsympathetic to Marxism as a project and, even more unusually in recent Vygotskian interpretation, critical of a whole set of assumptions in twentieth-century ideas of psychology as a science. Joravsky contrasts the record of psychology and literature, the one laying claim to 'impersonal knowledge of human beings as a natural species', the other expressing 'the tormented or comic search for a self worth telling about'. He gropes, in a different place, 'for the reason why the boldest psychologists in the most liberal periods of Russian history – pre- as well as post-revolutionary – have been quite tame politically, have provoked only a little ideological controversy compared to most creative imaginative writers' (p 207). Joravsky, then, interprets Vygotsky in ways which make the 'God-like arrogance' of positivist science, common to both Marxist and non-Marxist psychology, more significant than any differences which may exist between them.

I am tempted to picture Vygotskii, like the best literary artists, as a person in search of the essential self, but one turned increasingly away from the search by his determination to find the self in psychological science. Some future biographer, with full access to his papers, will perhaps discover how close to the man's inward life this guess may be. For present purposes the important issue is the collective mentality that he was assimilating, the functionalist ethos of professional psychologists in the twentieth century. In their congregation the component elements of personality are explained by the functions they serve, the whole is the sum of those functions, efficiency is the measure of the integrating function, and any questions about an essential person are turned aside as relics of a bygone metaphysical enquiry into the spirit or soul.

(Joravsky 1987: 206)

Joravsky's essay was published in 1987. His reading must be regarded therefore as an intervention in the work of recent American commentators on Vygotsky, of whom James Wertsch and Michael Cole are the clearest examples. Cole and his colleagues re-edited the work published in *Mind in Society* in 1978. James Wertsch has been seeking to bring together American and Soviet psychology at least since the 1970s and has published two books on Vygotsky in the 1980s (Wertsch 1985a,b). While I read Joravsky's text as an intervention, I read the approaches of Wertsch and Cole and their collaborators as an attempt to transform the climate of understanding of Marxist psychology among Western psychologists, in the interests of achieving a fully social psychology and, more far reaching yet, a unified social science.

But it is a project also influenced by debates of a different kind within the psychology of the Soviet Union. In Soviet deliberations, Marxism as an intellectual line of descent is not an issue. But a key interpretative problem is whether Vygotskian psychology adopted the right starting points for a Marxist psychology. The work of Wertsch and Cole is then characterized by a dual emphasis. To borrow a move made by the Russian psychologist V.V. Ivanov, describing *The Psychology of Art*, it has to be shown both that Vygotsky's is a Marxist *psychology* and that it is a *Marxist* psychology (Ivanov 1971).

The two requirements carry different implications. Accented towards the West, the emphasis is placed on the sociocultural account of the development of higher mental functions and on the account of the sign as a psychological tool, for these are the basic concepts in Vygotskian psychology, with their roots in a Marxist ontology which needs to be explained. On the same ground is the connection made between Vygotsky's explanatory concern with ontogenesis and Marx's historical method.

Accented towards Soviet psychology and towards arguments within Marxism, the methodological choices made by Vygotsky in translating a Marxist explanatory approach into a specific psychology are what matters. Since fundamental orientations can be assumed, what then become issues for debate are the principles through which Vygotskian psychology is realized: especially the selection of particular 'units of analysis', the explanatory principle of 'activity' and the extent to which Vygotskian psychology does bridge psycho-physiological and socio-semiotic levels. To interpret these arguments it is necessary to move inside Marxism as an intellectual framework and inside the traditions of Soviet psychology.

VYGOTSKY AS METHODOLOGIST IN SOVIET DEBATE

In this Soviet oriented debate, I want to pause briefly in the argument put by the Soviet psychologists, V.V. Davydov and L.A. Radzikhovskii, which is included in Wertsch's collection: *Culture, Communication and Cognition* (Davydov and Radzikhovskii 1985, in Wertsch 1985b). I isolate this argument because it seems to me to be among the most powerful and illuminating examples of Vygotskian interpretation which I have encountered in the last few years. At the same time, the piece is fiendishly difficult to read. If I am deceiving myself into an entirely private version of what it says, I hope there may be some use at any rate in making the attempt to offer an account of this version.

The argument of Davydov and Radzikhovskii is for a continuity between the theoretical and methodological works of the mid-1920s and the substantive psychological investigations illustrated in *Mind in Society* and in *Thought and Language*. They make the case for regarding 'Crisis in Psychology' not just as a piece of general philosophical analysis of the warring schools but as setting a framework of theoretical and methodological principles which Vygotsky in his own psychology seeks to meet. These include identification of the way in which broader philosophical concerns relate to the governing explanatory principle of a psychological theory and a distinction between the principle of explanation and the object of study.

I shall have to say more about the context of these two points if I am to bring out the interpretative force with which they are invested. They arise in the 'Crisis in Psychology' (Vygotsky 1982) in the following way. A substantial part of the intention in this work is a critical review of Western psychologies to date, with a view to formulating the principles on which a unified Marxist psychology might proceed. Vygotsky's conclusion is that Western psychologies are each grounded in an identifiable and limited set of explanatory principles which control the forms of explanation which they can give and the nature of the problems which they are able to pose. These principles may originate in the study of a particular set of problems but, as they are developed into psychologies, they merge with philosophies and with general world views. Pursued to their conclusion, all existing psychologies may be interpreted as variants either of scientific naturalism or philosophical idealism.

At the same time, if Marxist psychology is to develop a third way, the gap between Marxist theory and explanatory psychological principles will need to be accepted. Psychological theories bear a close relation to philosophical world views and may be interrogated from their vantage points. But the two are not reducible to each other. Thus a Marxist psychology cannot be just a simple extrapolation of Marxist historical materialism to the psychological sphere. It will require the development of an independent set of psychological explanatory principles. Such principles should be compatible with historical materialism, certainly. But they will stand between the philosophical level and explanation of actual behaviour. As important, they will be comparable with those in other psychologies, but will transcend them.

Vygotsky also makes a further methodological distinction between explanatory principles and the object of study. This distinction, as I understand it, is about operationalizing explanatory principles, ensuring that they truly explain phenomena and do not merely assume what should be explained. Davydov and Radzikhovskii (1985) explore this distinction in an essay also written at this time: 'Consciousness as a Problem in Psychology' (1925). In analysing the moves made by Vygotsky, they show how Vygotsky set out to resolve the debate about consciousness in Soviet psychology by treating consciousness as an object of study rather than as a disputed principle in psychology. The analysis is too intricate to give in detail but offers too powerful an insight into Vygotskian psychology just to be passed over in a general way. I shall therefore try to explain the analysis a little further.

It is necessary to recall the context. As many have described it, an important undertaking for Soviet psychologists in the 1920s was the development of an alternative to the mentalist/introspective psychology which had been the dominant mode before the revolution and still had some representatives. This psychology assumed consciousness in its founding explanatory principles, since its methods required the introspection on data by experimental subjects. It was actually constituted therefore in a division between higher and lower faculties and between body and mind.

As is also well-known, the attack on this psychology came from many quarters – from reflexology, from behaviourism, from some aspiring versions of a Marxist psychology (though of a reductive kind not favoured by Vygotsky). Vygotsky's solution, of course, leads ultimately to his sociocultural account of the formation of higher mental processes and to the analysis of the role of the psychological sign. The interest of Davydov and Radzikhovskii's article is that they move back before this development of a concrete psychology to Vygotsky's methodological and theoretical concerns. They show that what was crucial in Vygotsky's approach to the problem of consciousness was the development of a distinction between the explanatory principle of a psychology and its object of study.

Vygotsky's critique differed from others in seeing that it was a methodological problem, not acknowledged in mentalist/introspective psychology, that study of consciousness posed. In this tradition, consciousness, the object of study, was not distinguished from the assumption of consciousness, in the formative, explanatory principles. In other critiques than his, from whatever quarter, it was assumed that consciousness could only be studied in a mentalist/introspective way. These critiques then had no alternative but to drop the problem of consciousness altogether. Vygotsky instead identified the problem as one of finding a way of making consciousness the object of study, of studying it in different ways.

As Davydov and Radzikhovskii put it,

> As he already saw then, it is necessary to give consciousness a different methodological status. It is necessary to place it in the position of an object of independent study . . . For this, in turn, it was necessary to find a new explanatory principle in psychology. In other words it was necessary to identify a stratum of reality that determines consciousness. This involved beginning with a *nonreductionist* reconstruction of consciousness. Such is the main task that Vygotsky broached as a result of his analyses of the problem of consciousness, and this was also the main result of that analysis. The resolution of this problem became one of the basic tasks in all of Vygotsky's scientific work.
>
> (Davydov and Radzikhovzkii 1985: 46–7)

This methodological account, added to the illuminating interpretation of Wertsch, Cole and Kozulin and others, throws sharply into relief the experience I have in reading Vygotsky. There are three points to emphasize. First, it alerts me to the formal (methodological), as well as substantive, dimension of his psychology. I find recurrent in Vygotsky this shuttle between empirical interest and the conceptually, critically argued claim for this as the correct method of study. Second, the division between philosophical issues and world view, explanatory principles and object of study accounts for what I find in reading Vygotsky and seems to me excitingly to illuminate the form of Vygotskian analyses. Third, the methodological stress reclaims Vygotsky as a psychologist. This analysis shows Vygotsky as a thinker interested in more than just conceptual approaches and perspectives. Vygotsky began with a sociocultural philosophy of activity and development. What excited him was finding the points of entry by which this could be studied.

RE-READING *THOUGHT AND LANGUAGE*

I want to end by re-reading the first chapter of *Thought and Language* (Vygotsky 1986). The argument contains all the characteristic movements of Vygotsky's thought. Moreover, its content is synoptic.

As a preliminary, let me recall the textual context. In the work as a whole, Vygotsky will weave together the themes of 'nearly ten years' of intense exploration and will draw on empirical research of different origins. There is the work begun in the late 1920s which contrasts the role of tools with that of psychological signs in forming higher mental functions. To this, in the early 1930s, with colleagues, he has added the experimental study of concept development, the investigation of the relation of scientific and spontaneous concepts and an accompanying study of writing. Several different arguments and analyses and enterprises, evolved within a whole programme of research, are, then, to be included.

But *Thought and Language* is intended as a work for the general public, not as a technical research report for psychologist colleagues. So the empirical investigations are integrated within two pivotal arguments. In the first, Vygotsky will be concerned with the specific ontogenesis of verbal thought. He will want to explain how verbal thought arises, how this is achieved developmentally, how speech and thinking, in origin separate, come together. In the second, he will move beyond the ontogenetic origins of verbal thought to aspects of later development. The part played by the word in guiding thinking towards adult forms of conceptualization and behavioural control will then come into central focus.

In the unfolding scheme of these two arguments, several alternative starting points in other psychologies emerge as helpful but incomplete. There are old arguments with Gestalt psychologists around the contributions of tools and sign in problem-solving which will recur. But central will be Stern's recognition of the powers conferred by language (but neglect of the ontogenesis of verbal thought) and Piaget's appreciation of the developmental nature of children's thinking (but subordination of the role of language in this). Vygotsky's critique will identify these as his main antagonists. It is worth adding a word more about these critiques, since they throw into relief the arguments which follow.

Vygotsky's criticism of Stern is that he assumes the very point which should be explained: how children come to perceive the intellectual power of language, the matter of ontogenesis. With Piaget, the issue is different. It is also more fundamental than has sometimes been appreciated, for it centres round more than a different explanation of egocentric language.

In place of Piagetian operations and the reflexive unfolding of epistemological logic, Vygotsky will want to assert the guiding force of language and with this the importance of the culture and the teaching of formal concepts. These are matters in which major arguments are at issue, reflecting substantial differences in orientation in the two psychologies. A point which Joravsky makes is well taken: that Vygotsky's review of Piaget's work is not especially likeable (now that the full text is available) and reflects pressures on him to indicate his distance from Western psychology. But to minimize differences between Piagetian and Vygotskian psychologies seems to me mistaken.

THE METHODOLOGICAL ARGUMENT

Vygotsky embarks on this complex set of arguments and reports by reflecting on the word. The question I want to ask is: why? The answer given by Vygotsky is methodological. This is at any rate the argument which occupies the opening pages of his first chapter. Vygotsky begins the chapter by posing a contrast between the present work and other modes of analysis. 'The atomistic and functional modes of analysis prevalent during the past decade treated psychic processes in isolation' (1986, p 1), he remarks. Instead, a move beyond this separate treatment is needed, towards 'a clear understanding of interfunctional relations'. He continues by tying this distinction to the study of language and thought.

These former investigations, he notes, have polarized along two lines. A look at the results will show that 'all theories offered from antiquity to our time range between identification, or fusion, of thought and speech on the one hand, and their equally absolute, almost metaphysical disjunction and segregation on the other'. The difficulties to which either form of reduction necessarily lead are then briefly exemplified by Vygotsky. With these in mind, he closes on the key point. This is to identify the nature of the mistake which has been made.

One might have supposed the issue here to be principally conceptual. But it is the methodological point which Vygotsky makes. The mistake is not a matter of where, conceptually, different investigators have started out. The fault of previous investigators 'lies in their methods of analysis'. Essentially, there are two modes of analysis possible in the study of psychological structures: one analysing complex psychological wholes into elements, the other the method of analysis into units, which 'retain the properties of the whole'.

> What is the unit of verbal thought that is further unanalysable and yet retains the properties of the whole? We believe that such a unit can be found in the internal aspect of the word, in word meaning.
>
> (Vygotsky 1986: 5)

Vygotsky is not saying, then, that it is through the word that human knowledge is created. He is arguing for a focus in psychology not an account of human nature or a form of philosophical idealism. There is at this point a sharp distinction to be made and an argument against just a Kantian reading. But then nor is he arguing for a politics of culture. Vygotsky's Marxism is not centrally interested in ideology, but in how to bring together the two psychologies in a third, Marxist way which allows for an object of study which explanation can get to. If we miss the methodological point, we shall miss a key implication of Vygotskian thought: that the difficult part about higher mental processes is to find the point of entry for studying them.

So, Vygotsky transforms Von Humboldt's emphasis on the word's inner form into a site in which the interaction between language and thought can be studied. He is not implying in this that words are all that matter. He is indicating a way forward that meets appropriate methodological criteria. It is an interest in breaking new ground which motivates the chapter and with which Vygotsky now marches forward in utterly exciting ways.

THE PROBLEM TRANSFORMED

Words look like the names of things. Most – not all – look as if they refer to particular objects. They look to be the materials of thinking, not to affect thought itself. First, acquire words, so to speak, then think in them. Or think about ideas, then put these thoughts into words. Vygotsky finds his way through this philosophical tangle in a different, specific way: 'A word does not refer to a single object, but to a group or to a class of objects. Each word is already a generalization' (Vygotsky 1986: 6). The keynote for Vygotsky's conception of thought and language is in that recognition of the word as 'already a generalization', for if a word is already a generalization it is also already a thought.

The recognition that words refer to classes and categories runs as one key thread throughout what Vygotsky has to say subsequently in *Thought and Language*. To grasp the investment which Vygotsky places in the idea is quite important. If words refer, by and large, to classes, it follows that in constructing a class *as a class* an act of thought has already occurred. Word meanings are not natural but have been constructed.

The point psychologizes language. Words are in the language. They relate to each other contrastively, as every Saussurean knows. But thought is in the language too, because words are not just categories but generalizations. They have got there through an act of mind, in history. It follows that in children's learning words do not just pop out of language or out of daily life and into their heads. To grasp and use a word is to grasp a generalization. There is a gathering, intense excitement to following Vygotsky's logic, as he moves on from the argument about modes of analysis, to spelling out the implications of this insight for the study of thought and language but also for the focus of psychological investigation more generally.

To follow Vygotsky, as this logic unfolds, is to move from a point about the nature of words to arguments about the nature of human mind and about psychology. The transition is made by distinguishing between thought and sensation. Vygotsky goes on to talk of a qualitative difference, 'a dialectical leap not only between total absence of consciousness (in inanimate matter) and sensation but also between sensation and thought'.

> There is every reason to suppose that the qualitative distinction between sensation and thought is the presence in the latter of a generalized reflection of reality, which is also the essence of word meaning, and consequently that meaning is an act of thought in the full sense of the word.
>
> (Vygotsky 1986: 6)

We are in touch at this point with fundamental themes in *Thought and Language* and more generally with some shaping dimensions of Vygotsky's whole psychology.

James Wertsch characterizes Vygotsky's psychology rightly, I believe, when he talks of three shaping dimensions which are constantly present in his approach: concern for genetic explanation, the emphasis on a sociocultural account of development, the argument for the semiotic mediation of higher mental processes (Wertsch 1985a). Wertsch's point is that all three dimensions need to be in mind when reading and interpreting Vygotsky. Lose the connection between them and you lose the complexity of the argument. I give the reminder in approaching the last stage of Vygotsky's opening chapter. Let me pause for just one more moment in review before allowing Vygotsky to tie the final knot.

We have come a long way from Vygotsky's initial distinction between different modes of study. The key unit for study is the word. A word presupposes generalization. Word meaning, therefore, is not independent of thought. It involves an act of mind. But at the same time as belonging to the realm of thought, word meaning belongs equally to the realm of language. Vygotsky, at this point, can talk therefore of having found in word meaning the unit of analysis which 'preserves the unitary nature of the process under study: the process, that is, of verbal thought'. The analysis is already echoing with characteristic resonances about culture, semiotic mediation, development, psychology, justified by the argument for having found a way of studying these.

If there is a dialectical leap between sensation and verbal thinking, then it follows that no analysis of thinking in which language is ignored will do justice to human thought. It follows that the higher mental faculties characteristic of human thought require a different form of study from that appropriate in animal psychology or at the level of lower, minimal units of human behaviour. If word meaning belongs in the public, sociocultural sphere of language but also requires an act of thought, a generalization, then words are at the interface of the cultural and the individual. Vygotsky's analysis has taken us from words towards the outline of a sociocultural theory of development in which distinctive priority will be attached to the mediating, semiotic power of language.

> The conception of word meaning as a unit of both generalizing thought and social interchange is of incalculable value for the study of thought and language. It permits true causal-genetic analysis, systematic study of the relations between the growth of the child's thinking ability and his social development.
>
> (Vygotsky 1986: 9)

The knot is tied. What will lie ahead will be the causal-genetic analysis, principally of the development of concepts. What is also being claimed is support for a theory of the role of the semiotic in development, emerging from a methodological search and from attention to the nature of the word. The problem of thought and language has been transformed.

PSYCHOLOGIES AND EDUCATION

Those of us who work in education have need of psychologies. Psychologies insert into the educational debate learning, identity, development, children, us as teachers. Psychologies stand, potentially, between children and schools and governments. Psychologies have it in them to question mechanisms of control, misleading versions of mind and body, the dominance of hegemonic fragments and ideas. They may lead us towards freedom. They may point us forward, out of the past. I have taken it virtually for granted here that all psychology is properly social psychology and that psychologists have a proper concern with the political. At the same time, I have been reaching towards the feeling, without ever quite being able to express it, that to equate the political and the psychological is reductive.

The substance of Vygotsky's psychology has been, here, a secondary concern. That is because I have also largely taken for granted the key analyses of tools and signs, of inner speech, of the links between phylogenetic and ontogenetic explanation, of the evolutionary, involutionary and revolutionary courses of development, of conceptual development and the distinction between development and learning. Setting out these is for another place and has been well done by others, as I hope that I have sufficiently registered. But these powerful, substantive themes in Vygotsky's psychology can be given different inflections in alternative interpretations. I have therefore tried to link the goal of Vygotskian interpretation to the goal of a version of reading in psychology, which takes account of its historical nature. The two-sided hope which I have for such a version of reading is that it will, on the one hand, indicate the potential for readings of different kinds and, on the other, allow for clarity about differences and contribute to the growth of historical, interpretative psychological discourse.

But historical interpretation is one thing; realizing the aims of a psychology another. In my reading of the first chapter of *Thought and Language*, I have found myself wanting to redress this balance, provoked into taking some account of Vygotsky as a searching psychologist by the article by Davydov and Radzikhovskii. To read Vygotskian psychology as the continuing search for a method both brings the work together and leaves it open-ended. To learn from this search and to take it forward also hovers as an exciting possibility.

REFERENCES

Ash, M. G. and Woodward, W. R. (eds) (1987) *Psychology in Twentieth-century Thought and Society*, Cambridge, Cambridge University Press.

Britton, J. N. (1970) *Language and Learning*, London, Allen Lane.

Bruner, J. S. (1986) *Actual Minds, Possible Worlds*, Cambridge, MA, Harvard University Press.

Bullock Report (1975) *A Language for Life*, London, HMSO.

Cassirer, E. (1955) *The Philosophy of Symbolic Forms*, vol. 1, New Haven and London, Yale University Press.

Cole, M. and Scribner, S. (1978) 'Introduction' to L.S. Vygotsky, *Mind in Society*, Cambridge, MA, Harvard University Press.

Davydov, V. V. and Radzikhovskii, L. A. (1985) 'Vygotsky's theory and the activity-oriented approach in psychology', in J. V. Wertsch (ed.) *Culture, Communication and Cognition: Vygotskian Perspectives*, Cambridge, Cambridge University Press.

Foucault, M. (1970) *The Order of Things*, London, Tavistock Publications.

Foucault, M. (1972) *The Archaeology of Knowledge*, London, Tavistock Publications.

Hall, S., Hobson, D., Lowe, A. and Willis, P. (eds) (1980) *Culture, Media, Language* (Birmingham Centre for Contemporary Cultural Studies, University of Birmingham), London, Hutchinson.

Hoare, Q. and Nowell-Smith, G. (eds) (1971) *Selections from the Prison Notebooks of Antonio Gramsci*, London, Lawrence & Wishart.

Holub, R. C. (1984) *Reception Theory: A Critical Introduction*, London, Methuen.

Iser, W. (1974) *The Implied Reader*, Baltimore, Johns Hopkins Press.

Ivanov, V. V. (1971) 'Commentary' (commentary on *The Psychology of Art*), Cambridge, MA, MIT Press.

Joravsky, D. (1987) *L. S. Vygotskii: The Muffled Deity of Soviet Psychology*, in M. G. Ash and W. R. Woodward (eds) *Psychology in Twentieth-century Thought and Society*, Cambridge, Cambridge University Press.

Kozulin, A. (1984) *Psychology of Utopia*, Cambridge, MA, MIT Press.

Kozulin, A. (1986) 'Vygotsky in context' (introduction to revised edition of *Thought and Language*), Cambridge, MA, MIT Press.

Langer, S. K. (1960) *Philosophy in a New Key* (3rd edn), Cambridge, MA, Harvard University Press.

Langer, S. K. (1967) *Mind: An Essay on Human Feeling*, vol. 1, Baltimore, Johns Hopkins Press.

Luria, A. R. (1976) *Cognitive Development: Its Cultural and Social Foundations*, Cambridge, MA, Harvard University Press.

Luria, A. R. (1979) *The Making of Mind: A Personal Account of Soviet Psychology*, edited by M. Cole and S. Cole, Cambridge, MA, Harvard University Press.

Miller, J. (1990) *Seductions: Studies in Reading and Culture*, London, Virago.

Rorty, R. (1989) *Contingency, Irony and Solidarity*, Cambridge, Cambridge University Press.

Vygotsky, L. S. (1925) 'Consciousness as a problem in the psychology of behaviour', in K. N. Kornilov (ed.) *Psikhologiya i marksism* (*Psychology and Marxism*), Moscow-Leningrad, Gosizdat. (Translated as 'Consciousness as a problem in the psychology of behaviour', *Soviet Psychology* 27 (4), 3–35.

Vygotsky, L. S. (1925/1971) *The Psychology of Art*, Cambridge, MA, MIT Press.

Vygotsky, L. S. (1926) *Pedagogicheakaya Psikhologiya* (*Pedagogical Psychology*), Moscow, Rabotnik Prosvesheniya.

Vygotsky, L. S. (1978) *Mind in Society*, edited by M. Cole and S. Scribner, Cambridge, MA, Harvard University Press.

Vygotsky, L. S. (1934/1986) *Thought and Language* (translation revised and edited by A. Kozulin), Cambridge, MA, MIT Press.

Vygotsky, L. S. (1982) 'Istoricheskii smysl psikhologichesko krizisa' ('The historical significance of the crisis in psychology'), in L. S. Vygotsky *Sobranie Sochinenii* (*Collected Essays*), vol. 1, Moscow, Pedagogika.

Wertsch, J. V. (1985a) *Vygotsky and the Social Formation of Mind*, Cambridge, MA, Harvard University Press.

Wertsch, J. V. (ed.) (1985b) *Culture, Communication and Cognition: Vygotskian Perspectives*, Cambridge, Cambridge University Press.

Williams, R. (1977) *Marxism and Literature*, Oxford, Oxford University Press.

Chapter 2

Some implications of Vygotsky's work for special education

Peter Evans

No book that considered the work of Vygotsky for the present education scene would be complete without attempting to draw out some of the more important implications for special education. The very fact that Vygotsky worked throughout much of his professional life in the area of problem children would suggest that his contribution in this area should be as profound as in the others on which he worked. It is my view that Vygotsky's ideas provide the basis of a very useful approach to understanding some of today's key issues relating to the practice of special education. These issues are first, how to develop the curriculum and pedagogy for children with special educational needs and, second, how to understand the potential benefits of integration of the disabled into the mainstream. But before considering these points in more detail it is necessary to begin with some background.

SPECIAL EDUCATIONAL NEEDS IN THE 1990S

Special education throughout the world has undergone substantial changes and developments over the past twenty years. There are two highly significant issues. First, in very many countries, although not all, every child is considered to be educable. This principle includes those with the most profound handicaps. In practice this means that all children are taught by trained teachers and administered by the same authorities that are responsible for other aspects of educational provision. A development such as this provides the context for all teachers to need to receive some training in educational matters that relate to *all* children – an important first step to integration.

The second crucial issue has been the abandoning of categories of handicap for educational decision-making. In the UK for example, up to the 1981 Education Act, handicapped children were categorized according to their major disability, e.g. deafness, partial sight, physical handicap, mental handicap, and educational provision tended to follow this categorization; children with physical disability, for instance, went to schools for the physically disabled whatever their educational needs. It had long been recognized that this classification system was unsatisfactory (e.g. Gulliford 1971) for educational purposes but it was not until the Warnock Report (1978) and the ensuing legislation in 1981 that categories were officially abolished. The Education Act of 1981 formally introduced the idea of all children being on a continuum of educational ability and those with special educational needs were those whom schools could not educate effectively without additional support. Thus, slowly the idea that some children were different to the extent of being 'subnormal' (the terminology in use up to the mid–1970s) has been completely abandoned, although it has to be said that no satisfactory educational theory has emerged to take the place of the categorical 'medical' model. There is, however, a general acceptance that it is up to schools as systems to adapt themselves to meet the needs of all children.

It will perhaps surprise readers to know that many of the recent developments noted above with regard to our understanding of special educational needs are consonant with much of Vygotsky's thinking. Vygotsky rejected the biological approach that was popular in the Soviet Union of the time (e.g. Pavlov 1927), and opposed the view that the development of the abnormal child obeyed its own particular laws. He argued instead that the laws of development were the same for *all* children. He emphasized in particular the importance of the social aspects of learning and in this way laid the ground for an educational approach which would emphasize not only pedagogy but also a means for developing and improving pedagogical skills.

Vygotsky criticized the use of IQ tests for the screening of children which grouped together children on the basis of their weaknesses who, if viewed from their positive aspects, would otherwise have nothing in common. (This is the argument that educators now use for the rejection of categories of disability and the reconceptualization in terms of special educational needs.) He argued for what we would now call a 'compensatory' approach (e.g. Wedell 1980), which took into account not only the severity of the difficulty but also the effectiveness of the pedagogic strategy used to help to overcome the problem. Furthermore, he pointed to the distinction that would in present times be made between impairment and disability by recognizing that the underdevelopment of, e.g. speech and thinking in the deaf, or spatial orientation in the blind, were secondary problems. That is to say, they are examples of disabilities that are mediated by the original impairment but which could be overcome by the appropriate compensatory pedagogy.

Vygotsky's views then, as expressed in the 1920s and 1930s, have, sixty to seventy years later, a very modern ring to them. They have the potential to provide a theoretical basis for furthering our understanding of educational practice especially for children with special educational needs.

RELEVANT THEORETICAL CONSTRUCTS

In the next part of this chapter I want to focus on Vygotsky's major theoretical constructs that are important for the development of pedagogy for children with special educational needs. It will only be necessary to describe the concepts briefly since they are covered in detail elsewhere in this book (see Chapter 5).

Vygotsky was brave enough to place education at the forefront of the development and socialization of the child. He recognized that what was necessary was a theory which focused on how to get the child from his present state of development or learning to a point in the future which was commensurate with the sociohistorical realities of the culture or science of the time. In doing this emphasis was placed on the key role that teachers (as well as other adults and children) play in mediating the world for the child. It appears in his second fundamental psychological law:

> any function appears twice on the scene in the cultural development of the child, on two levels, first the social and then the psychological, first among people . . . then within the child himself.
>
> (see Davydov and Zinchenko, this volume, p. 102)

As Davydov and Zinchenko go on to indicate this psychological law is manifested particularly in the domain Vygotsky called the 'zone of proximal development'.

The general sense of this 'zone' is that at a certain stage in his development, a child can resolve a certain range of problems only under the guidance of adults and in collaboration with more intelligent comrades, but cannot do so independently. Thus

> pedagogy should be oriented not toward yesterday but toward tomorrow in child development. Only then will it be able to create, in the process of education, those processes of development that are present in the zone of proximal development.
>
> (Davydov and Zinchenko, this volume, p. 102)

Although it may be noted that Davydov and Zinchenko point out that 'procedures for organizing this activity have been rather neglected in our pedagogy'(p. 103).

CURRICULUM RESEARCH FOR PUPILS WITH MODERATE LEARNING DIFFICULTIES

I want to turn now to a research project that was carried out by myself and colleagues (Evans, Ireson et al. 1987; Redmond, Evans et al. 1988) in the field of children with moderate learning difficulties (MLD) that develops some of the ideas described above but within the current context. In Vygotskian terms this project was concerned with how teachers could create a zone of proximal development (ZPD) with their pupils (e.g. Belmont 1989) and what implications this would have for the school system.

An important feature of Vygotsky's approach was the emphasis that he placed on the role of socio-historical factors in education. Education, he believed, has a key role to play in helping the child to organize the knowledge and experience that has developed during the history of mankind. Vygotsky described this in terms of a systemic or structural approach through which consciousness becomes organized in terms of the socio-history of the particular culture.

In modern mainstream schools much of this structure is represented in the minds of teachers, through their own education, and in textbooks and other curriculum materials that are written at a level which enables the teacher and pupil to engage with the task in a meaningful way by creating the ZPD. However, for children with MLD (in IQ terms (I use this description with some caution) those lying roughly between 50 and 75) and who are failing to learn successfully, the teaching materials that are generally available are not at a level or in a form to allow a ZPD to be readily created between teacher and pupil and additional resources need to be provided. But the question remains as to how effective teaching resources are to be developed.

This problem is especially acute in special schools for children with MLD where relevant materials must be written by the teachers who work in those schools. Special schools, then, make a particularly interesting field of study, because often, effectively in isolation, many of them have had to invent their own curriculum materials. These materials have to be meaningful to children of a wide range of ability and age (i.e. younger than 5 to over 16). In addition these schools have had to determine a process for the development of their teaching resources.

The very few available descriptions of schools that have worked systematically in this way have focused largely on the approaches that they developed for working with pupils in the classroom (Ainscow and Tweddle 1979; Robertshaw 1990). Furthermore these methods were highly influenced by work broadly speaking in the behaviourist tradition. As a consequence the reports tend to use terms such as 'behavioural objectives' and the link to operant psychology is identifiable in the way in which the teaching programmes are put into practice.

There is, however, a broader approach that may be taken to this issue. Skilbeck (1984), for example, has argued that curriculum development that also focuses on objectives is a school-based enterprise of collaboration and structured decision-making. My colleagues and I used this latter approach to investigate more closely the whole school organizational factors that are involved in curriculum development in special schools and later in ordinary schools. The work has been reported elsewhere (Evans, Ireson *et al.* 1987; Redmond, Evans *et al.* 1988; Ireson, Evans *et al.* 1989) and will be described here in outline only.

Based on Skilbeck's whole school approach which emphasized the planning, development, implementation and evaluation of the curriculum, semi-structured interviews were carried out with head teachers and teachers of ten schools for children with MLD in the UK. Accounts of these interviews were written up and verified by the teachers. They were then analysed by qualitative methods described by Miles and Huberman (1984). From these analyses statements relating to various levels of the working of the curriculum seemed to fall naturally into a systems model which relates aims and goals of the school, classroom practices, evaluation and decision-making in a systematic way. Included also are issues relating essentially to factors external to the school (see Figure 2.1).

Figure 2.1 reveals five categories in an area called INTENTION. *Philosophic orientation* was created for the expression, especially by headteachers of a philosophic position with respect to what the school was trying to achieve. The potential for integration was commonly expressed. Some curriculum intentions were stated in terms of *aims and goals*, whereas others were in terms of *objectives* of a wide range, some being behavioural and others being akin to goals. *Curriculum content* was often mentioned as were positive *attitudes and values* that schools wished to develop in their pupils.

The area of FORMULATION, intermediate between INTENTION and IMPLEMENTATION, may be seen through the school's curriculum documentation.

IMPLEMENTATION comprises four categories. *Teaching arrangements* refers to the ways in which pupils are brought together. *Method* refers to methods or techniques used at class, group or individual level and *resources* to curriculum materials or the lack of them, that are of central significance to the schools. The category *individualization* covers issues relating to individual programmes of work.

The area of RECORDING has three categories. *Records* refers to a list of records used. *Pupil progress* relates to the progress of the children and *continuity and progression* is the way the school ensures curriculum continuity for each child. Information from Recording was used by teachers in classrooms, at least in some schools, and for this reason the IMPLEMENTATION and RECORDING areas are linked together by an arrow that is intended to indicate that these two areas can operate independently of the rest of the school.

On the other hand, information from Recording may be used in the next area, EVALUATION of the curriculum. Here *evaluation* refers to information that the school is using to make judgements about the curriculum and *correspondence* refers to the extent to which the curriculum received by pupils corresponds to that taught. Information from these various categories is used in *curriculum decision-making* which covers the extent of teacher involvement in decisions about the curriculum.

Many teachers mentioned training courses and thus a category of *staff development* was constructed. This category also holds

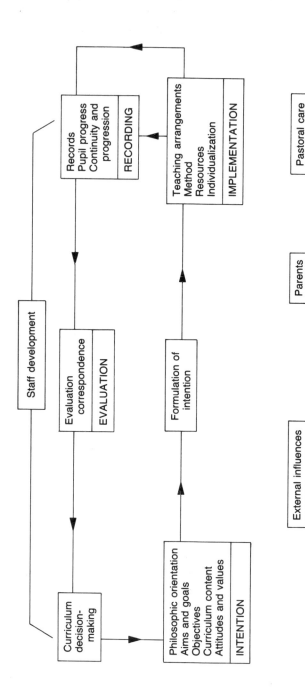

Figure 2.1 A model of school-based curriculum development in special education. The figure shows some of the interrelationships of categories of data in the curriculum development process as derived from ten special schools for children with moderate learning difficulties. The model is intended to represent a co-ordinated interdependent and heterarchical system which has classroom practice at its core (IMPLEMENTATION and RECORDING) but which is supported by and influences other aspects of the system.

comments on curriculum meetings and staff discussion which were also perceived as staff development.

Three other areas also emerged. *External influences* refers to the impact, for instance, of the school psychological service and the local education authority as well as other influences on the curriculum. The category of *parents* includes comments about the child's home background. *Pastoral care* is self-explanatory.

This model is seen as representing a co-ordinated interdependent and heterarchical system which has classroom practice at its core (Implementation and Recording) but which is supported by and influences other aspects of the system.

Although the model described here was derived from data collected in special schools the work has been replicated in both primary and secondary schools with essentially the same outcomes (see Ireson, Evans *et al.* 1989).

A VYGOTSKIAN INTERPRETATION

The work described above was not derived from any particular theoretical perspective but the descriptions do lend themselves rather well to a Vygotskian interpretation. There are a number of points. First of all there is a structured system which has as one of its main goals the creation of a successful learning environment not only for its pupils but also for the teachers. Furthermore, the system is responsive to this goal through a number of feedback loops which allow modifications to be made to the working of the system in order to achieve the main goals more effectively. Here one can mention the development of individual programmes of work which are written to be responsive to individual pupil needs. At the level which includes decision-making, evaluation, etc. the model allows for the development of the context in which the teachers may determine the curriculum in order to achieve better the first goal of improving teaching programmes for the pupils.

Clearly within this approach the aim is to provide an ever-increasing understanding of the teaching-learning process in conjunction with the content of the curriculum and its goals. This knowledge may then be passed on and utilized and modified during teaching.

In this way systematic attempts are made by all teachers to work with individual children by entering the ZPD at each teaching session. In practice this appears in the form of individual teaching programmes and their planning which has been derived through a process often described as hypothesis testing teaching (e.g. Pearson and Lindsay 1986). That is to say, the teacher begins to teach the child with a particular goal in mind and then modifies this through a systematic series of interactions during which the child's learning is monitored, until the pupil can be seen to be making progress. When success has been achieved a new goal is selected and the process begins again. This is not as rigid a process as it may sound so briefly described here (for a much fuller description see Robertshaw 1990). In reality it gives the teacher considerable freedom not only to modify the teaching for each pupil, as that particular teaching session develops and demands, but also to point out weaknesses in the original sequencing or structuring of the curriculum. From the pupils' perspectives internalization of the learning (the second level of Vygotsky's learning process leading to independent functioning) is demonstrated through the ability to transfer the learning to new situations. This process of generalization indicates the abstraction of rules and the beginnings of the development of internal consciousness and higher cognitive functioning (Evans 1986).

Through this process the curriculum is changed and developed to meet the needs of the pupils more fully. It is important to note that the teachers themselves are engaged in the creative task, through action research, of developing the curriculum. Since they are part of the construction of the system and understand its nature they are in a better position to use it flexibly. A system of development such as the one described here also helps teachers to develop and to understand the learning processes of their pupils.

School systems that develop in this way create large amounts of paperwork and lengthy descriptions of the curriculum. It has been pointed out elsewhere (Ainscow and Tweddle 1979) that these documents, although time-consuming to create, serve as useful communication devices for teachers to be able to discuss the curriculum, its sequences and structure as well as pupil progress.

It is worth emphasizing here a key point which is not just a nuance or nice distinction but a fundamental issue which concerns the derivation of the teaching objectives. This is worth stressing since there has been so much criticism of objectives models in education, especially those derived from behavioural analyses.

Evans (1988) has pointed out that it is essential to understand the origins of the objectives that are being used to guide the education that pupils receive. At one extreme there are objectives-based curriculum materials which are *imposed* on schools. These have an *external* locus of control. An example that can be cited are the direct instruction materials of Engelmann and Carnine (1982). These materials have been developed and written outside of schools and require teachers to follow scripts and to use particular teaching methods. Although often highly successful, in general terms the materials are frequently rejected by schools and their authorities, partly because of their perceived tendency to deskill teachers, but partly too because education authorities may lose control over a traditionally important input into curriculum content.

At the other end of the continuum are objectives-based models that are derived by the school and thus have an *internal* locus of control. In contrast to the imposed systems, curricula developed in this way are 'owned' by the school and the teachers in it and the content reflects the local culture. But perhaps the crucial issue is that because the teachers have developed the materials themselves they have a unique insight and understanding of their working and can modify them in the light of experience – a process which is reflected in the model presented in Figure 2.1 and which is a fundamental tenet of Vygotsky's activity theory.

It is worth re-emphasizing that curriculum development work of this sort that requires detailed understanding of the ways in which different pupils structure material as they learn, and to which teachers must be especially sensitive, as in the case of those with special educational needs, cannot be cut short by the purchase of curriculum packages. Teachers must go through the process themselves and to this extent they *do have to* reinvent the wheel.

Thus from a Vygotskian perspective it seems reasonable to propose that what is emerging through the development of written objectives and records of pupil progress is a language system of the teaching-learning-content triad which can act as a tool or a sign for the discussion of development and change. Again to refer to Davydov and Zinchenko's chapter, they quote Vygotsky: 'A sign exists outside the organism like a tool, and is separated from the individual; it is essentially a social organ or a social device' (this volume, p. 103).

Furthermore a sign is a means of communicating between people: 'Any sign, in terms of its real origin is a means of communication; and we may even say, further, that it is a means of communication of specific mental functions of a social nature' (Vygotsky, quoted in Davydov and Zinchenko, this volume, p. 103).

In fact Vygotsky was not alone in proposing the idea that external signs could function as tools for purposes of communication. G.H. Mead (1934) made a similar suggestion within the context of symbolic interactionism. Working from this perspective Evans (1988) has suggested that statements of written objectives may be likened to 'artifacts' of a culture. That is to say they reflect the 'producer's' understanding of the process and are open to refinement as that understanding develops with use.

In both the Vygotskian and Meadian approaches described above, objectives that are derived through action research by the teachers themselves from the process of teaching and discussion have special functions. One of them is to enhance communication between teachers and pupils, but they also serve to provide a sound basis for communication between teachers and teachers and teachers and others. In this way they serve as tools for learning for pupils, teachers and third parties.

I have pointed out above that special schools in the UK represent particularly interesting educational micro-cultures that have developed independently, very often in isolation, with very different philosophical traditions both from each other and mainstream schools. If these different traditions and practices are important, as Vygotsky would argue, then different school cultures would be expected to exert different impacts on the pupil. This hypothesis was tested by Daniels (1988) with MLD special schools. Working within the framework determined by Bernstein (e.g. Bernstein 1977) he demonstrated that different MLD special school organizations and teaching methods were associated with different descriptions by the pupils of everyday visual materials such as pictures of space rockets or the countryside.

Thus there is some evidence that different school cultures do have a differential impact on the cognitions of the pupils. For this reason close consideration needs to be given to the organization and operational methods of such schools to help to prevent the development of idiosyncratic learning structures which could prove incompatible with those of the mainstream culture and thus inhibit successful transition and integration at the end of the school period.

INTEGRATION OF THE DISABLED INTO THE MAINSTREAM

The history of special education has stemmed from an intellectual tradition in which children with disabilities were essentially seen as different from those without. In most countries of the world with advanced education provision this 'disease' orientation has led to the formation of special school provision. As has been indicated, the view of children with disabilities as being somehow different from the others is one with which, at least from the point of view of learning and education, Vygotsky profoundly disagreed, since he emphasized similarity and a continuum in development.

In current times this conceptualization is seen most strongly in the integration movement which has become the dominant issue in special education since, in most societies, people with disabilities do not have the same chances as the non-disabled in a wide range of aspects relating to normal life such as in education, where they are often segregated, or in work, where they suffer a higher incidence of unemployment. In spite of much research which attempts to demonstrate preferences for integrated or non-integrated settings across a range of variables such as academic progress or social acceptance, there is really no theoretical model on which to pin the data or really much idea about how mainstream schools could go about developing their structures in order to teach the whole range of pupil ability.

If schools are viewed as micro-cultures (House 1981), which is the stance that has been adopted in this chapter, then it is clear that Vygotsky's theories that emphasize the importance of culturally organized human activities should be in a position to make a contribution to the integration debate. Shotter (1989) has pointed out that within the Vygotskian position the most important emphasis is not:

> knowledge in forms of inner representations of things or states of affairs . . . but instead it is a knowledge of the different ways (and means) in which we might organise and relate ourselves to our circumstances. In other words what children have to learn

is not first about the things in their world and what to do with them, but how *to be* speakers and listeners of a particular kind, how to be observers, rememberers and imaginers, requesters, storytellers, commanders, obeyers etc. and how to be those in ways that makes sense to others.

(Shotter 1989: 189)

One of the obvious implications of this position is that the forms of communication that are used to teach and interest children are of paramount importance (Wertsch 1990) and if this is the case and, given the segregation and even isolation that exists within the special school system where children's social and educational experiences are far from 'normal', it is likely that children brought up in special schools will develop a culturally different way of thinking than those in the mainstream schools where methods and curriculum are more homogeneous.

In recent years, as indicated above, there has been in many forms of special education a particular interest in the use of powerful instructional methods derived from behaviour modification principles in order to teach skills of various kinds. Whatever the virtues of these approaches, and there are many, one of the problems that they present is the provision of education through a form of experience including communicative style which is substantially different from that which most children would receive in the mainstream school. From a Vygotskian perspective these children would be acquiring a different consciousness based in a different socio-history from those children in mainstream schools and this of itself could prevent later integration of these schools' alumni. However speculative this proposition may be, the fact is that the question of the balance between improved skills and what is an essential affinity for others through shared experience is not one which is currently given much air-time.

Of course the same argument applies to children brought up in the ordinary school system who have little interaction with the disabled and are therefore prevented from building this experience into their consciousness.

Perhaps the most vivid example of these processes at work is with the case of deaf people who have received a segregated education for many centuries. They have developed sign languages as a means of communication which are, of course, opaque to most non-deaf citizens. In recent years the deaf in some countries have rejected integration feeling instead that their interests are best served by maintaining their own culture.

CONCLUSIONS

This chapter has discussed the significance of aspects of Vygotsky's theory for some current issues in special education. It has pointed to the important role that school systems may play in developing teacher understanding of the learning difficulties faced by children so that adaptations to the content of both curriculum and pedagogy can be made in the light of pupils' particular needs.

The key issue here is how the teacher can acquire the necessary knowledge of the subject area in a flexible enough form to be able to transfer to the pupil culturally acceptable structures of knowledge using reasonably homogeneous teaching methods.

Thus what does seem to matter within a culture is that children receive similar knowledge bases and methods of teaching so that they can be part of that society, accepted and active contributors. The implementation of this view would of necessity involve the integration of disabled pupils into the mainstream of schools and life.

The attraction of Vygotsky's theory lies in the fact that it addresses constructively the educational problems posed by children with special needs by looking for solutions within the systems that support the child. This is, of course, a very up to date perspective and that of itself makes the theory of interest. But as I have tried to show, Vygotskian theory goes beyond this by providing mechanisms through which the dynamics of educational systems can be better understood.

Although a great deal of work needs to be carried out to establish the limitations of the theory there can be no doubting its heuristic value. In the area of special education there are few other serious challengers.

REFERENCES

Ainscow, M. and Tweddle, D. (1979) *Preventing Classroom Failure*, Chichester, Wiley.

Belmont, J. M. (1989) 'Cognitive strategies and strategic learning; the socio-instructional approach', *American Psychologist* 44, 142–8.

Bernstein, B. (1977) *Class, Codes and Control (Vol. 3) Towards a Theory of Educational Transmissions*, 2nd revised edn, London, Routledge & Kegan Paul.

Daniels, H. (1988) 'An enquiry into different forms of special school organization, pedagogic practice and pupil discrimination', *Collected Original Resources in Education* 12 (2).

Davydov, V. D. and Zinchenko, V. P. (1992) 'Vygotsky's contribution to the development of psychology', in H. Daniels (ed.) *Charting the Agenda: Educational Activity After Vygotsky*, London, Routledge.

Education Act (1981) London, HMSO.

Engelmann, S. and Carnine, D. W. (1982) *Theory of Instruction Principles and Practice*, New York, Irvington.

Evans, P. (1986) 'The learning process', in J. Coupe and J. Porter (eds) *The Education of Children with Severe Learning Difficulties*, Beckenham, Croom Helm.

Evans, P. (1988) 'Towards a social psychology of special education', DECP conference proceedings, Leicester, BPS.

Evans, P. L. C., Ireson, J., Redmond, P. and Wedell, K. (1987) *Curriculum Research for Pupils with Moderate Learning Difficulties*, DES Project Report No. MLD (87) 2, London, DES.

Gulliford, R. (1971) *Special Educational Needs*, London, Routledge & Kegan Paul.

House, E. R. (1981) 'Three perspectives on innovations: technological, political, and cultural', in R. Lehming and M. Kane (eds) *Improving Schools – Using What We Know*, London, Sage.

Ireson, J., Evans, P., Redmond, P. and Wedell, K. (1989) 'Developing the curriculum for children with learning difficulties: towards a grounded model', *British Educational Research Journal* 15, 141–54.

Mead, G. H. (1934) *Mind, Self, and Society: From the Standpoint of a Social Behaviourist*, edited and with an introduction by C. W. Morris, Chicago, University of Chicago Press.

Miles, M. B. and Huberman, A. M. (1984) *Qualitative Data Analysis: A Sourcebook of New Methods*, London, Sage.

Pavlov, I. P. (1927) *Conditioned Reflexes*, Oxford, Oxford University Press.

Pearson, L. and Lindsay, G. (1986) *Special Needs in the Primary School: Identification and Intervention*, Windsor, NFER-Nelson.

Redmond, P., Evans, P., Ireson, J. and Wedell, K. (1988) 'Comparing the curriculum development process in special (MLD) schools: a systematic qualitative approach', *European Journal of Special Needs Education* 3, 147–60.

Robertshaw, M. (1990) 'The role of a special school in the amelioration of mental handicap', in P. L. C. Evans and A. D. B. Clarke (eds) *Combatting Mental Handicap: A Multidisciplinary Approach*, Bicester, AB Academic Publishers.

Shotter, J. (1989) 'Vygotsky's psychology: joint activity in a developmental zone', *New Issues in Psychology* 7, 185–204.

Skilbeck, M. (1984) *School-based Curriculum Development*, London, Harper & Row.

Warnock Report (1978) *Special Educational Needs*, Cmnd 7212, London, HMSO.

Wedell, K. (1980) 'Early identification and compensatory interaction', in R. M. Knights and D. J. Baker (eds) *Treatment of Hyperactive and Learning Disordered Children*, Baltimore, University Park Press.

Wertsch, J. V. (1990) 'A meeting of paradigms: Vygotsky and psychoanalysis', *Contemporary Psychoanalysis* 26, 53–73.

Chapter 3

The individual and the organization

Harry Daniels

INTRODUCTION

The last two years of Vygotsky's life were marked by the increasing emphasis in his writing on the analysis of the development of psychological systems in connection with the development of social behaviour. Minick (1987) traced the progression of Vygotsky's thinking through three phases and argued that in contrast to his earlier work, his writing in the period 1933–4 insisted that the analysis of the development of word meaning should begin with the analysis of the function of the word in communication. Here was the connection between the analysis of social and psychological systems. The intended analysis proceeds from that of specific forms of social practice through an analysis of the function of the word in mediating specific types of social interaction and communication, to an understanding of the development of the word.

The purpose of this chapter is to suggest that a general theory of cultural transmission is required if the goals set in the final phase of Vygotsky's writing are to be realized. Vygotsky provided an account of cultural transmission which articulates a concern for the interactional level but remains silent at the institutional/organizational level. One direction for the development of Vygotsky's work is to propose a form of analysis of the units of cultural transmission at the institutional/organizational level which subsumes an interactional account of the process of internalization for the individual. The framework used to explore this issue will be that of a consideration of the limitations of some of the original studies and the position that the work has come to occupy within psychological theory, followed by an examination of the conceptual compatibility of the model of cultural transmission developed by Basil Bernstein (1977). The bringing together of work within semiotics, new Vygotskian psychology and symbolic interactionist and structuralist sociology for the sake of the development of an overall theoretical perspective which articulates the process of the internalization of social/cultural factors mediated by sign systems is both theoretically exciting and of direct practical utility (Daniels 1989). An example of empirical work conducted within the proposed framework will be used to discuss possibilities for future developments of the original thesis.

METHODOLOGY

Both Wertsch (1985a) and Kozulin (1990) discuss the significance of Vygotsky's writings in terms of methodology. Their view is that Vygotsky's study of the general theoretical and metatheoretical issues that underlie any investigation of psychological phenomena constitutes his major contribution (Wertsch 1985a). This contribution remains remarkable particularly as it was made so far in advance of its time. Consequently it is of great importance to distinguish between the general framework and the practical implementation of his ideas and also to allow for changes in the methodological basis of his writing.

Minick has made a major contribution to our understanding of Vygotsky's writing through his translation of a complete version of *Thinking and Speech* (in Rieber and Carton 1987). As Kozulin (1990) points out, this widely cited text does not represent a coherent view of Vygotsky's ideas. The book, although published in 1934, is not entirely representative of the final stages of Vygotsky's work. Indeed some of the writing incorporated into this volume is drawn from the mid-1920s phase of his studies. It is, therefore, not an easy book to read. As Minick (1985) has shown, the stages of development of the work reflect shifts in priority and conceptual development. A compilation of Vygotsky's writing such as this requires a reading which is sensitive to the developments which are represented by the various chapters of the book.

Davydov and Radzikhovskii (1985) argue that basic to Vygotsky's methodology or metatheory is the insistence that psychological theory must involve the elucidation of the 'explanatory principle', the object of study (or analytic unit) and the dynamics of the relations between these two. Minick's (1985) analysis of three phases of Vygotsky's work enable a reader to gain a perspective on the development of Vygotsky's methodological writings. The first transition was from a focus on an analytic unit called the instrumental act in 1925–30, to an analytic unit of the psychological system in 1930. This was followed in 1933–4 by a refinement of the explanatory principle which became the differentiation and development of systems of interaction and action in which the individual participates (Minick, 1987). This final phase has remained obscure until very recently. It is evidenced in papers and lectures written in the last two years of his life. These sources are often difficult to obtain and remain elusive as his work was often left in the form of sketches rather than fully fledged arguments (Vygotsky 1983). This final phase of Vygotsky's work suggests the need to move towards a broad analysis of behaviour and consciousness which articulates and clarifies the social, cultural and historical basis of development.

ACTIVITY THEORY AND SEMIOTIC MEDIATION

Kozulin (1986) provides an illuminating discussion of the social history of Vygotsky's psychology. Starting with Vygotsky's suggestion that socially meaningful activity should serve as explanatory principle in regard to consciousness he proceeds to examine the way in which the concept of activity has been transformed during the period 1930 to 1970, the core of his argument being that the Kharkov group of psychologists, led by Leontiev, developed what became known as 'activity theory' as a response to immediate political circumstances. In a context in which the analysis of subjectivity was, to say the least, considered problematic, activity theory promoted the analysis of practical actions, and ignored, or at least tempered and restricted, the analysis of semiotic mediation. The concept of consciousness had a struggle to survive in the atmosphere of Soviet psychology, dominated as it was in the early part of the century by the reflexology of Bekhterev and the work of Pavlov. The work of Leontiev, undertaken in Kharkov in the years following Vygotsky's death, is seen by Minick (1985) to differentiate from the earlier thesis in two ways. First, Leontiev attempted to carry the analysis beyond the face-to-face social interactional level to a more macrosociological level. Second, he extended the analysis beyond word meaning itself and proposed a more general thesis which related individual functioning to the object world through a theory of activity. The gradual drift away from the analysis of semiotic mediation in Soviet psychology in the period 1935–9 was witnessed by claims that the structure of cognitive processes mirrored the structure of external activity and operations. The emphasis of the analysis became that of the mediation of reality to the individual by practical activity rather than semiotic means. Writers such as Leontiev thus insisted that it was practical action which should predominate in psychological analysis. In doing so, as Kozulin (1986) suggests, they fell foul of one of Vygotsky's own methodological cautions. The activity theorists were trying to explain activity through the analysis of activity.

> The concept of sign creates one of the interesting paths of activity . . . The fact that studies of the sign-mediated nature of mental functions have not developed further in the activity oriented approach can be considered a weakness that can be overcome in the near future.
>
> (Kozulin 1986: 266)

He expressed the hope that the 1980s would witness a renaissance of Vygotsky's work in which developments in activity theory were reconnected with the original methodological base. This influence has only recently been expressed in Soviet writing. Bozhovich argues a remarkably semiotic view of mediation far in advance of many of her Soviet contemporaries.

> Central to Vygotsky's concept was the notion that new, systematic structures are formed during the process of individual development. These new structures are the outcome of the subject's having *assimilated* the products of human culture.
>
> (Bozhovich 1977: 5)

The events of the last few years have allowed these issues to be discussed much more fully (see Davydov 1991).

When considering the social/cultural origins of higher mental functions it is also of importance to distinguish between the methods advocated by Vygotsky and those he actually used. A problem associated with the implementation of the methodology was with respect to the nature of the theory that describes or accounts for social factors.

SOCIO-INSTITUTIONAL FACTORS

In attempting to provide a non-reductionist account of social processes in the development of mental functions Vygotsky developed the notion of social processes being mediated by psychological tools and then internalized. A crucial point in relation to this chapter is with respect to the operational definition and description of social and cultural factors. Vygotsky provides an account of the social origins of higher mental processes with his general genetic law of cultural development.

> Any function in the child's cultural development appears twice, or on two planes. First it appears on the social plane, and then on the psychological plane. First it appears between people as an interpsychological category, and then within the child as an intrapsychological category. This is equally true with regard to voluntary attention, logical memory, the formation of concepts, and the development of volition. We may consider this position as a law in the full sense of the word, but it goes without saying that internalization transforms the process itself and changes its structure and functions. Social relations or relations among people genetically underlie all higher functions and their relationships.
>
> (Quoted in Wertsch 1990: 56)

Vygotsky also emphasizes the importance of this account for empirical study.

> We shall place this transition from a social influence outside the individual to a social influence within the individual at the centre of our research and try to elucidate the most important moments from which it arises.
>
> (Vygotsky 1978: 116)

It is important to note here that Vygotsky at one time acknowledged the operation of societal or social institutional forces and yet, as Wertsch (1985a) shows, did not fully develop a place for them in his empirical work. 'Vygotsky said very little about the principles that deal with social institutional phenomena' (Wertsch 1985a: 60).

Minick (1985) identified three ways of relating social and cultural factors with psychological development. He termed them 'isolating, contextual and activity oriented' approaches. His purpose was to consider the way in which psychological processes were conceptualized and related to the external object world. In what he terms isolating approaches there is a conceptual boundary between the individual and the object world. Contextual approaches are those which, whilst avoiding conceptual isolation of the individual and object world, fail to include an analysis of activity. Only in what he terms activity oriented approaches are conceptual isolations between individual, objective world and activity avoided. In this extension of activity theory Minick (1985) attempts to locate the analysis of the development of mental functions in activities within the social world. In proposing this form of theoretical development, Minick recognizes that many attempts which make a claim to this position continue to acknowledge the role of semiotic mediation.

SYMBOLIC INTERACTIONISM AND SOCIAL CONTEXTS

Just as Mead (1934) concentrated on social factors in face-to-face social interaction, Vygotsky tended to ignore wider societal or social institutional principles in his experimental investigations. As Bruner (1984) noted, both Vygotsky and Mead studied social processes in small group interaction in terms of interpersonal dynamics and communication. Holzman-Hood (1985) agrees that at a superficial level there are many individual quotes that may be drawn from the writings of Mead and Vygotsky that appear to signify a more general level of concordance. However she argues that beyond a surface level of analysis lie significant conceptual differences. She positions Mead as a social behaviourist, an act which is not uncontroversial, and Vygotsky as a dialectical materialist.

> For Mead, the process of communication, of interpersonal interaction, is what social activity is all about . . . For Vygotsky, social does not mean interpersonal; social interaction is not what the child has to learn. The activities of human behaviour, at all stages of development and organization, are social products and must be seen as historical developments.
>
> (Holzman-Hood 1985: 357)

She proceeds to discuss the 'misreading' of the Soviet concept of activity with the Meadian concept of action. Again the analysis proceeds from questions concerning the position of the term 'social' within historical and cultural frameworks. Wertsch and Lee (1984) argue that many of the psychological accounts which attempt to discuss factors beyond the individual level of analysis 'tend to equate the social with the intersubjective'. Vygotsky offers a dynamic and wide-ranging model that explains the process of internalization of semiotically mediated social forces.

The problem of the creation of context in problem-solving situations has been formulated in many ways, for example in Bruner (1975) through the creation of intersubjectivity, or Nelson (1981) through the use of scripts which are tied to activities. In the small scale, the way in which adults 'scaffold' the child's extension of current skills and knowledge to a higher level of competence has been explored and explained using this framework (see Wood, Bruner and Ross 1976; Wood, Wood and Middleton 1978; Wood 1980; Rogoff and Gardner 1984). Revealing as these studies are, they are still liable to Wertsch's criticism of their lack of account of social institutional factors. Significant exceptions are to be found in Estonia (Minick 1985; Valsiner 1988). Tulviste and his colleagues (Tulviste 1978; Tamm and Tulviste 1980) have conducted research on the relationship between schooling and the development of certain types of reasoning skills. Of critical importance here is the understanding of the relation between the social conditions of learning and development. The view of Vygotsky's analysis presented by Tulviste on the organization of learning, is that adults are creating the possibilities for stages of development rather than that the possibilities are being defined within the biology of the child.

Clearly there are many unresolved issues in the extension of Vygotsky's ideas. The most important issue in this chapter is that of accounting for social institutional factors. Minick suggests that a way forward may be found through an attempt 'to identify the general principles through which socio-cultural factors influence the individual's psychological development' (Minick 1985: 53).

LANGUAGE AND SOCIAL DIALOGUES

In a way that parallels some of Vygotsky's notions, the focus on language as the vehicle of interaction and self concept as an antecedent to interaction provides symbolic interactionism with an understanding of the links between individual psychology and social structure. Similarly, for those employing phenomenological methods language assumes a position of prominence.

In their development and domestication of the phenomenological perspective Berger and Luckmann (1967) stress how linguistic categories embody and crystallize the sedimented experiences of shared cultural resources. Language is thus, par excellence, the medium of the social construction of reality.

(Atkinson 1985: 57)

Vygotsky was convinced that verbally mediated collaborative social action provides the foundation for the development of what he called 'conscious awareness' of word meanings and their relationships. He also argued that this conscious awareness of word meanings provides the foundation for new forms of thinking. For Vygotsky, speech was an important psychological tool, which was at one time a social and cultural element but also served to mediate social processes in the process of internalization. Such psychological tools not only function externally/socially, they mediate or regulate *internally* the action of mental processes.

Vygotsky distanced himself from the suggestion that the social context of development was simply the objective environment. As has been sketched so far, Vygotsky was concerned to use a genetic/developmental analysis to understand how higher mental functions are mediated, internalized results of social interaction.

Wertsch (1985a) summarizes the four major points that are the foundation of Vygotsky's account of internalization.

1 Internalization is not a process of copying external reality on a pre-existing internal plane rather it is a process wherein an internal plane of consciousness is formed.
2 The external reality at issue is a social interactional one.
3 The specific mechanism at issue is the mastery of external sign forms.
4 The internal plane of consciousness takes on a 'quasisocial' nature because of its origins.

(Wertsch 1985a: 66–7)

Here it is impossible to reduce an explanation of social processes to principles that apply to individual psychological phenomena or to explain individual psychological phenomena as direct, internalized copies of social interactional processes. There are dialectical relations between social and individual levels which allow for levels of explanation without direct reduction of one to another. The active social positioning of the child within a particular practice was seen as part of the process of the construction of the context. Shotter (1989) discusses Vygotsky's concern with 'What happens in a zone at the boundaries between people's activities and the activities of others in their surroundings.'

> This talk of boundaries and their fluid nature in Vygotsky's psychology emphasises . . . How people respond to those around them and make for themselves in their transactions, by the boundaries they establish an 'organised setting' or situation, into which they must direct their future activity.
>
> (Shotter 1989: 192)

Shotter also discusses the tensions within social psychology between approaches which involve the analysis of the effects of environmental change and those which study individual creativity. He makes a plea for a 'two way flow' psychology.

> A prosthetic *outflow* of activity from people toward their already partially structured surroundings in which they can 'give' or 'lend' them further structure . . . and an *inflow* of activity in the other direction back from an already partially structured environment into the people within it, one that they must interpret hermeneutically to grasp the nature of the situation within which their current activity is 'grounded' and the relations between these two processes.
>
> (Shotter 1989: 190)

Even apparently the most individual and autonomous actions are situated in a context which must itself be viewed as an active participant in the structuring of their activities. Wertsch (1985a) sketches the evolution of Vygotsky's early view of psychological tools into a semiotically oriented account 'placing greater and greater emphasis on the meaningful and communicative nature of signs'. Bruner (1984) claims that this process was influenced by Vygotsky's association with linguists and literary intellectuals such as Bahktin, Jakobson and Voloshinov. In attempting to move the development of the unit of analysis in neo-Vygotskian psychology forward, Radzikhovskii (1987) is one of many Soviet writers who have recently revived the discussion of the contribution made by M. M. Bakhtin.

Vygotsky and Bakhtin were contemporaries who, although they probably never met, developed concepts and arguments within which a high degree of compatibility is to be found. Interestingly their work, as Kozulin (1990) notes, has also undergone similar periods of obscurity and rediscovery. As would seem fitting, indeed necessary, within their respective theoretical positions their own work has been recreated and transformed within a variety of social settings.

> There are, it should be pointed out, many Bakhtins; there is Bakhtin the revolutionary, Bakhtin the Marxist, Bakhtin the anti-Stalinist, Bahktin the populist and Bahktin the crypto-Christian. There is a left reading of Bahktin (Fedric Jameson, Terry Eagleton, Tony Bennett, Ken Hirschkop) and a liberal reading (Wayne Booth, Michael Holquist, Katerina Clark, Gary Saul Morson). The last few years have witnessed, in fact a kind of posthumous wrestle over the political soul of Bakhtin. As an extraordinarily complex, contradictory and at times enigmatic figure, Bakhtin has been open to appropriation by the most diverse ideological currents.
>
> (Stam 1988: 116–17)

There are distinct parallels here between Vygotsky's thinking and the dialectical philosophy of Voloshinov (1973) for whom experience, consciousness and individuality are only possible through the medium of the sign which itself 'emerges only in the process of interaction between one individual consciousness and another . . . the sign and its social situation are inextricably fused' so that 'consciousness becomes consciousness only in the process of interaction' (Voloshinov 1973: 11, 37, 48).

This body of writing on the multi-layered social dialogues inherent in social interaction may be seen as influential on the development of Vygotsky's ideas, in his attempt to create a system of analysis of the process of internalization of mediated social and cultural actions. As noted above, there has been a conspicuous dearth of analysis in this framework which accounts for anything but the immediate social circumstances of a working dyad or triad. The problem that remains is as to the nature of a model for articulating situation definitions. What distinguishes one form of activity or discourse from another and how are these differences to be described and their consequences for individuals investigated?

Wertsch *et al.* (1984) showed how differential experience with various activity settings resulted in dissimilar interpretations of an experimental situation. Hundeide (1985) has shown, in a study of the tacit background of children's judgments, how participants in an activity, in part, create the setting. These 'taken for granted background expectancies' reflect in part the sociocultural experience that the individual brings to the situation.

> one needs a framework that takes into account the historical and cultural basis of individual minds: the collective institutionalized knowledge and routines, categorization of reality with its typifications, world view, normative expectations as to how people, situations, and the world are and should be, and so forth. All this is tacit knowledge that has its origin beyond the individual, and it is this sociocultural basis that forms the interpretive background of our individual minds.
>
> (Hundeide 1985: 311)

There is a certain gentle irony here in that this statement reflects the point of departure of much sociological work. Shibutani (1962) offered a comment that serves as a useful point of departure for the next section.

> The failure to make the connection between Meadian social psychology and the sociology of knowledge on the part of the symbolic interactionists is of course related to the limited diffusion of the sociology of knowledge in America, but its more important theoretical foundation is to be sought in the fact that both Mead himself and his later followers did not develop an adequate concept of social structure. Precisely for this reason, we think, is the integration of the Meadian and Durkheimian approaches so very important.
>
> (Shibutani 1962: 213)

SOCIAL THEORY

Valsiner (1988) positions Vygotsky's work within a framework of European intellectual influence, drawing heavily on French and German psychology and philosophy. As with so many aspects of Vygotsky's work the interpretation of the basis of his work is a matter of controversy. On the one hand, Valsiner argues that

Vygotsky drew on the philosophical writings of Marx in a reflective and carefully considered manner.

> Vygotsky's acceptance of Marxist philosophy was not that of
> an ardent follower. Instead he was an active creator of Marxist
> psychology. This can be observed in his rare but appropriate
> use of Marxist philosophy. The demagogical use of Marxist
> worded slogans in trying to solve issues facing Soviet psy-
> chology was conspicuously absent from Vygotsky's writings.
>
> (Valsiner 1988: 125)

On the other hand, Kozulin (1990) suggests that the wider theoretical context of Vygotsky's work is dominated by two issues,
the first being mediation, which Kozulin relates to a Hegelian
philosophical base, and the second being the social nature of
human cognition, a notion which Kozulin relates to the work of
Durkheim. Kozulin (1990) argues that Vygotsky turned to the
French sociological school led by Durkheim rather than to Marx
for a social theory of human cognition. The analysis of the role
and function of collective representations formed the focus of this
discussion. In a recent interview Davydov (1991) argued that
whilst Vygotsky's interpretation of social determinism draws
heavily on Marx, it is enriched by writers within the French
sociological school. Davydov's suggestion is that a complete view
of Vygotsky's social vision must be informed by both German
and French sources.

BERNSTEIN'S THEORY OF CULTURAL TRANSMISSION

It is clear from reviews by Atkinson (1985), Moore (1984), Diaz
(1984) and Tyler (1983, 1984) and the work of Bernstein himself
that he directly addresses the issues of concern in this chapter.

> Essentially and briefly I have used Durkheim and Marx at the
> macro level and Mead at the micro level, to realize a socio-
> linguistic thesis which could meet with a range of work in
> anthropology, linguistics, sociology and psychology.
>
> (Bernstein 1972: 160)

Bernstein's thinking was influenced profoundly by his acquaint-
ance with the various philosophical and anthropological authors

on language and symbolism – including Cassirer and Whorf. To this was added the work of the Russian psychologists Vygotsky and Luria.

(Atkinson 1985: 14)

Whilst it appears, as Atkinson (1985) notes, that Bernstein epitomizes an essentially macrosociological point of view, 'It is undoubtedly true that in Bernstein's general approach there is little or no concern for the perspectives, strategy and actions of individual social actors in actual social settings' (Atkinson 1985: 32). On the one hand Durkheim's notion of collective representation allowed for the social interpretation of human cognition, on the other it failed to resolve the issue as to how the collective representation is interpreted by the individual. This is the domain so appropriately filled by the later writings of Vygotsky. The fact that Bernstein has utilized Mead and Vygotsky in the formulation of his model allows for the exploration of interpersonal relations at the face-to-face level in the classroom. Many of the symbolic interactionist and Vygotskian inspired insights noted above can be subsumed into his model, which affords the wider social dimension a central place in a general thesis. The implications of the macrosociological, social psychological and psychological studies of times will require reformulation in the light of this extended social perspective. In that wider social institutional factors will have been reduced to lower levels of explanation, there is the potential within such studies for the distortion of results. In the same way psychological studies of learning which ignored contextual constraints confounded and confused interpretation of results.

A consideration with respect to Bernstein's relation to structuralist theory is raised by Atkinson:

Given the structuralist character of his thought, it is perhaps odd that in the development (under-developed though it is) of the psychological analogues of the sociology, Bernstein explicitly acknowledges no great debt to Piaget; this despite the fact that Piaget's project is itself structuralist.

(Atkinson 1985: 59)

It is certainly true that Piaget was structuralist; however, it is doubtful whether his work can be seen as a 'psychological analogue' of Bernstein's sociology. It is argued here that the work of

Vygotsky and his followers provides the psychological analogue required rather than Piaget's version of structuralist psychology. The subject is constituted, in Piaget's structuralism, through the construction of knowledge, logical structures or operations, rather than as in Bernstein's thesis through social relations. It is argued here that Vygotsky's approach lacks that which Bernstein explicitly has set out to provide – a theoretical framework for the description and analysis of the changing forms of cultural transmissions: 'I wanted to develop a different approach which placed at the centre of the analysis the principles of transmission and their embodiment in structures of social relationships' (Bernstein 1977: 3).

BERNSTEIN'S SOCIOLOGY OF THE SCHOOL

Bernstein's work on the school shows his continuous engagement with the interrelations between changes in organizational form, changes in modes of control and changes in principles of communication. Essentially (if embryonically) the analysis of the early papers focuses upon two levels: a structural level and an interactional level. The structural level is analysed in terms of the social division of labour it creates and the interactional level with the form of social relation it creates. The social division of labour is analysed in terms of strength of the boundary of its divisions, that is, with respect to the degree of specialization. Thus within a school the social division of labour is complex where there is an array of specialized subjects, teachers and pupils, and it is relatively simple where there is a reduction in the specialization of teachers, pupils and subjects. Thus the key concept at the structural level is the concept of boundary, and structures are distinguished in terms of their boundary arrangements and their power supports and legitimations (Bernstein 1991).

The interactional level emerges as the regulation of the transmission/acquisition relation between teacher and taught: that is, the interactional level comes to refer to the pedagogic context and the social relations of the classroom or its equivalent. The interactional level then gives the principle of the learning context through which the social division of labour, in Bernstein's terms, speaks. The solution to linking the structural and interactional levels in such a way that these levels *up to a point* are in relation of free variation, was to distinguish in the school three message systems: curriculum, pedagogy (practice) and evaluation. Curriculum referred to what counted as legitimate knowledge and the latter was a function of the organization of subjects (fields), modules or other basic units to be acquired; pedagogy (practice) referred to the local pedagogic context of teacher and taught and regulated what counted as a legitimated transmission of the knowledge; evaluation referred to what counted as a valid realization of the knowledge on the part of the acquirer.

Evaluation was given no separate analysis (until much later) and it was considered to be dependent on the organization of the curriculum and the form of pedagogic practice. Curriculum was to be analysed not in terms of contents but in terms of relation *between* its categories (subjects and units).

Pedagogic practice again was not to be analysed in terms of its contents but in terms of the control over the selection, sequencing, pacing and criteria of communication in the transmitter/acquirer relation. It is apparent that the curriculum is regarded as an example of a social division of labour and pedagogic practice as its constituent social relations through which the specialization of that social division (subjects, units of the curriculum) are transmitted and expected to be acquired.

Bernstein uses the concept of classification to determine the underlying principle of a social division of labour and the concept of framing to determine the principle of its social relations and in this way to integrate structural and interactional levels of analysis in such a way that, up to a point, both levels may vary independently of each other.

Classification

Classification is defined at the most general level as the relation between categories. The relation between categories is given by their degree of insulation. Thus where there is strong insulation between categories, each category is sharply distinguished, explicitly bounded and having its own distinctive specialization. When there is weak insulation then the categories are less specialized and therefore their distinctiveness is reduced. In the former case, Bernstein speaks of strong classification and in the latter case Bernstein speaks of weak classification.

Framing

The social relations generally, in the analyses, are those between parents/children, teachers/pupils, doctors/patients, social workers/ clients, but the analysis can be extended to include the social relations of the work contexts of industry or commerce. Bernstein considers that from his point of view all these relations can be regarded as pedagogic.

> Framing refers to the control on communicative practices (selection, sequencing, pacing and criteria) in pedagogical relations, be they relations of parents and children or teacher/ pupils. Where framing is strong the transmitter explicitly regulates the distinguishing features of the interactional and locational principle which constitute the communicative context . . . Where framing is weak, the acquirer is accorded more control over the regulation.
>
> Framing regulates what counts as legitimate communication in the pedagogical relation and thus what counts as legitimate practices.
>
> (Bernstein 1981: 345)

In that the model is concerned with principles of regulation of educational transmission at any specified level, it is possible to investigate experimentally the relation between principles of regulation and the practices of pupils. Relations of power create and maintain boundaries between categories and are described in terms of classification. Relations of control revealed in values of framing condition communicative practices. It becomes possible to see how a given distribution of power through its classificatory principle and principles of control through its framing are made substantive in agencies of cultural reproduction, e.g. families/schools. The form of the code (its modality) contains principles for distinguishing between contexts (recognition rules) *and* for the creation and production of specialized communication within contexts (realization rules).

> Through defining educational codes in terms of the relationship between classification and framing, these two components are built into the analysis at *all levels*. It then becomes possible in one framework to derive a typology of educational codes, to show the interrelationships between organizational and knowledge properties to move from macro- to micro-levels of analy-

sis, to relate the patterns internal to educational institutions to the external social antecedents of such patterns, and to consider questions of maintenance and change.

(Bernstein 1977: 112)

The analysis of classification and framing can be applied to different levels of school organization and various units within a level. This allows the analysis of power and control and the rules regulating what counts as legitimate pedagogic competence to proceed at a level of delicacy appropriate to a particular research question.

INSTRUCTIONAL PRACTICES AS SOCIAL CONTEXTS

In the most recent translation of Chapter 6 of *Thinking and Speech* Vygotsky claims a particular function of speech in instruction within schooling.

> The instruction of the child in systems of scientific knowledge in school involves a unique form of communication in which the word assumes a function which is quite different from that characteristic of other forms of communication . . .
> 1) The child learns word meanings in certain forms of school instruction not as a means of communication but as part of a system of knowledge.
> 2) This learning occurs not through direct experience with things or phenomena but through other words.
>
> (in Rieber and Carton 1987: 27)

Participation in specific forms of social practice is linked with the development of word meaning. In order to understand the development of word meaning the characteristics of particular communication practices must be understood. This revealed his emphasis during the 1933–4 period on the analysis of psychological characteristics in connection with social action and culture. 'The incorporation of signs into the structure of a mental function (mediation through signs) links that function to culture' (Davydov and Zinchenko 1989: 33). Davydov and Zinchenko (1989) quote from an as yet untranslated section of Vygotsky's *Psychological Investigations*, published in Moscow in 1956, as part of their assertion that instruction, in the widest sense, constitutes the individual.

If correctly organised education will allow the child to develop intellectually and give birth to a whole series of processes of development that would become impossible without education. Education is thus an internally necessary and universal aspect of the process of development in the child of the historical characteristics of man, not his natural characteristics.

(Davydov and Zinchenko 1989: 76)

Thus, Vygotsky argues that the forms of instruction in scientific concepts of formal schooling (i.e. mathematics, the natural sciences) involve the child in new ways of using words in communication. Vygotsky saw the psychological characteristics of the scientific concept as inseparable from the unique use of words in the social interaction that occurs between teachers and pupils in formal school instruction (Minick 1985: 107). If socio-institutional effects of schooling are to be considered within a Vygotskian framework then one approach is to compare the effects of a different forms of organization of subjects of instruction. This calls for a description and analysis of structures and of effects. Bernstein provides the structural level of analysis and Vygotsky furnishes the theoretical framework which can account for the position of the individual.

EMPIRICAL STUDIES

The major focus of an experimental study conducted within this theoretical orientation was on the relation between school and classroom organization and pupils' ability to realize criteria of communicative competence generated by specific discourses in schools displaying variation in organizational form.

Daniels (1988) tested the relation between different classification and framing values, recognition and realization rules and different specializations of meanings in a study of pupils' discriminations and realizations of science and art texts in schools differing in their organization, pedagogic practice and external relation. It was shown that pupils' discriminations and realizations of such texts were related to the classification and framing values of the school's organization and pedagogic practice.

This study was concerned with the transmission of selected criteria of communicative competence within schools. The intention was to demonstrate how different contexts generate different

criteria of competence and to develop measures of these differences. Schools studied were selected on the basis of the variation
they displayed with respect to a number of organizational features. The organization of subjects in the curriculum, whether
integrated or separate, and the organization of teachers, whether
relatively autonomous or highly controlled within the school,
were the features which aroused the initial interest in these
schools. The implications of the organizational structure of the
school for pupil talk in specified subjects became the focus of the
major empirical investigation. The sample was thus of possible
forms of organization, not of all schools. Subjects entered into
different relations with each other in different schools. The
research question asked whether such subject insulations would
influence the communicative competence of pupils. As it was
degree of insulation *between* school discourses which was coded
in the descriptions of schools, then differences *between* the performances of each child within each discourse was taken as a
valid dependent variable. It was expected that the stronger the
framing of the pedagogic practice, the more likely the pupils
would be to acquire the criteria of competence expected by the
teacher. Clearly this competence may be acquired through many
channels. However, it is clear that one of the main agents of
control is the teacher. Thus teachers were asked to differentiate
between children's statements made within different discourses.
The study produced data that was in accord with the predictions.

In a related study, arrangements through the production, selection and combination of children's painting were shown to act as
a relay of the deep structure of the pedagogic practice of particular
schools. From this perspective schools may be considered as generators of a specialized semiotic. The meaning of these signs for
the participants in the practice of schooling then becomes the
object of study. The study of wall displays indicated that children
from different schools 'saw' different meanings in the same displays. This study took measures of school modality. Although
somewhat crude these were measures of the discursive, organizational and interactional practice. Measures were then taken of
the pupils' recognition and realization rules with respect to visual
relay of aspects of their pedagogic practice. A relationship was
revealed. A connection was made between the rules the children
used to make sense of their pedagogic world and the modality
of that world (Daniels 1989). This study of a non-verbal relay

confirms the general view of the earlier study of verbal discourse (Daniels 1988).

The measures taken in these studies were crude and conclusions must remain tentative. Despite these reservations they do suggest that the social organization of the schooling of children is an issue which demands serious investigation. There is a clear need to develop systems of enquiry that enable and permit the empirical investigation of the implications of placing children in particular school environments. If progress is to be made towards the construction of a system of semiotic analysis of schooling that understands individual learning within activities that are organized acts of cultural transmission then at least two levels of development are required. At a theoretical level there is a need to refine and develop models of socio-institutional organization in such a way that allows for the empirical investigation of individual positioning. Similarly social models of learning require balanced accounts of the effects of the semiotic mediation of the organization of activity.

There is much to be done.

REFERENCES

Atkinson, P. (1985) *Structure and Reproduction: An Introduction to the Sociology of Basil Bernstein*, London, Methuen.

Berger, P. L. and Luckman, T. (1971) *The Social Construction of Reality*, Harmondsworth, Penguin.

Bernstein, B. (1972) 'Social class, language and socialization', in P. P. Giglioli (ed.) *Language and Social Context*, Harmondsworth, Penguin.

Bernstein, B. (1977) *Class, Codes and Control Volume 3, Towards a Theory of Educational Transmissions*, 2nd revised edn, London, Routledge & Kegan Paul.

Bernstein, B. (1981) 'Codes, modalities and the process of cultural reproduction: a model', *Language in Society* 10, 327–63.

Bernstein, B. (1991) Personal communication.

Bozhovich, L. I. (1977) 'The concept of cultural historical development of the mind and its prospects', *Soviet Psychology* 16 (1), 5–22.

Bruner, J. (1975) 'The ontogenesis of speech acts', *Journal of Child Language* 2, 1–20.

Bruner, J. (1983) 'Language, mind and reading', in H. Goodman, A. A. Oberg and F. Smith (eds) *Awakening to Literacy*, London, Heinemann.

Bruner, J. (1984) 'Vygotsky's zone of proximal development: the hidden agenda', in B. Rogoff and J. Wertsch (eds) *Learning in the 'Zone of Proximal Development'*, New Directions for Child Development no. 23, San Francisco, Jossey Bass.

Daniels, H. (1988) 'An enquiry into different forms of special school organization, pedagogic practice and pupil discrimination', *Collected Original Resources In Education* 12 (2).

Daniels, H. (1989) 'Visual displays as tacit relays of the structure of pedagogic practice', *British Journal of Sociology of Education* 10 (2), 123–40.

Davydov, V. V. (1991) Interviewed by H. Daniels at the Academy of Pedagogical Sciences, Moscow, March 1991.

Davydov, V. V. and Radzikhovskii, L. A. (1985) 'Vygotsky's theory and the activity oriented approach in psychology', in J. V. Wertsch (ed.) *Culture, Communication and Cognition: Vygotskian Perspectives*, Cambridge, Cambridge University Press.

Davydov, V. D. and Zinchenko, V. P. (1989) 'Vygotsky's contribution to the development of psychology', *Soviet Psychology* 27 (2), 22–36.

Diaz, M. (1984) 'A model of pedagogic discourse with special application to the Columbian primary level of education', unpublished PhD thesis, University of London, Institute of Education.

Holzman-Hood, L. (1985) 'Pragmatism and dialectical materialism in language development', in K. E. Nelson (ed.) *Children's Language*, New Jersey, Lawrence Erlbaum Associates.

Hundeide, K. (1985) 'The tacit background of children's judgments', in J. C. Wertsch, *Vygotsky and the Social Formation of Mind*, Cambridge, MA, Harvard University Press.

Kozulin, A. (1986) 'The concept of activity in Soviet psychology: Vygotsky, his disciples and critics', *American Psychologist* March, 264–74.

Kozulin, A. (1990) *Vygotsky's Psychology: A Biography of Ideas*, London, Harvester Wheatsheaf.

Mead, G. H. (1934) *Mind, Self and Society from the Standpoint of a Social Behaviourist*, Chicago, University of Chicago Press.

Minick, N. J. (1985) 'L. S. Vygotsky and Soviet activity theory: new perspectives on the relationship between mind and society, unpublished PhD thesis, Northwestern University, USA.

Minick, N. (1987) 'The development of Vygotsky's thought: an introduction', in R. W. Rieber and A. S. Carton (eds) *The Collected Works of L. S. Vygotsky Volume 1*, New York, Plenum Press.

Moore, R. (1984) 'Education and production: a generative model', unpublished PhD thesis, University of London.

Nelson, K. (1981) 'Social cognition in a script framework', in J. H. Flavell and L. Ross (1981) *Social Cognitive Development*, Cambridge, Cambridge University Press.

Radzikhovskii, L. A. (1987) 'Activity: structure, genesis, and unit of analysis', *Soviet Psychology* 25 (4).

Rieber, R. W. and Carton, A. S. (eds) (1987) *The Collected Works of L. S. Vygotsky, Volume 1*, New York, Plenum Press (includes *Thinking and Speech*).

Rogoff, B. and Gardner, W. (1984) 'Adult guidance of cognitive development', in B. Rogoff and J. Lave (eds) *Everyday Cognition: Its Development in Social Context*, London, Harvard University Press.

Shibutani, T. (1962) 'Reference groups and social control', in A. Rose (ed.) *Human Behaviour and Social Processes*, London, Routledge & Kegan Paul.

Shotter, J. (1989) 'Vygotsky's psychology: joint activity in a developmental zone', *New Ideas in Psychology* 7 (2), 185–204.

Stam, R. (1988) 'Michael Bakhtin and left cultural critique', in A. E. Kaplan (ed.) *Postmodernism and its Discontents: Theories and Practices*, London, Verso.

Tamm, T. and Tulviste, P. (1980) 'Theoretic syllogistic reasoning – regressing when not used?' *Acta et Commentationes Universitatis Tartuensis* 522, 50–9, Tartu, Tartu University Press.

Tulviste, P. (1978) 'On the origins of theoretic syllogistic reasoning in culture and in the child', *Acta et commentationes universitatis Tartuensis* 474, 3–22, Tartu, Tartu University Press.

Tyler, W. (1983) 'Complexity, and control: the organizational background of credentialism', *British Journal of Sociology of Education* 3 (2).

Tyler, W. (1984) 'Organizations, factors and codes: a methodological enquiry into Bernstein's theory of educational transmissions', unpublished PhD Thesis, University of Kent.

Valsiner, J. (1988) *Developmental Psychology in the Soviet Union*, Brighton, Harvester Press.

Voloshinov, V. N. (1973) *Marxism and the Philosophy of Language*, translated by L. Matejka and I. R. Titunik, New York, Seminar Press.

Vygotsky, L. S. (1978) *Mind in Society: The Development of Higher Psychological Processes*, edited by M. Cole, V. John-Steiner, S. Scribner and E. Souberman, Cambridge, MA, Harvard University Press.

Vygotsky, L. S. (1981) 'The genesis of higher mental functions', in J. V. Wertsch (ed.) *The Concept of Activity in Soviet Psychology*, Armonk, NY, Sharpe.

Vygotsky, L. S. (1983) 'From the notebooks of L. S. Vygotsky', *Soviet Psychology* 21 (3), 3–17.

Wertsch, J. V. (1979) 'From social interaction to higher psychological processes. A clarification and application of Vygotsky's theory', *Human Development* 22, 1–22.

Wertsch, J. V. (ed.) (1981) *The Concept of Activity in Soviet Psychology*, Armonk, NY, M. E. Sharpe.

Wertsch, J. V. (1985a) *Vygotsky and the Social Formation of Mind*, Cambridge, MA, Harvard University Press.

Wertsch, J. V. (ed.) (1985b) *Culture, Communication and Cognition: Vygotskian Perspectives*, Cambridge, Cambridge University Press.

Wertsch, J. V. (1990) 'A meeting of paradigms: Vygotsky and psychoanalysis', *Contemporary Psychoanalysis* 26 (1) 53–73.

Wertsch, J. V. and Lee, B. (1984) 'The multiple levels of analysis in a theory of action', *Human Development* 27, 193–6.

Wertsch, J., Minick, N. and Arns, F. J. (1984) 'The creation of context in joint problem solving', in B. Rogoff and J. Lave, *Everyday Cognition: Its Development in Social Context*, London, Harvard University Press.

Wood, D. J. (1980) 'Models of childhood', in A. J. Chapman and D. M. Jones (eds) *Models of Man*, Leicester, BPS.

Wood, D., Bruner, J. S. and Ross, G. (1976) 'The role of the tutor in problem solving', *Journal of Child Psychology and Psychiatry* 17, 89–100.

Wood, D., Wood, H. and Middleton, H. (1978) 'An experimental evaluation of four face-to-face teaching strategies', *International Journal of Behavioural Development* 1, 131–47.

Chapter 4

Continuing the dialogue
Vygotsky, Bakhtin, and Lotman

James V. Wertsch and Ana Luiza Bustamante Smolka

A fundamental tenet of Vygotsky's approach to human mental functioning is that 'the social dimension of consciousness is primary in time and in fact. The individual dimension of consciousness is derivative and secondary' (1979: 30). This is a claim that underlies Vygotsky's analyses of a range of phenomena such as egocentric and inner speech, concept development and the 'zone of proximal development', yet it is a claim whose full implications have yet to be fully appreciated. Our purpose in this chapter is to explore some of these implications with the ultimate aim of being able to provide some insight into issues of educational activity after Vygotsky.

Vygotsky's claims about the priority of sociality have often been overlooked or distorted. One reason for this is the fundamental difference between the setting in which Vygotsky lived and the setting in which his writings have often been interpreted (especially in the US). In particular, the individualistic assumptions that permeate much of contemporary psychology have shaped our discourse in ways that make it difficult to incorporate the full force of Vygotsky's ideas into existing theoretical discussion. Furthermore, we believe that Vygotsky himself failed to develop some of the implications of his ideas and that these shortcomings can be addressed by invoking ideas from other theorists such as the Soviet semioticians and literary scholars M.M. Bakhtin (1981, 1986; Voloshinov 1973) and Yu.M. Lotman (1988a, 1988b).

Vygotsky's claim that social, or 'inter-mental' functioning gives rise to individual, or 'intra-mental' functioning can be understood as one of three interrelated themes that run throughout his writings (see Wertsch 1985, 1991). The other two are his reliance on a genetic, or developmental method to examine all aspects of human mental functioning, and his claim that human social and psychological processes are fundamentally shaped by the mediational means, especially language, they employ.

As Wertsch (1985, 1991) has noted, Vygotsky's use of a genetic method has much in common with the ideas of other theorists such as Piaget (1923) and Werner (1961; Werner and Kaplan 1963). However, in contrast to the emphasis in much of contemporary developmental psychology, Vygotsky's genetic method did not focus exclusively on ontogenesis. Instead, he viewed our under-standing of developmental processes in this 'genetic domain' (Wertsch 1985) as part of a larger picture that must take into consideration the other genetic domains of phylogenesis, sociocul-tural history and microgenesis (see Vygotsky and Luria 1930).

With regard to the mediational means that shape human mental processes, Vygotsky made increasingly strong claims toward the end of his career (Minick 1987) that an understanding of language and other such tools provide the foundation for the rest of his approach. Under the general heading of mediational means Vyg-otsky paid special attention to 'signs' which are used to organize one's own or others' behaviours. Among the signs and sign sys-tems he mentioned are 'language; various systems for counting; mnemonic techniques; algebraic symbol systems; works of art; writing; schemes, diagrams, maps, and mechanical drawings; all sorts of conventional signs; and so on' (1981a: 137).

An essential aspect of Vygotsky's treatment of mediational means is that their incorporation into human action (including mental action) does not simply make this action easier or more efficient in some quantitative sense. Instead, their incorporation inevitably results in a qualitative transformation. In his view

> by being included in the process of behavior, the psychological tool [sign] alters the entire flow and structure of mental func-tions. It does this by determining the structure of a new instru-mental act, just as a technical tool alters the process of a natural adaptation by determining the form of labor operations.
>
> (Vygotsky 1981a: 137)

The notion of mediational means played such an essential role in Vygotsky's approach that it brings into question some of our basic assumptions about agency. Instead of assuming that agency can be assigned to the isolated individual as is usually the case in psychology, we would argue that Vygotsky's ideas call on us to assign agency to the 'individual-operating-with-mediational-means' (Wertsch 1991; Wertsch *et al.*, in press). Such an approach to agency emphasizes that mediational means always empower as well as restrict human action in specific ways, hence calling into question assumptions grounded in the 'unencumbered image of the self' and 'atomism' (Taylor 1985) that have guided so much of contemporary research in psychology.

Given the theoretical context provided by Vygotsky's themes concerning genetic method and mediational means, his comments about the analytic and genetic priority of the social dimension of consciousness take on new significance. In order to map this out, consider a more concrete formulation of his claim about the social origins of individual mental functioning – his 'general genetic law of cultural development'.

> Any function in the child's cultural development appears twice, or on two planes. First it appears on the social plane, and then on the psychological plane. First it appears between people as an interpsychological category, and then within the child as an intrapsychological category. This is equally true with regard to voluntary attention, logical memory, the formation of concepts, and the development of volition . . . [I]t goes without saying that internalization transforms the process itself and changes its structure and functions. Social relations or relations among people genetically underlie all higher functions and their relationships.
>
> (Vygotsky 1981b: 163)

This statement entails several points that are often not fully appreciated. First, it is significant that Vygotsky formulated his general genetic law of cultural development in terms of how one and the same mental function appears on two planes. His comment about internalization warns against the notion that the intra-mental processes are simple and direct copies of inter-mental processes; the relation is instead one of genetic transformation and the *formation* of an internal plane of consciousness (Wertsch and Stone 1985). However, the functional parallel between inter-mental and intra-mental functioning (a parallel that emerges from using similar mediational means on both planes) is a central tenet in his approach, and it calls into question some basic assumptions in contemporary psychology about the nature of mental processes. Specifically, it points to Vygotsky's assumption that mental processes do not occur solely, or even fundamentally in individuals.

The contrast this provides with assumptions underlying contemporary research in psychology is reflected in the terms we use. In contemporary Western psychology, terms such as 'cognition', 'memory', and 'attention' apply exclusively to processes carried out on the intra-mental plane. The strength of this individualistic assumption is reflected in the fact that investigators have recently felt it necessary to create new labels such as 'socially shared cognition' (Resnick et al. 1991) and 'socially distributed cognition' (Hutchins 1991). 'Socially shared' and 'socially distributed' must be used as modifiers in contemporary discourse because the underlying assumption is that *unless marked to the contrary* terms such as 'cognition' automatically apply to the individual. This is specifically the kind of assumption that Vygotsky was not making in his approach. In his view the line between individual and social functioning as well as the primacy attached to the former in most psychological accounts are not assumptions around which one can organize an adequate account of human mental functioning.

A second aspect of Vygotsky's general genetic law of cultural development that we find worth noting is his statement that 'Social relations or relations among people genetically underlie all higher functions and their relationships' (1981b: 163). In Vygotsky's view, even when mental processes are carried out by the isolated individual they remain a 'quasi-social' (1981b: 164). His use of the term 'inner speech' where we might today speak of 'information processing' or 'cognitive processes' reflects this assertion, and claims by semioticians such as Ivanov (1974) that inner speech is best understood as inner dialogue highlights it even more clearly.

However, several implications of Vygotsky's claims about social relations or relations among people are not well developed in his writings. From the perspective of 'Vygotsky the methodologist' (Davydov and Radzikhovskii 1985) these have to do with issues such as class consciousness and the commodification of the individual – that is, issues raised in the broad philosophical and social theoretic background that framed Vygotsky's writings. In his actual writings Vygotsky wrote primarily from the perspective of 'Vygotsky the psychologist' (Davydov and Radzikhovskii

1985) and focused on issues of concrete social interaction, perhaps involving dyads or other small groups.

The result is that even though Vygotsky's talk of 'social relations' sounds quite similar to phrases employed in the Marxist texts from which he was drawing, his empirical studies almost always were restricted to dyadic or small group social interaction. In our view this constitutes a shortcoming in Vygotsky's approach. It is a point at which his theoretical and empirical research did not fulfil the overarching agenda he had proposed for a cultural-historical or sociocultural (Wertsch 1991) approach to mind.

THE DIALOGICALITY OF BAKHTIN

We believe that an effective way to delineate the connections between inter-mental and intra-mental processes on the one hand and cultural, historical and institutional settings on the other is to draw on some ideas from the Soviet semiotician, literary scholar and philosopher Bakhtin (1981, 1984, 1986; Voloshinov 1973). Even though Bakhtin and Vygotsky were contemporaries, there is no concrete evidence that they met or even read one another's works. However, the themes that were 'in the air' at the time which both of them wrote resulted in a great deal of overlap and complementarity in their approaches.

Fundamental to Bakhtin's account of human social and mental processes was the notion of 'dialogicality'. In his view any utterance produced by humans can be understood only by under-standing its relationship to other utterances. As authors such as Todorov (1984) and Holquist (1990) have noted, 'alterity', or 'otherness' is a fundamental property of what it means to speak and to be human in Bakhtin's approach.

For Bakhtin, dialogicality is a much broader notion than that usually associated with the term 'dialogue' in contemporary social science. In general, it concerns the various ways in which two or more voices come into contact. He outlined several ways in which this contact occurs. In the 'primordial dialogue of dis-course' (Bakhtin 1981: 275) voices come into contact in the kind of face-to-face turn-taking interaction usually associated with the notion of dialogue. From this perspective essential aspects of an utterance may be understood as an answer to another voice's utterance, an anticipation of another's utterance and so forth.

One of the ways in which the primordial dialogue of discourse is manifested is in the process of 'understanding', or what is sometimes today termed 'comprehension'. In Bakhtin's view understanding is a process wherein the utterances of a listener come into contact with and confront the utterances of a speaker. The listener's utterances may be in the form of internal as well as external speech. The resulting view is one in which:

> For each word of the utterance that we are in process of understanding, we, as it were, lay down a set of our own answering words. The greater their number and weight, the deeper and more substantial our understanding will be.
>
> Thus each of the distinguishable significative elements of an utterance and the entire utterance as a whole entity are translated in our minds into another active and responsive context . . . Understanding strives to match the speaker's word with a *counter word*.
>
> (Voloshinov 1973: 102)

A second way in which utterances may come into contact is reflected in the practice of one voice's taking over another voice's words or expressions. For example, in parody a single concrete voice produces an utterance, but it incorporates the expressions of another voice in such a way that this second voice can be heard as well, resulting in a 'multi-voiced' utterance. Thus if a speaker repeats the utterances of a well-known politician by producing these utterances with a different intonation or in contexts that differ from those in which the original utterances occurred, the parodic effect (be it humour, sarcasm or whatever) derives from the simultaneous presence of *two* voices. Indeed, it is only if one hears both voices that a parodic effect is produced.

Parody is a form of multi-voicedness that illustrates the kind of phenomena at issue when one is concerned with a basic question arising out of Bakhtin's work. This is the question, 'Who is doing the speaking?' The Bakhtinian answer is, 'At least two voices.' At first glance this question and this answer may seem to be relevant only to a relatively esoteric set of phenomena such as parody. However, when one considers other forms of dialogicality in Bakhtin's writings, it becomes clear that multi-voicedness is an essential part of *any* utterance. The point where this emerges most clearly is in connection with Bakhtin's treatment of 'social languages' and 'speech genres'.

For Bakhtin, a social language is 'a discourse peculiar to a specific stratum of society (professional, age group, etc.) within a given social system at a given time' (Holquist and Emerson 1981: 430). Any national language may be used in connection with several social languages, and a social language may invoke more than one national language. Hence national languages and social languages can, at least to some extent, be considered independently of one another. As examples of social languages Bakhtin mentioned 'social dialects, characteristic group behavior, professional jargons, generic languages, languages of the authorities of various circles and of passing fashions, languages that serve the specific sociopolitical purposes of the day' (1981: 262).

In Bakhtin's view, a speaker always invokes a social language in producing an utterance, and this social language shapes what the speaker's individual voice can say. This process of producing unique utterances by speaking in social languages involves a specific kind of dialogicality or multi-voicedness that Bakhtin termed 'ventriloquation' (Bakhtin 1981; Holquist and Emerson 1981), or the process whereby one voice speaks *through* another voice or voice type as found in a social language.

> The word in language is half someone else's. It becomes 'one's own' only when the speaker populates it with his own intention, his own accent, when he apropriates the word, adapting it to his own semantic and expressive intention. Prior to this moment of appropriation, the word does not exist in a neutral and impersonal language (it is not, after all, out of a dictionary that the speaker gets his words!), but rather it exists in other people's mouths, in other people's concrete contexts, serving other people's intentions: it is from there that one must take the word, and make it one's own.
>
> (Bakhtin 1981: 293–4)

Bakhtin's treatment of social languages suggests that they have no particularly obvious or regular overt markers attached to them. There often is nothing in the form, such as a distinct dialect or vocabulary or the use of unique tense and aspect forms, that distinguishes one social language from another. When considering other social speech types, however, Bakhtin posited the existence of clear surface marking. This is spelled out in most detail in connection with his ideas about 'generic languages' or 'speech genres'.

Bakhtin recognized that the study of such genres was in its infancy, noting that 'No list of oral speech genres yet exists, or even a principle on which such a list might be based' (1986: 80). However, he did occasionally provide sample lists of the kind of phenomena he had in mind, lists that included military commands, everyday genres of greeting, farewell and congratulation, salon conversations about everyday, social, aesthetic and other subjects, genres of table conversation, intimate conversations among friends and everyday narration. According to Bakhtin:

> A speech genre is not a form of language, but a typical form [i.e. a type] of utterance; as such the genre also includes a certain typical kind of expression that inheres in it. In the genre the word acquires a particular typical expression. Genres correspond to typical situations of speech communication, typical themes, and, consequently, also to particular contacts between the *meanings* of words and actual concrete reality under certain typical circumstances.
>
> (Bakhtin 1986: 87)

In contrast to social languages, which Bakhtin conceptualized as belonging to a particular group of speakers, speech genres are characterized primarily in terms of belonging to 'typical situations of speech communications'. The two phenomena and the two sets of criteria may be analytically distinct, but in concrete reality they are often thoroughly intertwined. For example, speakers from certain social strata, or groups (e.g. the military) are typically the ones who invoke certain speech genres (e.g. military commands).

In Bakhtin's view, the production of any utterance entails the appropriation of a speech genre.

> We speak only in definite speech genres, that is, all our utterances have definite and relatively stable typical *forms of construction of the whole*. Our repertoire of oral (and written) speech genres is rich. We use them confidently and skillfully *in practice*, and it is quite possible for us not even to suspect their existence *in theory*. Like Molière's Monsieur Jourdain who, when speaking in prose, had no idea that was what he was doing, we speak in diverse genres without suspecting that they exist.
>
> (1986: 78)

Thus, in Bakhtin's account it is no more possible to produce an utterance without using some speech genre than it is possible to produce an utterance without using some national language such as English.

As we have argued elsewhere (Wertsch 1991), Bakhtinian constructs such as dialogicality, social language and speech genre provide concrete mechanisms for extending Vygotsky's claims about the social origins and social nature of human mental functioning. Specifically, they make it possible to clarify some of the links between inter-mental and intra-mental functioning on the one hand and cultural, historical and institutional settings on the other. This linkage comes into focus when social languages and speech genres are considered as mediational means. Such mediational means are quintessentially sociocultural in nature and hence naturally 'import' the sociocultural into the mental. This contrasts with Vygotsky's treatment of word meaning as a unit of analysis where the relation to sociocultural setting is suggested but not elaborated. Thus it is by invoking some of Bakhtin's ideas about social languages and speech genres that we can provide the sociocultural grounding called for by Vygotsky the methodologist but not provided by Vygotsky the psychologist.

VOICES IN CONTACT AND THE FUNCTIONAL DUALISM OF TEXTS

In order to pursue this line of enquiry, it is essential to identify some specific speech genres and social languages or at least the dimensions along which they can be distinguished. This is essential if one wishes to specify how mental functioning is shaped by the various mediational means employed. We shall examine this issue by focusing primarily on speech genres.

As Wertsch (1991) has noted, Bakhtin did relatively little in the way of building a typology of speech genres. However, he did make some general comments about criteria or dimensions that could be employed to distinguish one such genre from another. The central criterion that concerned him was how voices come into contact, a criterion that is the key to understanding the 'compositional structure' of the utterance (Bakhtin 1986). Bakhtin saw this property of dialogicality as characterizing virtually every utterance. In his view 'utterances are not indifferent to one another and are not self-sufficient; they are aware of and mutually reflect one another' (1986: 91). This awareness and reflection can occur in many ways. For example, 'others' utterances can be repeated', 'they can be referred to', 'they can be silently presupposed' or 'one's responsive reaction to them can be reflected only in the expression of one's own speech' (1986: 91).

Bakhtin's claims about the necessity of understanding meaning, utterances and other semiotic phenomena from the perspective of how voices come into contact (i.e. their 'dialogic interanimation') have been explicated in a variety of ways. One author who has made several important contributions to this discussion is the semiotician, Yu. M. Lotman. An extremely interesing way in which Lotman has dealt with this issue can be found in his idea of the 'functional dualism' of texts. This notion provides the foundation for an important dimension along which speech genres can be seen to vary.

Lotman sees virtually all texts as fulfilling two basic functions: 'to convey meanings adequately, and to generate new meanings' (1988a: 34). These may be termed the 'univocal' and the 'dialogic' functions of text, respectively. In Lotman's account *both* functions are characteristic of almost all texts, hence the notion of functional dualism. However, he also notes that one or the other function tends to dominate in most cases. In instances where the main emphasis is on the accurate transmission of information, the univocal function dominates.

> The first function is fulfilled best when the codes of the speaker and the listener most completely coincide and, consequently, when the text has the maximum degree of univocality. The ideal boundary mechanism for such an operation would be an artificial language and a text in an artificial language.
>
> (Lotman 1988a: 34)

Lotman notes that this univocal text function has been at the core of language study. One of the reasons for this is that 'it is this aspect of a text that is most easily modeled with the means at our disposal' (1988a: 35). The means he had in mind are of course the mediational means that appear in the form of concepts and theories used by linguists, communication scientists and others. The overwhelming tendency to presuppose the univocal function in these approaches has resulted in a situation where this function has 'at times . . . been identified with a text as such, obfuscating the other aspects' (1988a: 35).

In contrast to this first, transmission-like function of a text, a function which 'requires maximal semiotic ordering and structural uniformity of the media used in the process of reception and transmission' (Lotman 1988a: 41), the second function of text is grounded in the kind of dialogicality that lay at the centre of Bakhtin's analyses.

> The second function of text is to generate new meanings. In this respect a text ceases to be a passive link in conveying some constant information between input (sender) and output (receiver). Whereas in the first case a difference between the message at the input and that at the output of an information circuit can occur only as a result of a defect in the communications channel, and is to be attributed to the technical imperfections of this system, in the second case such a difference is the very essence of a text's function as a 'thinking device'. What from the first standpoint is a defect, from the second is a norm, and vice versa.
>
> (1988a: 36–7)

Lotman argues that this second, dialogic function of text is more interesting than the univocal function for the semiotic study of culture. Instead of focusing on the transmission of meaning or on the 'conduit metaphor' of communication (Reddy 1979) it points the way to understanding the generation of meaning, a process that can occur on the intra-mental as well as the inter-mental plane of functioning.

Lotman's account of functional dualism implies that when a text is heavily orientated toward serving a dialogic function, it cannot be adequately understood in terms of constructs which focus on the univocal function. This is so because such constructs presuppose that a single, univocal message is transmitted from sender to receiver, whereas Lotman and Bakhtin view the process as involving multiple, dialogically interanimated voices from the outset. As noted earlier, for Bakhtin 'Understanding strives to match the speaker's word with a *counter word*' (Voloshinov 1973: 102).

Many of the properties of the dialogic function reflect the fact that 'The main structural attribute of a text in this second function is its internal heterogeneity' (Lotman 1988a: 37).

> . . . in its second function a text is not a passive receptacle, or bearer of some content placed in it from without, but a generator. The essence of the process of generation, however, is not only an evolution but also, to a considerable extent, an interaction between structures. Their interaction in the closed

world of a text becomes an active cultural factor as a working semiotic system. A text of this type is always richer than any particular language [i.e. either a social or a national language] and cannot be put together automatically from it. A text is a semiotic space in which languages interact, interfere, and organize themselves hierarchically.

(1988a: 37)

Lotman's account of the functional dualism of texts provides useful criteria for distinguishing one speech genre from another. Specifically, it suggests that speech genres can be distinguished into general categories on the basis of the extent to which the univocal function or the dialogic function is foregrounded. A focus on the univocal function (i.e. on information transmission) is associated with minimal contact between voices and with a quite restricted way in which this contact can occur. One voice functions to send information and another functions to receive it (although in accordance with Bakhtin's account of understanding, this receiving voice can never be entirely passive). In speech genres organized around the univocal function of text, then, there is little room for the receiving voice to question, challenge or otherwise influence the sending voice.

In contrast, speech genres grounded primarily in the dialogic function of text assume that each voice will take the utterances of others as thinking devices. Instead of viewing others' utterances as static, untransformable packages of information to be received and perhaps 'stored', they are viewed as providing one move in a form of negotiation and meaning generation. In general, the possibilities for voices to come into contact are much greater and much richer in the case of the dialogic function of text than for the univocal function. Instead of being viewed as containers of information to be transmitted, received and stored, utterances are viewed as open to challenge, interanimation and transformation.

THE SPEECH GENRE OF CLASSROOM INTERACTION

As noted earlier, the essence of a speech genre is to be associated with a particular set of cultural, historical and institutional settings. It is such settings that provide the 'typical situations of speech communication' mentioned by Bakhtin (1986). Since speech genres are also the mediational means that shape inter-mental and intra-mental processes in this view these processes are inherently shaped by the sociocultural setting in which they occur. In order to make this rather abstract claim a bit more concrete, we turn in this section to some illustrations. These illustrations both come from interaction in formal instructional settings. How-ever, they focus on different speech genres used in these settings, speech genres distinguished on the basis of Lotman's distinction between the univocal and dialogic functions of text.

Our first example comes from discourse in a kindergarten class-room in a middle-class US suburban public school. It is a tran-script of a videotape made during the final part of the school year. The form of interaction reflected in this example has been extensively documented and analysed by Mehan (1979) in his account of 'learning lessons'. It takes the form of a teacher's Initiation followed by a pupil's Reply followed in turn by the teacher's Evaluation. This 'I-R-E' sequence appears to be widely used in classroom discourse throughout the world. This excerpt goes as follows.

(1) T: How long will it take for the chicks to hatch?
(2) Jen: Eight days.
(3) T: OK.
(4) T: How many days have the eggs been in the incu-
            bator?
(5) Jen: Three days.
(6) T: Yes, good.

From the perspective of Lotman's account of functional dual-ism, a striking fact about I-R-E sequences is tht they are grounded in the univocal function of texts. The focus in an interchange is on the transmission of information from the teacher to the pupil and from the pupil to the teacher. As Lotman notes in this case any 'difference between the message at the input and that at the output of an information circuit can occur only as a result of a defect in the communications channel, and is to be attributed to the technical imperfections of this system' (1988a: 36–7).

If the pupil misunderstood the teacher or vice versa, the correct procedure would be to repeat or clarify the message somehow so that accurate transmission would occur. In no case is an utterance by the teacher or pupil viewed as a thinking device or a generator of new meanings. For example, at no point would it be appropriate for a pupil to respond to a teacher's Initiation by noting that the question is very interesting and raises further issues. Or conversely, the teacher's Evaluation of the pupil's Reply is typically in simple positive or negative terms. The Reply is not taken as utterance that can serve as a thinking device or as the beginning of a negotiation capable of generating new meanings. Hence this first example illustrates a kind of classroom discourse in which the univocal function of utterances is foregrounded.

In our second example the dialogic function is foregrounded. This example comes from the instructional discourse of a kindergarten classroom in a Brazilian public school. The teacher in this classroom is a participant in an ongoing collaborative project between teachers and researchers designed to find better ways to meet the needs of pupils from low-income families. This collaborative effort is motivated by the claim that

> The social practice in school settings reflects society's structure and functioning, so the access to institutionalized knowledge 'via' school is not sufficient to change or to overcome the reproductive and selective character of formal eduction. Yet, while we hear a generalized claim for democracy and joint collaborative work, the social practice in school settings is marked by authoritative discourse and individualized work.
>
> (Smolka 1990: 2)

One of the goals of this project is to change the forms of discourse found in formal instructional settings in such a way that they will better serve low-income pupils' needs. As others such as Tharp and Gallimore (1988) have done, the goal is to transform classroom discourse such that it is not so alien and alienating to children as they begin their schooling.

The discourse we shall examine comes from a kindergarten classroom for children of low- and middle-income families. The 27 children in this classroom were generally assumed by teachers and the principal to have learning and/or behavioural disorders. The full day programme (8 am to 4:30 pm) these children attended is not the regular programme in the local school system, and children in this programme already carry a certain stigma.

The teacher in this interaction session had participated as a teacher-researcher in extensive discussions about how to understand and change classroom discourse. It was her fifth year of teaching kindergarten. Her interaction style differed markedly from that of other teachers in this setting who relied much more heavily on the kind of I-R-E sequence outlined in our first illustration and on lecturing and pupil seatwork. This second illustration is a transcript of a videotape of a session that took approximately 15 minutes.

(1) T: Ronaldo, yesterday when you didn't come, and the day before yesterday, lots of different things happened here in the classroom.
(Ronaldo, ontem, que voce nao veio, e antes de ontem, aconteceu um monte de coisa diferente aqui na classe.)

(2) Pri: So neat!
(Legal!)

(3) T: One of the things is that somebody found a different thing. Who wants to tell him?
(Uma coisa que aconteceu e que alguem encontrou uma coisa diferente. Quem quer contar pra ele?)
[several children raise their hands]

(4) Raf: I. [raising his hand]
(Eu.)

(5) T: Rafa, tell Ronaldo what happened.
(Rafa, conta pro Ronaldo.)

(6) Raf: We found a toad.
(A gente achou uma pererreca.)

(7) Jul: A toad.
(Uma pererreca.)

(8) T: A toad?
(Uma pererreca?)

(9) Raf: A frog!
(Um sapo!)

(10) T: We . . . haven't we discussed this yesterday and didn't you guys say it was not a toad . . . ?
(A gente . . . A gente nao discutiu isso e voces nao falaram que nao era pererreca . . . ?)

(11) Cai: It is a frog!
(E um sapo!)

(12) Jul: A frog!
(Um sapo!)

(13) Raf: It looks like a frog, this animal there!
(Parece um sapo, esse bicho ai!)

(14) T: It was a frog?
            (Que ere sapo?)
(15) Eli: But it is a little toad.
            (Mas e emo pererequinha.)
(16) Chi: It is not.
            (Nao e.)
(17) Adr: It is.
            (E.)
(18) T: Look what we found, Ronaldo.
            (O. o que a gente encontrou, Ronaldo.) [gets the
            jar with the frog and sets it in the centre of the
            circle]
(19) Jul: A toad is a baby frog!
            (Perereca e filho de sapo!)
(20) Bru: Show . . . let Ronaldo see it.
            (Mostra . . . deixa a Ronaldo ver.)
(21) Eli: But it is a little, little toad full of little spots!
            (Mas e uma pererequinhazinha cheia de pintinha!)
(22) Adr: Our toad was just like that!
            (A nossa perereca era assim tambem!)
(23) Jul: A toad? A toad is a baby frog!
            (Perereca? Perereca e filho de sapo!)
(24) T: A toad is a baby frog?
            (Perereca e filho de sapo?)
(25) Children (many voices): No!
                              [Nao!]
                              No!
                              [Nao!]
                               .
                               .
                               .

(26) T: {inaudible} are different.
            ({inaudible} sao diferentes.)
(27) Sul: They are of the same family.
            (Sao da mesma familia!)
(28) Chi: . . . locked in the jar . . .
            (. . . presa no vidro . . .)
(29) Eli: . . . she has little yellow paws . . .
            (. . . ela tem patinhas amarelas . . .)
(30) Adr: . . . little spots.
            (. . . pintinhas.)

(31) T: . . . of the same family.
             (. . . da mesma familia.)

(32)   Children (many voices): {unclear}

(33) T: No, the toad is different.
             (Nao, a perereca e diferente.)

(34) Children (many voices): {unclear}

(35) T: See, Ronaldo, one of the things is this frog.
             (Viu. Ronaldo, uma coisa que a gente encontrou e
             esse sapo.)

(36) Jul: Toad.
             (Perereca.)

(37) T: Now, I have found out something to tell you about
             the frog, which I found out yesterday, and I didn't
             know before. Yesterday, I asked a person who is a
             biologist and who read a lot about . . .
             (Agora, eu tenho uma coisa pra falar do sapo, que
             eu descobri ontem, que eu nao sabia. Ontem, eu
             perguntei pra uma pessoa que e biologo, e que leu
             muito ja de . . .)

(38) Raf: Frog.
             (Sapo.)

(39) T: Frogs.
             (Sapos.)

(40) Eli: Toad.
             (Perereca.)

(41) T: . . . he studied a lot about frogs and then he told
             me the following: that it doesn't do any good to
             catch bugs and throw them inside, dead bugs,
             because she doesn't see to eat, she doesn't see them.
             She sees what is flying, what is moving. Then she
             eats. What is . . .
             (. . . ja pesquisou muito de sapo e ai ele me disse
             o seguinte: que nao adianta nada cata bicho e
             taca la dentro, bicho morto, porque ela nao vai
             ver pra comer, ela nao enxerga. Ela ve o que ta
             voando, o que ta se mexendo eai que ela come. O
             que ta . . .)

(42) Jul: She is jumping!
             (Ela pula!)

(43) T: Yeah . . . what runs, what flies, then she gets it.
             What is dead . . .

(E, o que ta andando, assim, o que ta voando, ai
ela pega, o que ta morto . . .)

(44) Jul: She jumps!
(Ela pula!)

(45) T: . . . say she never sees, that she is going to die here
of hunger cause it doesn't do any good to put dead
bugs there . . .
(. . . diz que ela nunca ve, que ela vai morrer aqui
de fome porque nao aiianta a gente colocar bichinho
morto la . . .)

(46) Jul: O Christ!
(O Cristo!)

(47) T: . . . cause she doesn't eat.
(. . . porque ela nao come.)

(48) Jul: Where is Siri today?
(Onde que ta aquele Siri?)

(49) T: We can even see . . .
(A gente pode ate ver . . .)

(50) Bet: and that crab?
(e aquele siri?)

(51) T: . . . the bugs we put here yesterday, look.
(. . . os bichos que a gente colocou ontem, o.)

(52) Raf: All dead!
(Tudo mortinho!)

(53) T: . . . they are still here. She didn't eat yet.
(. . . tao aqui ainda. Ela nao comeu.)

(54) Eli: . . . has little green and yellow paws . . .
(. . . tem patinha verde e amarela . . .)

(55) T: Then this person told me the following: that we
could keep the t . . . // him for a couple of days
here, inside, but after that we should open the jar
so he could live. Otherwise, he is going to die here.
(Entao, essa pessoa me disse o seguinte: que a gente
podia ficar uns dois dias aqui com a p . . . // aqui
com ele, aqui dentro, e depois disso precisava abrir
pra ele poder viver. Ou senao ele vai morrer aqui.)

There are several interesting points to notice about the interaction in this case. In contrast to the I-R-E sequence examined
in the first illustration where the focus was on the accurate transmission of information back and forth between teacher and pupil,

there is much more interanimation of voices in this case. This is not to say that the accurate transmission of information is unimportant. It is simply to say that in addition to serving this univocal function utterances also serve a dialogic function, in addition to transmitting information they serve as thinking devices, as generators of new meanings.

One of the most obvious ways in which this is manifested is in the seemingly endless dispute over whether the animal in the jar is a frog or a toad. Instead of simply declaring what the animal is and transmitting this information to the children, the teacher did not close this off as a matter for discussion. At certain points (e.g. utterances 33 and 34) the teacher does assert that it is a frog, but even then she does not do so by making the assertion in the form of an 'authoritative word' (Bakhtin 1981). Such an assertion would be made in a voice not open to contact or question.

Instead of insisting that the children accept her assertion that the animal is a frog, the teacher engages them in dialogue intended to lead them to distinguish between toads and frogs (utterances 8, 14, 24, 31) and to remind them of previous discussions in which they themselves concluded that the animal was a frog (utterance 10).

The degree to which the speech genre invoked in this discussion is characterized by the contact and interanimation of voices is reflected in several additional facts. One of the most striking is in the teacher's use of pronouns from utterances (41) through (55). In utterances (41) through (53) the teacher used the feminine gender pronoun (ela) that would be appropriate for referring to a toad (perereca) instead of the masculine gender pronoun (ele) that would be appropriate for referring to a frog (sapo). For a native speaker of Portuguese this is obviously not some kind of simple grammatical error. Rather, it is grounded in the interanimation of voices characteristic of this segment of the interaction. Even though the teacher had stated that the animal was a frog, her use of pronouns reveals the 'infiltration' (Voloshinov 1973) of pupils' voices who insisted that it was a toad. The teacher produced the concrete utterances (41), (43), (45), (47) and (53), but it is possible to hear the voices of students in her use of pronouns (and elsewhere for that matter). The result is that these utterances are multi-voiced in a specific way.

This multi-voicedness is grounded in a confusion that the teacher pauses over, recognizes and corrects in utterance (55). In our view it reflects the kind of openness with which she approached discussion with the students. She was so open to debate that her voice began to take on aspects of certain of the pupils' perspectives. Without noticing it, she began to appropriate the perspective of pupils who insisted that the animal was a toad. This reflects the general tendency for the discourse in this example to be characterized by the incorporation of others' utterances into one's own. Of course this did lead the teacher in the end to change her mind about the identity of the animal in the jar. Once she recognized her mistake (see utterance 55) she immediately corrected it. However, it does reflect the kind of openness to others' voices that is characteristic of the entire interchange.

CONCLUSION

Most observers would agree that the form of inter-mental functioning found in our two illustrations are strikingly different. The interaction organized around the I-R-E sequences emphasized the univocal function of utterances and involved minimal contact and interanimation of voices. The interaction from the Brazilian project reflected an emphasis on the dialogic function of utterances and involved rich and relatively unusual forms of contact between voices. In terms of the distinctions we laid out earlier, they reflect the use of two different speech genres.

In accordance with Vygotsky's general genetic law of cultural development we would hypothesize that the different forms of inter-mental functioning associated with these speech genres would result in different forms of intra-mental functioning. Some observers might view the difference between our illustrations simply as a difference between good and bad teaching (although there might be different opinions about which is which). In this view one could expect maximum intra-mental benefits from one form of interaction and minimal benefits from the other.

However, instead of trying to understand the difference between the two forms of inter-mental functioning in terms of a simple ranking, it may be more appropriate to understand them in terms of the qualitatively different intra-mental outcomes they produce. This would be more in accord with recent suggestions by investigators such as Damon and Phelps (1987) and Rogoff (1990) that different forms of inter-mental functioning might benefit different forms of intra-mental functioning and that some kind of mixed exposure is natural and appropriate.

Furthermore, in trying to understand the difference between the two forms of inter-mental functioning we presented in our illustrations it is essential to take into consideration the quite different backgrounds and socialization histories of the pupils involved. When considering the interaction from this perspective, it is interesting that a number of Vygotskian inspired studies have indicated that at least for pupils experiencing major difficulties in formal school settings it may be quite useful and productive to make major changes in the forms of inter-mental functioning in which they are expected to participate. This is the common factor to successful intervention studies such as those conducted by Tharp and Gallimore (1988) and Palinscar and Brown (1984, 1988).

What unites these studies with the procedures employed in the Brazilian classroom outlined earlier is that important changes were made in the speech genres employed by teachers and pupils. What distinguishes the new speech genres from the ones these pupils otherwise encountered in formal instruction is an emphasis on the dialogic function. Instead of taking others' utterances as untransformable packages of information to be received, they were encouraged to take them as thinking devices, as a kind of raw material for generating new meanings.

If such studies and if a general desire to teach pupils to be active thinkers rather than passive recipients of facts suggest that there should be a massive shift in schools in the speech genres employed, why doesn't it happen? After all, at least since the time of Dewey, if not Plato, there have been calls for change in educational discourse similar to what we have suggested here. In order to answer this question we need to return to the issues we raised at the outset of our chapter. Specifically, we need to return to the issue of how Vygotsky's claim that 'the social dimension of consciousness is primary in time and in fact' (1979: 30) can be extended to the sociocultural level. Instead of stopping with an analysis of how intra-mental functioning has its roots in inter-mental functioning, it is clear that we need to proceed to ask questions about why intra-mental functioning is organized as it is, and the key to this is understanding how inter-mental functioning shapes and is shaped by the cultural, historical and institutional settings in which it occurs.

If we pursue this line of reasoning it becomes clear that inter-mental functioning is not always structured in accordance with what would be efficacious in producing the desirable intra-mental outcomes we overtly espouse. As authors such as Bourdieu (1984) and Smolka (1990) suggest, the structure of discourse in formal instructional settings may have as much to do with producing and reproducing the cultural capital and hence the relative social position of groups as it has to do with cognitive growth. As a result, if we are to understand Vygotsky's claim about the priority of sociality as Vygotsky the methodologist rather than Vygotsky the psychologist would have desired, we will have to incorporate sociocultural issues into our accounts to a much greater degree than we have. The beauty of Vygotsky's approach is that it is open to such elaboration; its shortcoming is that Vygotsky himself did not explore these issues. It is precisely such issues that we view as being extremely important for undertaking the processes of understanding and shaping educational activity after Vygotsky.

NOTE

The writing of this chapter was assisted by a grant from the Spencer Foundation to the first author and by a grant from the Fulbright Commission to the second author. The statements made and the views expressed are solely the responsibility of the authors.

REFERENCES

Bakhtin, M. M. (1981) *The Dialogic Imagination: Four Essays by M. M. Bakhtin*, edited by M. Holquist; translated by C. Emerson and M. Holquist, Austin, University of Texas Press.

Bakhtin, M. M. (1984) *Problems of Dostoevsky's Poetics*, edited and translated by C. Emerson, Minneapolis, University of Minnesota Press.

Bakhtin, M. M. (1986) *Speech Genres and Other Late Essays*, edited by C. Emerson and M. Holquist; translated by V.W. McGee, Austin, University of Texas Press.

Bourdieu, P. (1984) *Distinction: A Social Critique of the Judgment of Taste*, translated by R. Nice, Cambridge, MA, Harvard University Press.

Damon, W. and Phelps E. (1987) 'Peer collaboration as a context for cognitive growth', Paper presented at Tel Aviv University School of Education annual symposium, June.

Davydov, V. V. and Radzikhovskii, L.A. (1985) 'Vygotsky's theory and the activity-oriented approach to psychology', in J.V. Wertsch (ed.)

Culture, Communication, and Cognition: Vygotskian Perspectives, New York, Cambridge University Press.

Holquist, M. (1990) *Dialogism: Bakhtin and his World*, London, Routledge.

Holquist, M. and Emerson, C. (1981) 'Glossary for M. M. Bakhtin', in *The dialogic imagination: Four essays by M. M. Bakhtin*, edited by M. Holquist; translated by C. Emerson and M. Holquist, Austin, University of Texas Press.

Hutchins, E. (1991) 'The social organization of distributed cognition', in L.A. Resnick, R. Levine and A. Behrend (eds) *Perspectives on Socially Shared Cognition*, Washington, DC, American Psychological Association.

Ivanov, V. V. (1974) 'The significance of M. M. Bakhtin's ideas on sign, utterance, and dialogue for modern semiotics', in H. Baran (ed.) *Semiotics and Structuralism: Readings from the Soviet Union*, White Plain, NY, International Arts and Sciences Press, Inc.

Lotman, Yu. M. (1988a) 'Text within a text', *Soviet Psychology* 26 (3), 32–51.

Lotman, Yu. M. (1988b) 'The semiotics of culture and the concept of a text', *Soviet Psychology* 26 (3), 52–8.

Mehan, H. (1979) *Learning Lessons*, Cambridge, MA, Harvard University Press.

Minick, N. J. (1987) 'Introduction to L. S. Vygotsky', in *Thinking and Speech*, edited and translated by N. Minick, New York, Plenum.

Palinscar, A. S. and Brown, A. L. (1984) 'Reciprocal teaching of comprehension-fostering and comprehension-monitoring acivities', *Cognition and Instruction* 1 (2), 117–75.

Palinscar, A. S. and Brown, A. L. (1988) 'Teaching and practicing thinking skills to promote comprehension in the context of group problem solving', *Remedial and Special Education* 9 (1), 53–9.

Piaget, J. (1923) *Le Langage et la pensee chez l'enfant*, Paris. Published in English as *The Language and Thought of the Child*, New York, Harcourt Brace, 1926.

Reddy, M.J. (1979) 'The conduit metaphor: a case of frame conflict in our language about language', in A. Ortony (ed.) *Metaphor and Thought*, Cambridge, Cambridge University Press.

Resnick, L.A., Levine, R. and Behrend, A. (1991) *Perspectives on Socially Shared Cognition*, Washington, DC, American Psychological Association.

Rogoff, B. (1990) *Apprenticeship in Thinking: Cognitive Development in Social Context*, New York, Oxford University Press.

Smolka, A. L. (1990) 'School interactions: an analysis of speech events in Brazilian public school settings', paper presented at the Boston University Child Language Conference, October.

Taylor, C. (1985) *Human Agency and Language. Philosophical Papers 1*, Cambridge, Cambridge University Press.

Tharp, R. G. and Gallimore, R. (1988) *Rousing Minds to Life*, New York, Cambridge University Press.

Todorov, T. (1984) *Mikhail Bakhtin: The Dialogic Principle*, translated by W. Godzich, Minneapolis, University of Minnesota Press.

Voloshinov, V. N. (1973) *Marxism and the Philosophy of Language*, translated by L. Matejka and I. R. Titunik, New York, Seminar Press. (Originally published in 1929.)

Vygotsky, L. S. (1979) 'Consciousness as a problem in the psychology of behavior', *Soviet Psychology* 17 (4), 3–35.

Vygotsky, L. S. (1981a) 'The instrumental method in psychology', in J. V. Wertsch (ed.) *The Concept of Activity in Soviet Psychology*, Armonk, NY, Sharpe.

Vygotsky, L. S. (1981b) 'The genesis of higher mental functions', in J. V. Wertsch (ed.) *The Concept of Activity in Soviet Psychology*, Armonk, NY, Sharpe.

Vygotsky, L. S. (1987) *Thinking and Speech*, edited and translated by N. Minick, New York, Plenum.

Vygotsky, L. S. and Luria, A. R. (1930) *Etyudy po istorii povedeniya: Obez'yana, primitiv, rebenok* (Essays on the history of behavior: Ape, primitive, child), Moscow and Leningrad, Gosudarstvennoe Izdatel'-stvo.

Werner, H. (1961) *Comparative Psychology of Mental Development*, New York, International Universities Press.

Werner, H. and Kaplan, B. (1963) *Symbol Formation*, New York, John Wiley & Son.

Wertsch, J. V. (1985) *Vygotsky and the Social Formation of Mind*, Cambridge, MA, Harvard University Press.

Wertsch, J. V. (1991) *Voices of the Mind: A Sociocultural Approach to Mediated Action*, Cambridge, MA, Harvard University Press.

Wertsch, J. V. and Stone, A. (1986) 'The concept of Vygotsky's account of the genesis of higher mental functions', in Culture, Communication and Cognition, ed. Wertsch, J. V., New York, Cambridge University Press.

Wertsch, J. V., Tulviste, P. and Hagstrom, F. (in press) 'A sociocultural approach to agency', in E. Forman, N. Minick and C. A. Stone (eds) *Knowledge Construction and Social Practice: Institutional and Interpersonal Contexts of Human Development*, New York, Oxford University Press.

Chapter 5

Vygotsky's contribution to the development of psychology

V. V. Davydov and V. P. Zinchenko

Lev Semonovich Vygotsky is one of the greatest psychologists of the first half of the twentieth century. He entered science on the wave of its post-revolutionary transformations and contributed much to the creation of a Marxist psychology. Fifty years have passed since his death, but he remains one of the leaders in theory in the great school of Soviet psychologists, and has had considerable influence on all of world psychology.

Vygotsky was in science for a very short time, about ten years. These were years of intense, brilliant and fruitful creativity. He worked in the most varied areas of psychology: he wrote talented works on the methodology and history of psychology; on general, developmental and educational psychology; on the psychology of art; on the psychology of abnormal development; and on clinical neurology (see Vygotsky 1968, 1982–84). But there is one area in which his scientific interests were concentrated: the development of human consciousness, the development of the human mind. Vygotsky created a fundamental theory of human mental development that is still of considerable practical significance for upbringing and education.

Vygotsky was born on 5 (17) November 1896, in the city of Orsha, to a clerk's family. He graduated from the law faculty of Moscow University in 1917 and, at the same time, from the history and philosophy faculty of the A.L. Shanyavskii University. He worked as a schoolteacher in the city of Gomel'. In 1924 Vygotsky moved to Moscow, where he began to work at the Institute of Psychology, and then at the Institute of Defectology, which he founded. He gave a series of lectures on Defectology. He died in Moscow on 11 June 1934, at the age of 38.

During the years of his scientific activity, Vygotsky gathered around him a group of young scholars who later came to constitute the greatest scientific school in Soviet psychology, one that included Luria, Leont'ev, Bozhovich, Gal'perin, Zaporozhets, Zinchenko, El'konin and other psychologists. These scholars developed their own, now widely known, psychological theories, which rested on the common foundation that Vygotsky had created. Today his students' students are working in psychology. While preserving the heritage of Vygotsky's school, they are endeavouring to deepen the principal ideas of the founder of this scientific school in accordance with contemporary needs.

It is usually said that Vygotsky's output represents a unique phenomenon in the history of psychology. When he appeared on the scientific scene, he was an unknown young man; yet he proceeded to criticize profoundly the fundamental postulates of psychology and to counter them with a number of serious theoretical ideas the experimental development of which opened up new horizons in psychology. In our view, the 'Vygotsky phenomenon' has a set of unique causes the examination of which will explain its historical legitimacy.

Vygotsky entered the human sciences in the years of preparation, realization and consolidation of the first results of the greatest social revolution in history, which freed the workers from the chains of class that has restricted their intellectual development for many centuries. His world outlook was developed in the revolutionary years, and reflected the fundamental and most advanced social-ideological influences related to understanding the essential forces of man and the laws of his historical development and all-round formation under the conditions of the new socialist society. This thought was presented in full form in the dialectical materialist philosophy of which Vygotsky had profound mastery and on which he based his own word view.

In his student years, and then as a teacher, Vygotsky immersed himself deeply in the study of the history of philosophy, and was attracted by the ideas of Spinoza. During these same years, he began to study the philosophy of Marxism. A man of extraordinary capacities, Vygotsky worked at the same time in some of the humanities: in literary criticism, theater, linguistics, the psychology of art and, as mentioned above, in philosophy. Hence, when he took up theoretical problems of psychology, he had already attained the level of humanist knowledge of his contemporaries. In the last years of his life, he was deeply engaged in the study of physiology and medicine and was concerned with questions of neurology.

The breadth of his knowledge enabled Vygotsky to create a psychological theory with deep roots in Russian and Soviet culture. This must be kept in mind if his works are not to seem enigmatic and isolated. Vygotsky was, in our view, an orthodox and legitimate representative of the most important and, in many respects, remarkable period in the history of our native culture and science. Here we give a few examples, to give a better idea of the atmosphere of enquiry and creativity in which Vygotsky lived and worked.

For instance, the idea of the symbolic and sign basis of consciousness that Vygotsky developed was related to the theory and practice of Russian symbolism, which was displayed most distinctly in poetry, theater and the cinema. Symbolism is in opposition to naturalism in art, as is clearly evident in the works and poetry of V. Ivanov and A. Belyi, in the books, plays and movies of V. Meierkhol'd and S. Eisenstein. For Vygotsky, a first-rate connoisseur of art, this opposition assumed the form of a scientific protest against naturalism in psychology.

The problem of the development of the mind was the key to the theory of Vygotsky and his school. The evolutionary biologists V.A. Vagner and A. N. Svertsev, contemporaries of Vygotsky, presented some noteworthy ideas in this area. The first insisted that the psychology should have much closer links with general biology and the theory of evolution, but expressed fear that psychology's excessively close relations with physiology might deform it and lead its enquiry down a false path (today we can say that such fears were not unwarranted). Svertsev turned to the realities of the mind to explain the evolutionary process, believing that the mind was a factor in evolution. Vygotsky's statements that the biological significance of the mind was a necessary consideration in scientific psychology were along the same line (1982–84, vol. 1: 76). In those same years, a new antihomeostatic line of thought began to form in physiology itself. We have in mind primarily the works of Ukhtomskii and Bernstein. These scientists presented the idea that there is a special class of functional rather than anatomic-morphological organs in the individual, among which they ranked dominants, an integral image, movement, etc. Today this area of research in physiology is called the 'physiology of activity'. It is completely compatible with Vygotsky's idea that not so much the physiology of psychology as physiological physiology (which must not be confused with the classic psychophysiology of the sense organs) is important for the development of psychology. Vygotsky himself viewed higher mental functions as functional systems or organs of the individual. Today, the physiology of activity and the theory of activity developed by Vygotsky's school are coming ever closer together.

The problem of thought and language and the origin and functions of the consciousness occupied an important place in Vygotsky's scientific enquiries. Such well-known scholars as G.G. Shpet, N. Ya. Marr and M.M. Bakhtin worked in these areas of psychology as well. All were interested in the problem of the origin of language, rightly considering it the foundation of consciousness. Shpet was one of the first to develop the idea of the functional structure of a word, distinguishing between its external and internal forms and stressing the role of transitions between them. Marr investigated the genesis of language and linked its origin to the implementation of practical actions with objects and with symbolic (gestural-kinetic) forms of reflecting and expressing those actions. Bakhtin developed the idea of dialogism and the polyphony of consciousness.

These scholars undoubtedly had a substantial influence on the development of Vygotsky's idea of the formation of human consciousness. In his work we find the problem of the external and the internal, the idea of the relationship between facts and sounds, the notion that the existential and the symbolic layers of consciousness genetically precede its strictly reflexive layers and, finally, a conception of dialogism and the polyphony of consciousness.

Vygotsky was personally acquainted with many of the above representatives of science, culture and art (some were his friends), and others he knew from their publications. If we describe the cultural background of his life, it is certainly not to suggest that he simply borrowed a number of ideas from his predecessors and contemporaries, though of course there was also this. In science it cannot be otherwise. But what is important to us is that the reader feel the spirit of the times and the atmosphere of enquiry of those times; it is important to show that the problem of human activity and consciousness was a concern of many outstanding representatives of science and culture. Each of them was original in establishing his own area of research, and only now, knowing the retrospective and contemporary state of these currents, can we see how deep were the relations among them. But however close they might have been, Bakhtin remains Bakhtin, Bernstein remains Bernstein, and Vygotsky is Vygotsky. The task of thinking through and understanding these relations and of effecting a possible synthesis of the ideas developed concerning human activity and consciousness of outstanding representatives of art, philosophy, linguistics, physiology, evolutionary biology and psychology is the most interesting task for the historians of science.

We have pointed out the general cultural and general scientific roots of Vygotsky's psychological theory. These are related to our domestic tradition. However, in pre-revolutionary Russia, psychology was much less developed than it was in the West. This is especially true with regard to experimental psychology. Vygotsky actively assimilated the experience of world psychology, and what he assimilated was transformed into a creative new rendition of the theories of behaviourism, Gestalt psychology, functional and descriptive psychology, developmental psychology, the French sociological school and Freudianism. Vygotsky published the results of this work in numerous prefaces to Russian editions of books by Western psychologists, in historical critical essays, and in his fundamental work (*The Historic Meaning of the Crisis in Psychology*) which was published after his death (1982–84, vol. 1). He always constructively criticized the various theories. Vygotsky adopted an attentive and careful attitude toward the factual experimental material accumulated in the different currents and schools of Western and Russian psychology.

But Vygotsky was not a collector of facts. He regarded them through the prism of his own thought, which he never considered complete. Because of this relation to facts, he was able to rethink this huge mass of material and present it in a harmonious system in his lectures, articles and books. Of course, this work could not have been done by the scientist if he had not had distinct methodological points of reference. Vygotsky was not only a theoretical psychologist and experimental psychologist: he was also a specialist in the methods of psychology.

Let us once more stress that Vygotsky was a convinced adherent of dialectical and historical materialism. He was one of the creators of Marxist psychology. It is useful to emphasize this very important circumstance, borrowing the words of the contemporary American philosopher and historian of science S. Toulmin, who wrote:

> Vygotsky was more than happy to call himself a Marxist . . . The general frame provided by a 'historical materialist' philosophy gave him the basis he needed for developing an integrated account of the relations between developmental psychology and clinical neurology, cultural anthropology and the psychology of art – an account that we in the West can afford to take very seriously today.
>
> (Toulmin 1978/79: 57)

However, for Vygotsky, Marxist philosophy was not a dogma or a theory in which one could find the answers to all the concrete question of psychology. These answers can be obtained only on the basis of careful, scientific, psychological study of human activity and consciousness. But having mastered Marxism, a psychologist can learn a general method of scientific enquiry that should also be based on many years of scientific experimental work in psychology. 'I do not want to discover what the mind is on the cheap, by culling a few quotations,' wrote Vygotsky. 'I want to learn, by Marx's formal method, how a science is constructed and how to approach the study of the mind' (1982–84, vol. 1: 421).

A scientist must pay for such an investigation of the mind with his sweat; he must seek a theory that will help him to understand the human mind and consciousness. The Marxist dialectical method of knowledge enables a scientist to find a theory without distorting psychological reality to the benefit of the most plausible or authoritative conceptual schema. That was Vygotsky's position.

Without going into the essence of his methodology, let us merely say that it made a substantial contribution not only to psychology but also to the general methodology of science. We have in mind Vygotsky's notions of the systemic structure of consciousness, which he formulated even before the systems movement, usually associated with the name of Bertalanffy, began in science. In many of his works, Vygotsky clearly presents the essence of a systemic (structural) approach to an analysis of human consciousness. He combined the principle of system with the idea of development.

Let us here give the essence of Vygotsky's main scientific achievement – the theory of human mental development, or cultural-historical theory, based on the above-enumerated fundamental general psychological ideas, on a profound analysis of factual material in developmental psychology and the history of science systems, and on the experimental data of his colleagues. The main postulates of this theory may be formulated as follows:

1 The basis of man's mental development is a qualitative change in his social situation (or his activity).
2 The original form of activity is its expanded performance by a person on an external (social) level.
3 New mental structures forming in man derive from internalization of the initial form of his activity.
4 Various sign systems play an essential role in the process of internalization.

Let us examine what these postulates mean. Vygotsky regarded the problems of human mental development mainly as they pertain to childhood, in which this process is most intense and most explicit. In his analysis of the development of the mind of a child, he introduced a very important concept, the 'social situation of development', which

> is the initial starting point for all the dynamic changes taking place in development during this period. It defines completely the forms and the path the child follows as he acquires more and more new personality traits, taking them from social activity, the principal source of development. This is the path by which the social becomes the individual.
> (Vygotsky 1982–84, vol 4: 258–9)

Qualitative changes in the social situation in which a child lives and acts lead to substantial changes in his mind, i.e. to its development.

Determining the social sources of the child's mental development enabled Vygotsky to formulate an original approach to the problem of periods in this process: a specific psychological age corresponds to each concrete social situation in development, and the alternation of situations creates conditions for the transition to the following age period.

Refining the concept of a social situation of development, Leont'ev showed that the child's relation to social reality, realized through his activity, is tied into this situation because 'when we study the development of the mind of the child, we must begin with an analysis of the development of his activity as it takes place in the particular concrete conditions of his life' (1956/83, vol. 1: 285). Vygotsky's claim that human mental development, with its social sources, is mediated by man's relation to those sources (or, more accurately, by his own activity in social reality) is of major theoretical importance since it enables us to surmount the view that the effect of the social environment on man in itself determines the development of man's consciousness and mind. Actually, there is a special, unique reality between this influence and consciousness that must be taken into account if we are to understand the internal connections between social reality and the development of human consciousness, i.e. the reality of man's own activity in it.

The history of psychology has given birth to concepts that see human mental development as a completely independent process taking place in accordance with its own immanent laws, independent of learning and upbringing (which only accelerate or retard this process). Education and upbringing are adapted to mental development and, so to speak, follow in its tracks. One such concept has been developed by the greatest psychologist of our century, Piaget.

Vygotsky examined some of these concepts and wrote that in them 'child development is represented as a process subject to natural laws and taking place as a kind of maturation, whereas education is seen as some purely external use of the capacities that emerge during the process of development' (1982–84, vol. 2: 225). Vygotsky ironically observed that with such a concept of the relationship between development and education, education is 'the tail behind child development', guided not by tomorrow, but by yesterday, by 'the child's weakness, not his strength' (1982–84, vol. 2: 225).

But according to Vygotsky's own theory, education and upbringing are social means for organizing a life situation that promotes the child's mental development.

If correctly organized education will allow the child to develop intellectually and give birth to a whole series of processes of development that would become impossible without education. Education is thus an internally necessary and universal aspect of the process of development in the child of the historical characteristics of man, not his natural characteristics.

(Vygotsky 1956: 450)

This brings up the question, 'What is the real reason for such contradictory views of the relationship between education and human mental development? In our view, it is due to the fundamental difference in the socio-historical practice of mass education between bourgeois and socialist societies. In bourgeois society, the system of mass education has a multitude of diverse restrictions, and in fact often has a weak influence on the mental development of children; this fact was grasped, for example, in Piaget's theoretical concepts.

But the construction of a system of truly democratic education in socialist society has demonstrated the tremendous role of upbringing and education in the mental development of children of the working masses. From the very first years of existence of Soviet power, many educators (e.g. S.T. Shatskii) conducted extensive experimental work aimed at organizing education in such a way as to enable it to have an essential influence on the development of the mind of the child. This historical fact was correctly perceived by scholars with a dialectical materialist concept of the social origins of human mental development, in particular, Vygotsky, and is reflected in his theory as well.

The subsequent concretization of the general postulates of this theory in the works of the followers and students of Vygotsky has demonstrated that education and upbringing are means of organizing the process of man's assimilation of socio-historically developed capacities, which are reproduced by the individual in the course of his mental development. Education and upbringing (assimilation) are necessary and universal forms of this development. Hence, development and education are not two independent processes, but are related as the content and form of the same process. This approach to the problem eliminates the parallelism in the conception of the relationship between development and education that is evident in some trends in psychology and educational science.

The initial form of activity, defining the social situation of human development, is collective accomplishment of that activity.

First, a person (in particular, a child) is part of some joint activity distributed among members of some group and having an extensive external expression. But then the person begins to perform the activity individually on the basis of the mental functions he developed as he was participating in joint activity. Vygotsky formulated the following postulate, which pinpoints a fundamental psychological law: 'Any function appears twice on the scene in the cultural development of the child, on two levels, first the social, and then the psychological, first among people . . . then within the child himself . . .' (1982–84, vol. 3: 145).

This law is manifested particularly in the domain Vygotsky called the 'zone of proximal development', in which the internal relationship between education and mental development is reflected. The general sense of this 'zone' is that at a certain stage in his development, a child can resolve a certain range of problems only under the guidance of adults and in collaboration with more intelligent comrades, but cannot do so independently. The problems resolved by the child initially under guidance and in collaboration with others he will then carry out completely independently. As Vygotsky wrote, 'Development from collaboration and development from learning are a basic fact in the child's life. The whole significance learning has for development is based on this . . .' (1982–84, vol 2: 250).

Vygotsky repeatedly noted that the possibilities of genuine education and upbringing depend not so much on the already existing characteristics of the child as on the characteristics that are in the zone of proximal development. He wrote: 'Pedagogy should be orientated not toward yesterday, but toward tomorrow in child development. Only then will it be able to create, in the process of education, those processes of development that are at present in the zone of proximal development' (1982–84, vol 2: 251).

A person's transition from joint collective accomplishment of an activity to individual accomplishment Vygotsky calls 'internalization'. New mental functions or new structures are born and take shape in a person for the first time in this process. 'Functions first form in a group in the form of relations among children, but later they become mental functions of the individual' (1982–84, vol 3: 146–7).

Sign systems (the language system, system of mathematical symbols, etc.) play an important role in the process of internalization; they are the real bearer of human culture, the means by which individual activity and individual consciousness are socially determined. The incorporation of signs into the structure of a mental function (mediation through signs) links that function to culture. On the one hand, a sign is always supra-individual and objective since it belongs to the cultural world, but on the other, it is individual since it belongs to the mind of a particular person. As Vygotsky thought, a sign is first and foremost a social instrument, a kind of 'psychological tool' for man.

Vygotsky wrote: 'A sign exists outside the organism like a tool, and is separated from the individual; it is essentially a social organ or a social device' (1982–84, vol. 3: 146). In addition, a sign is a means of communication between people. Vygotsky observed: 'Any sign, in terms of its real origin is a means of communication; and we may even say, further, that it is a means of communication of specific mental functions of a social nature' (1982–84, vol. 1: 116).

According to Vygotsky, signs enable man to create imaginary models of objects and to operate with them, planning ways to solve different kinds of problems. Operating with signs means planning through the organization of an integral activity. But planning is the most important component of human consciousness. Hence, signs are one of the important foundations of the formation and functioning of consciousness.

For Vygotsky, determination of individual consciousness follows this schema: collective (social activity – culture-signs-individual activity – individual consciousness. Study of the development of individual consciousness requires examining the transformation of all aspects of this schema.

Vygotsky's theory of psychological development, briefly outlined above, continues to have tremendous importance for educational practice. For instance, it can be used to construct and design education and upbringing that focus principally on the development of different types of activity that will enable children to reproduce the corresponding socially evolved needs and aptitudes. If we consider the possibilities of this theory in cultivating functions of individual consciousness in children, it is necessary, first, to create appropriate conditions for their performing various types of joint activity, which will later be internalized (we might point out that procedures for organizing this activity have been rather neglected in our pedagogy).

Complete internalization of joint activity by children requires that this activity be mediated by signs whose content fully captures the history of the culture the child is assimilating (in modern school education, the developmental and historical aspects of the culture assimilated by the children are still very poorly dealt with).

These examples show, in our view, that this theory has considerable potential in applied pedagogy. General pedagogy, teaching methods and special methods, should take into account and utilize this potential to deal effectively with practical problems.

What is the present state of Vygotsky's theory, and what is the 'zone of proximal development' of his line of thought? Many ideas concerning his theory have been brilliantly developed by Vygotsky's students and colleagues. For example, Leont'ev created a psychological theory of activity and consciousness; Luria developed theoretical foundations of neuropsychology and remedial learning and described the historical development of cognitive processes; A.V. Zaporozhets created a theory of development of voluntary movements; and D.B. El'konin developed a periodization of the child's mental development. Much can be said about the works of other followers of Vygotsky as well.

First, Vygotsky's school is not very often mentioned as a *cultural-historical* school; much more frequently references are to the psychology theory of activity developed in this school. This is, in a certain sense, as it should be, since for many years representatives of this school worked mainly on problems of action and activity (e.g. the problems of the structure of activity, the structure of perceptual, mnemonic and intellectual actions, etc.), which undoubtedly was a great achievement of the representatives of Vygotsky's school. Hence, the psychological theory of activity is a new and legitimate stage in the development of cultural-historical theory.

The problems of symbolic mediation of mental functions, the transition from joint activity to individual activity, and the zone of proximal development remained, for quite some time, in obscurity. But these and other problems of the cultural-historical theory must be studied intensively on the basis of new ideas in activity theory.

Now, following the publication of the six-volume collection of Vygotsky's works, the theory of the cultural-historical development of consciousness, in the form in which Vygotsky himself presented it, has acquired a second life.

Vygotsky's name today is most renowned in psychology (see

Tul'viste 1989). A number of Western psychologists base their research on Vygotsky's theoretical notions. A few years ago an international conference on his scientific work was held in the USA.

Now let us say a few words about Vygotsky as a person. According to our teachers, he was a good person, passionate and exacting of both himself and others. Knowledge, feeling and will were harmoniously intermingled in him, which made him a true scholar, one whose life and works served as a model for many generations of Soviet psychologists. Here are some words in which the consciousness, personality and activity of the great scholar shine through:

> The mere attempt to approach the soul scientifically, the effort of free thought to comprehend the mind, however much it has been obscured and paralyzed by mythology . . . is where the entire future path of psychology lies, since science is the path to truth, though it progresses through errors. And this is the road of our science as well, struggling, overcoming errors, improbable difficulties and an inhuman struggle with thousand-year-old prejudices. We do not want to be Ivans who do not remember their birth; we do not suffer delusions of grandeur, thinking that history began with us; we do not want history to give us a clean and lustreless name: we want a name on which the dust of centuries has settled. Therein we see our historical right, an indication of our historical role, and our aspiration to make psychology a science. We must see ourselves within the context of, and in relation to, what has preceded us; we base ourselves on that even when we deny it.
>
> (1982–84, vol. 1: 428)

These words reflect a deep respect for many centuries of the history of psychology and of the scientists who created it. The name of Vygotsky, who made such a great contribution to the study of this very complex phenomenon of nature and history, human activity and human consciousness, demands the same respect.

NOTE

Reprinted from *Soviet Psychology* 27 (2). Reprinted by permission of M.E. Sharpe Inc., Armonk, New York 10504.

REFERENCES

Leont'ev, A. (1956/83) *Selected Psychological Works*, 2 vols, Moscow, Progress Publishers.

Toulmin, S. (1978/79) 'Mozart in psychology', *New York Review of Books* 25, 57 (published in the USSR in *Voprosy Filosfii* 10, 136).

Tul'viste, P.E. (1989) 'Discussion of Vygotsky's works in the USA', *Soviet Psychology* 27 (2), 37–52.

Vygotsky, L.S. (1956) *Selected Psychological Investigations*, Moscow, Progress Publishers.

Vygotsky, L.S. (1968) *The Psychology of Art*, Moscow, Progress Publishers.

Vygotsky, L.S. (1982–84) *Collected Works*, 2 vols, Moscow, Progress Publishers.

Chapter 6

Peer interaction and the development of mathematical understandings
A new framework for research and educational practice

Geoffrey B. Saxe, Maryl Gearhart, Mary Note and Pamela Paduano

The argument that interactions with peers play an important role in cognitive development is longstanding in the psychological and educational research literatures. Indeed, several different research traditions including the co-operative learning (e.g. Johnson and Johnson 1975; Slavin 1983a; Johnson, Johnson and Stanne 1985), collaborative problem-solving (e.g. Damon 1984; Doise and Mugny 1984; Bearison *et al.* 1986) and the more recently culturally oriented approaches (e.g. Cobb *et al.*, in press a, b; Nicolopoulou and Cole, in press) have produced a sizeable body of theoretical analysis and empirical evidence regarding the ways that children's peer interactions may influence their developing understandings. In this chapter, we offer a further contribution to existing approaches. We present a treatment of cognitive development recently put forth by Saxe (1991a) in which analysis of the roles of peers is embedded within a more comprehensive framework for understanding sociocultural processes in cognitive development. Saxe's approach builds upon prior constructivist treatments, most notably those of Vygotsky and Piaget, and has been used in the investigation of the mathematical understandings of remote Papua New Guinea highlanders (Saxe 1981, 1982, 1985; Saxe and Moylan 1982), young children's numerical practices and understandings in working and middle-class communities in New York (Saxe *et al.* 1987) and the development of mathematical understandings in candy sellers (Saxe 1989, 1991b) and straw weavers (Saxe and Gearhart 1990) in northeastern Brazil.

We begin by providing a summary of Saxe's framework, highlighting one aspect concerned with the relation of peer interactions to mathematics learning. We then consider the way other empirical research on peer processes is related to the framework, and we end by showing how the framework can serve as a basis for designing new educational practices that address the needs detailed in recent documents for mathematics curriculum reform (California State Department of Education 1990; National Council of Teachers of Mathematics 1989).

THE FRAMEWORK

Theoretical roots

Saxe's approach is rooted in both Vygotsky's (1978, 1986) and Piaget's (1970, 1977) constructivist treatment of cognitive development. Both of these theorists argued that children transform experience as a basis for the construction of new understandings and specified dialectical processes whereby children's prior knowledge guides their novel conceptual constructions. Neither theorist, however, adequately framed for empirical study the interplay between sociocultural processes and cognitive development and, as a result, neither theorist contributed a sufficiently complete analysis of the role of peer interactions in situated processes of cognitive development.

Piaget's theory focused on the logico-mathematical properties of a child's actions and the progressive transformation of these actions into operational structures from birth through adolescence. While his work defined fundamental changes in the formal properties of diverse forms of knowledge, it neglected a systematic treatment of social processes in cognitive development. In later works by Piaget and his followers, questions of social and cultural influences on rates of attainment of Piagetian stages of development emerged as an important concern (e.g. Piaget 1966, 1977; Dasen 1977; Doise and Mugny 1984), but these analyses treated social life largely as a catalyst for cognitive stage change rather than as interwoven with the character of individuals' intellectual constructions.

Vygotsky was more centrally concerned than Piaget with the ways that social and historical processes gave form to cognitive development. For Vygotsky, the child's natural and unmediated processes of cognition became redirected and mediated by forms of communicative discourse and culturally-linked semiotic and conceptual constructions that were produced in interaction with others. Thus, speech and other semiotic systems that first emerged interpersonally to serve social and communicative functions were transformed gradually by the child to serve intrapersonal functions of planning and problem-solving. While Vygotsky did contribute a global framework for the analysis of intrinsic relations between social and cognitive developmental processes, he did not elaborate a systematic empirical treatment of social interactional processes nor extend his model to analyses of cultural practices.

The three-component approach

In work with child candy sellers in Northeastern Brazil, Saxe (1989, 1991a) found that sellers displayed an interesting mathematics that was unlike the math children learn in school. Further, sellers' mathematics could not be adequately understood without detailed analyses of the organization of their practice and the social and cultural conditions in which the practice occurred – including interactions with peers. As a result, the framework constructed for earlier studies requires elaboration to incorporate more explicitly the roles of peers in mathematics.

In this chapter, we draw on Saxe's framework, targeting for our analysis peer interactions in everyday cultural practices like candy selling. Like Piaget's and Vygotsky's constructivist treatments, Saxe's approach has as its central assumption the view that children's conceptual developments are interwoven with their purposive goal-directed activities. Children's conceptual understandings serve to enable and constrain their construction of goals, and in their efforts to accomplish their goals, children generate new understandings.

Saxe's framework consists of three components, and the chapter presents a sketch of these, highlighting their utility for understanding peer processes and math learning. The first component is concerned with the dynamic processes of *goal formation* in everyday cultural practices; we focus in this chapter on the way peer interactions are interwoven with the emergence of mathematical goals. The second component is concerned with *cognitive developments* linked to children's goal-directed activities; we show how peer-influenced goals provide a context for children to construct new mathematical understandings. The third component is concerned with the *interplay* between children's learning across contexts and practices, and we focus on the ways that peer inter-actions may be interwoven with processes of 'transfer'.

For the bulk of this paper, we focus on Component 1, or emergent goals, discussing its link to Vygotsky's writings, its dimensions in Saxe's model and its implications for existing research on peer interaction and mathematics learning. Due to space limitations, we present more cursory reviews of Components 2 and 3. The interested reader is referred to additional sources for more in-depth treatment of these components (Saxe 1989, 1990, 1991a, in press).

COMPONENT 1: EMERGENT GOALS

Vygotsky argued that it was critical to conceptualize children's learning as occurring in a *zone of proximal development* (ZPD). Vygotsky defined the ZPD as a 'region' of sensitivity to instruct-ion – the distance between problem-solving that the child could accomplish unassisted and problem-solving for which assistance was useful to the child. Vygotsky's zone of proximal development has served as a useful representation of a complex phenomenon: it links social interactional processes with the constructive, form-building activities of the individual. However, Vygotsky's treat-ment was underdeveloped and did not include analyses of varied forms of social interactional processes nor their interrelatedness with broader cultural processes (see Wertsch 1984 for more on this concern). Saxe's first component builds upon Vygotsky's treatment to understand how children's cognitive goals shift and take form in children's everyday practices.

To represent the dynamic process of situated goal formation, Saxe developed new analytic categories. To illustrate, we use a prototypical situation concerned with peer interaction in price mark-up from the candy selling research to illustrate Saxe's four principal parameters, and we focus in the example on goals linked to mathematical problem-solving.

> Pedro, Joao and Luciano, ages 7, 9 and 9, have just purchased wholesale candy boxes and are pricing them for retail sale using the standard pricing convention of selling candy in ratio form (e.g. two chocolate bars for Cr$1000). Until recently, Pedro used price ratios dictated by older siblings; lately, his interest and engagement with the activity is changing. Pedro

now suggests to the older sellers that the prices for Lifesavers, purchased at 50 for Cr$10600, be set at one for Cr$1000 (at this retail price, the gross value of the 50-unit box is Cr$50000). After brief consideration, the older boys agree that one for Cr$1000 is a good price to make money, but comment that no one would buy. Through an extended process of calculation, in which one of the older children guides a joint effort of counting the Lifesaver packages three by three, incrementing a running total by Cr$1000, the older boys determine what the gross retail value for the box would be if they sold the packages for three for Cr$1000 (about Cr$16000). They compare the figure to the wholesale price and conclude that selling at three for Cr$1000 would yield an adequate profit.

Seven-year-old Pedro is a competent candy seller. Indeed, because of his young age, he elicits more sympathy from customers than his older peers, enabling him to sell at a comparatively high volume. His eagerness to contribute to mark-up computations notwithstanding, Pedro is dependent upon others in considering mark-up, and his goals and subgoals linked to mark-up computation have taken form in his interaction with his older peers, and are supported by the general structure of the candy selling practice and selling conventions that have emerged over the history of the practice. To understand the embeddedness of sociocultural processes in children's emergent goals in the example, we draw on the four-parameter model contained in Figure 6.1 (Saxe 1991b) in which the analysis of emergent goals is referenced to the general *structure* of the cultural practice, the *artifacts* used in the practice, the *prior understandings* children bring to bear on their practice, and to social interactional processes including *peer interactions*.

Peer interactions take form in cultural practices that have particular *structures*, and these structures are interwoven with the forms peer interactions take and the goals that emerge. For instance, the structure of the candy selling practice (parameter 1) is economic: it is a money-making activity in which children buy goods from wholesale stores, price their goods for retail sale, sell to customers in the street and then shop for a new box of candy. The case of Pedro, Joao and Luciano illustrates how sellers' peer interactions and emergent goals are linked to this economic organization. To make a profit, the boys are engaging in retail pricing

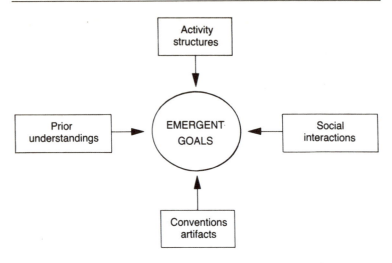

Figure 6.1 Saxe's four-parameter model of emergent goals.

calculations, attempting to balance speed of sale with profit per sale in interaction with one another, and their particular social interactions and the strategic forms they construct take on meaning with reference to this economic organization.

The *artifacts and conventions* of the practice (parameter 2) also influence the form interactions take and thereby the goals that emerge in the interactions. In the example, children are using price ratios and a currency system which are conventions and artifacts with an extended social history. The use of the price ratio convention requires the generation of unique forms of mathematical goals and subgoals which we see as sellers consider the ratio that would yield greater profit (one for Cr$1000 or two for $1000). Further, the inflated Brazilian currency system requires children to construct arithmetical goals involving very large values in their mark-up computations.

The mathematical environments that emerge in peer interactions are inherently linked to children's *prior understandings* (parameter 3). The knowledge children bring to practices enables and constrains their emergent numerical goals. In the example, we see that the 7-year-old understands that pricing entails constructing a ratio, similar to ratios he has used before or that he has observed other sellers using. In contrast, the older sellers conceive of the task as one of balancing speed of sale with amount of profit per sale in the creation of a retail price ratio. In each case, sellers' prior understandings of the task are interwoven with the form the interaction takes as well as the goals that emerge as each contributes to the discussion of mark-up.

Finally, *social interactions* (parameter 4), our targeted concern, are dynamic processes in which goals often shift and take form. In the mark-up interchange, Pedro begins with one retail price and, in proposing that price, creates a context for the reflection of the older sellers, a modification of their goal-directed activities. In their deliberations, they appropriate Pedro's suggestion, producing a solution strategy in which they co-ordinate the merits of quick sale with the merits of a sizeable profit per sale. In this way, Pedro becomes a contributing participant in the pricing computation, and his contributions are framed and sustained by more sophisticated mathematical operations and economic considerations.

REVIEW OF EMPIRICAL WORK ON PEER INTERACTION: IMPLICATIONS OF COMPONENT 1

Our selective review of empirical work on peer interactional processes and mathematics learning is focused on approaches that have defined the problem of peer interactions and cognitive development differently from one another and have used quite different methods of study. In the sketch of approaches to follow, we highlight the way existing research is related to processes of goal formation (Component 1).

The construct of 'emergent goals' is not one that is represented well in current work on peer interaction, though various studies do point to its potential utility. We have selected for review three approaches to research on peer processes, focusing on studies concerned with math learning. We identify the first two approaches as *co-operative learning*, exemplified by the work of Slavin (e.g. Slavin 1983a) or Johnson and Johnson (e.g. Johnson *et al.* 1985) and *collaborative problem solving*, exemplified by the work of Doise and Mugny (1984). The third body of work is concerned with understanding peer processes in a larger sociocultural context; we select for discussion peer interaction in an out-of-school practice (Nicolopoulou and Cole, in press) and a classroom practice (Cobb *et al.*, in press a and b). The borders that mark these three approaches are drawn by both the conceptual orientations of researchers as well as the chosen methods for study.

Co-operative learning: manipulating activity structures to influence student motivation and achievement

The co-operative learning literature is associated with such researchers as Johnson and Johnson (e.g. 1975, 1978, 1979) and Slavin (e.g. 1983a, 1983b, 1987). The guiding concern in this tradition is to create social contexts that enhance students' motivation to learn and most studies involve comparative manipulations of peer arrangements in classrooms to identify those that can facilitate learning. The subject matter to be learned is often an arbitrary choice by the researchers, and when mathematics is used, the content is typically factual or procedural (e.g. multiplication tables, arithmetical 'facts') as opposed to conceptual. The work originates from traditions very different from Saxe's, but it shares the concern to understand the way peer interactions are related to processes of learning.

In co-operative learning studies, researchers often manipulate or study students' interaction with reference to one or two principal variables – *group incentives* (rewards to teams of individuals for achievement gains *vs* rewards to individuals *vs* no rewards) and *task specialization* (no role responsibilities assigned to children within teams *vs* role responsibilities assigned within teams) (see Slavin 1983b). These manipulations are seen as altering the motivational conditions for learning. Consider first *Teams Games Tournaments*, a co-operative learning arrangement with team incentives but without task specialization. Children are assembled in teams of four or five students of mixed abilities and assigned a task such as the memorization of the multiplication tables. Team members are instructed to assist one another to learn the material, and to seek the teacher's assistance only when the group is collectively unable to solve a problem or to answer a question. *Teams Games Tournaments* supports team competition but within team assistance because of the team reward incentive structure. Each team receives a score which is the average of the scores of all its members weighted by students' prior ability. The team that ends with the greatest score receives an extrinsic reward.

The same co-operative incentive structure with task specialization is also possible. In Slavin's (1983a) modification of Aronson's (Aronson *et al.* 1978) Jigsaw Classroom task structure, interactions are co-operative both between and within groups. In this arrangement, all children of a primary team are assigned to different secondary teams. Curriculum units are partitioned into smaller learning units for secondary teams, each of which has the responsibility for ensuring that each secondary team member masters the material so that the different members can return to their primary teams to teach primary team-mates the learning unit. The objective is that at the completion of the exercise, each member of each primary team will have learned each of the units of the lesson.

In order to gain insight into peer processes within co-operative learning structures, a few investigators have audiotaped or videotaped children's small group activities (examples of studies that make use of mathematical content include Peterson and Janicki 1979; Swing and Peterson 1982; Webb 1982; Lindow *et al.* 1985; Peterson and Swing 1985). Webb (1982), for example, analysed interactions of students organized in a co-operative incentive structure (with no task specialization). She instructed groups of same and mixed ability to solve mathematical problems involving exponents. Interactional analyses focused on help-seeking and providing behaviours, and Webb examined relations among group composition (same *vs* mixed ability groupings), social interaction patterns and resultant group achievements. Webb's results showed that giving and receiving explanations were positively related to post-test measures of exponential problem-solving. Webb also found an interaction between group composition and student ability leading her to argue that group composition (homogeneous *vs* heterogeneous) in interaction with student ability may create conditions that differentially facilitate or inhibit help-giving and help-seeking behaviours. Specifically, Webb found that medium ability students performed better in homogeneous groups, whereas high and low ability students performed better in heterogeneous groups.

Implications of Saxe's emergent goals model for the co-operative learning approach

The co-operative learning research tradition has created some interesting distinctions among classroom activity organizations with constructs like task specialization and incentive structure. To date, however, systematic analysis of these activity organizations has been quite limited. Below, we consider these activity organizations and the implications of the four parameters of the Saxe Component 1 model for the analysis of each.

Task specialization

Assigning students differentiated roles within groups creates activity structures (parameter 1) that could support children's construction and accomplishment of mathematical goals. For example, in task-specialized groups, norms should emerge so that students in secondary teams value mathematical learning, and students in primary teams value communicating their learning effectively to primary team members.

The particular subject content that students are to learn and the representational and procedural forms available to students are artifacts (parameter 2) that children use as they construct and accomplish emergent mathematical goals in co-operative learning arrangements. If in a secondary team a group is engaged in learning the formula to describe a line in the Cartesian plane, analyses of subject matter in relation to processes of goal formation could reveal, for example, whether some secondary teams (or some team members) are engaged with mathematical goals involving the memorization of algorithms for graphing equations and others are engaged with more conceptual activities like understanding relations between the algebraic and graphical expressions of slope.

Children differ in the prior understandings (parameter 3) that they bring to co-operative learning situations, and therefore developmental analyses are necessary to understand ways in which children are structuring mathematical goals. It is likely we would find that, even though children are ostensively engaged with the same activity, children with different levels of prior knowledge are structuring mathematical goals of different levels of complexity.

Finally, we need to investigate the dynamic processes that link peer interactions (parameter 4) to situated subject matter-linked goals. For instance, in responding to a question about the mapping between a graphical and algebraic expression of slope, a child may construct subgoals in which she explores the effects of different values of m (in $y = mx + b$) on the graphical representation of the line. Or, through the give and take of an extended interaction in which the secondary team members are attempting to explain to one another the mapping between graphical and algebraic representations, we might see the emergence and refocusing of goals to include other goals, like the linking of the representation of a line in the Cartesian plane to a physical phenomenon like the relation between height and weight. In interactions like these, a child creates and addresses subject matter-linked goals that would not have been addressed had the need for explanation or justification not arisen.

Incentive structures

Incentive structures are designed either to lead children to pursue subject matter-linked goals more vigorously or to adopt subject matter-linked learning goals where they may not have existed. To understand how incentive structures in an activity organization become interwoven with children's subject matter-linked goals, we would need the same kinds of analyses indicated for task specialization above. We might note, as others have cautioned in different terms (e.g. Damon 1984; Hatano 1988), that students' learning could be undermined by incentives. In offering extrinsic rewards to teams or individuals for winning a competition, incentives could lead a student to avoid constructing mathematical goals that would require longer-term investigative activities; students may be motivated to acquire facts and procedures at the expense of deeper understandings.

Summary and critique

From the perspective of Saxe's four-parameter model, studies in the co-operative learning tradition have strengths: they are situated largely in the classroom, are examinations of some prototypical contexts of interaction in educational settings, are focused on traditional subject matter areas and are conducted over a sustained period of time. However, we see a neglect in this literature of a critical analysis of the development of mathematical understandings. There appears to be a tacit assumption held by many co-operative learning researchers that knowledge consists of facts and procedures to be mastered, and that more knowledgeable children can serve to help less knowledgeable children master the facts and procedures dictated by the curriculum. Because there is little examination of ways that children are structuring mathematical knowledge and no differentiated analyses of the ways in which children's construction of particular kinds of mathematical understandings are interwoven with peer processes, we end with weak treatments of mathematics learning in peer interaction.

Collaborative problem-solving: analysing socio-cognitive conflict

The collaborative problem-solving research literature shares with Saxe the view that knowledge is constructed by individuals. Accordingly, peers in interaction may present differing perspectives that may lead children to reconceptualize their own thinking. The studies we review are part of a Piagetian-inspired literature on the role of peer interaction in cognitive, social and moral development and has been elaborated by various researchers (see, e.g. Damon 1984; Doise and Mugny 1984; Bearison et al. 1986). We focus here on studies that have a somewhat indirect relation to mathematics learning (conservation, projective space), since studies from this tradition that focus on mathematics as defined by school practices are rare if not non-existent.

In a typical study, pairs of children are presented with a conceptual problem for which neither partner has sufficient understanding, and the focus is on the conceptual gains that children may make from working together. The activity contexts studied are laboratory settings, and tasks are often adaptations of assessment tasks developed either by Piaget for research on projective space (e.g. Doise et al. 1975; Mugny and Doise 1978) or conservation (e.g. Perret-Clermont 1980), or by cognitive psychologists for investigations of problem-solving, such as the Tower of Hanoi (Glachan and Light 1982). Like the co-operative learning literature, studies of peer collaboration are varied in their methods; some researchers limit themselves to post-test assessments, others focus on the interactional process and others include both.

Analysis of collaborative problem-solving is typically motivated by Piaget's equilibration model. The guiding thesis is that under certain conditions peer interactions can promote realizations of contradiction, and thus in peer interactions can emerge contexts in which children generate new understandings as they identify and resolve contradictions in their own reasoning. Consider, for example, a situation in which two children are presented with two same-shaped glasses that differ in size of cross-section; when lemonade is poured from one glass into the other, the lemonade rises higher in the second glass. If the children are asked to determine whether the two glasses contain the same amount or whether one contains more, they may disagree, perhaps one arguing that one glass contains more because the lemonade rises higher, the other that the second glass contains more because it is fatter. If children recognize a contradiction between their views, they may try to resolve it – perhaps by arguing that the increase in height is compensated by the decrease in cross-section, a new conceptual understanding.

Various methods have been used to study interactional processes in collaborative problem-solving. Some are documentations of the way in which prior understandings (pre-test scores for stage of reasoning) are related to outcomes of peer interactions. Results of this approach have shown that children who are assessed as transitional in their understandings of a targeted conception, like conservation, are more likely to profit from the collaborative episode than those who are not (e.g. Mugny and Doise 1978). Other researchers develop schemes to code interactional processes linked to the Piagetian equilibration construct (e.g. Ames and Murray 1982). Occurrences of conflict in perspectives are coded and then related to post-test scores, often a Piagetian stage assessment on a task. The findings of these socio-cognitive conflict studies display a complex picture: Some studies report positive associations, others do not and, in a recent study, Bearison *et al.* (1986) report a curvilinear relationship between a measure of socio-cognitive conflict and post-test scores for boys but not for girls.

Implications of Saxe's emergent goals model for the collaborative problem-solving approach

We see an important strength in the collaborative problem-solving literature: researchers (particularly those within the Piagetian tradition) use a well-explicated model of cognitive development to guide their analyses of relations between interactional and cognitive developmental processes. The central construct of socio-cognitive conflict derives from Piaget's equilibration model and is viewed as the critical process that occurs in peer interactions and contributes to children's constructions of new understandings.

This analysis has offered valuable insights into social processes entailed in cognitive developmental change, but it is incomplete from the perspective of Saxe's model of emergent goals.

In collaborative problem-solving research, the activity structures used (parameter 1) do not represent ones that commonly occur in the lives of children. Children typically participate in these studies as dyads for only one sitting, and there is limited opportunity for the development of shared norms regarding, for example, sanctioned means of expressing conflict or sanctioned avenues for resolution. Nevertheless, even in these short-term studies, we would imagine that peers have varying beliefs about conflict and varying investments in resolution that emerge in the activity setting. These beliefs and dispositions may be based upon children's prior expectations for behaviour in these settings as well as on implicit and explicit communications to children by experimenters. To date, we do not have needed analyses of children's beliefs about conflict and methods of resolution nor of children's investments in these activities.

In analyses of collaborative problem-solving, we also have little representation of the particular artifacts (parameter 2) peers use in accomplishing tasks in interaction. In what way do the particular materials students use influence the nature of the possibly conflicting ways that a task is represented? For example, during peer interaction in a conservation of length task, in what way does the introduction of an artifact like a ruler lead interactions toward particular kinds of conflicts? Do we observe new kinds of conflicts about how to measure linked to this historically produced artifact (e.g. the meaning of the calibrations, where the 0-point on the ruler should be aligned with the target, the relevance of measurement to the task at hand)? Do we observe interactions that provide insight into ways in which children's own constructive activities become linked to historically constructed means of problem-solving, like measurement with a standard ruler? In other terms we are asking, how do different kinds of materials support or hinder children's creation of particular analytic directions and lead to particular kinds of conceptual problems? Such analyses would contribute to a more complete understanding of the emergence of conflict in peer settings and the nature of the situated developmental processes that emerge in such settings.

Collaborative problem-solving researchers do usually assess students' stage of development prior to the peer interaction intervention. These analyses of children's prior understandings (parameter 3) provide a partial understanding of peers' construction and resolution of conflict-linked goals in peer collaborations. But further analyses are needed of students' understandings that emerge *in situ*, as peers are trying to make sense of their partners' viewpoint in relation to their own. We do not find in this literature in-depth treatments of case studies that would be required for this form of analysis.

In the dynamics of collaborative peer interactions (parameter 4), children engage in rationally driven disagreement about particular judgments, and conflict situations are interpreted as catalysts for change. We see a need for more differentiated analysis in which conflict is understood in terms of emergent goals. Suppose, in a number conservation task, children are presented with two equal arrays of a discontinuous quantity aligned in one-to-one correspondence; one array is then elongated and children are queried about the numerical relation between the two arrays. What are the emergent goals and subgoals as peers interact with one another in both the generation and resolution of conflict? If they disagree about the quantity of elements, does one: engage in verification activities, like counting, to prove to another the validity of a conviction? Attempt to reverse the transformation by returning the spatially deformed array back to its original configuration? Attempt to compute the equality of differences across dimensions in the transformed quantity (compensation between greater spatial separations by greater length)? In any of these efforts at justification, how is data appropriated by the other in the accomplishment of prior goals or in the formation of new ones?

Summary and critique

There is a need to move toward a more differentiated treatment of conflict. What is required is an understanding of the sociocultural dimensions of the activity setting, including the values and norms for peer interaction and conflict, the artifacts used and the dynamic processes of goal formation and resolution of socio-cognitive conflict. In addition, there is a need to develop research situations that reflect better the actual practices in which children participate.

Sociocultural approaches

In recent years, there has emerged a new approach to the study of peer interaction and math learning that incorporates social and cultural processes in the analysis of ongoing educational practices (e.g. Forman and McPhail 1989; Cobb *et al.*, in press a, b; Ellis and Gauvain, in press; Nicolopoulou and Cole, in press). In these studies we find concern to understand the cultural contexts in which peer interactions are situated and some fine-grained analyses of peers' use of discourse to create what Cobb *et al.*, for example, refer to as 'taken-to-be-shared understandings'. Below, we sketch two studies related to mathematics learning – one concerned with an out-of-school practice and the other concerned with classroom practices.

Out of school

Nicolopoulou and Cole (in press) argue for the importance of understanding institutional contexts in which collaborative learning interactions are situated. These researchers investigated the way in which an after-school educational programme, the Fifth Dimension, was implemented at two different sites, a Boys' and Girls' Club and at a library. The Fifth Dimension, developed by Michael Cole and Peg Griffin, was designed to support the development of computer literacy and general social and cognitive skills (including mathematics), and Nicolopoulou and Cole report some major consequences for peer collaborative activities as a function of the two different 'micro-cultures' that the two sites supported.

The Fifth Dimension is an activity structure consisting of educational software in various subject matter areas (about forty games and other computer-based activities at various complexity levels). While the computers are available to children on a small number of tables, the Fifth Dimension is designed as an imaginary twenty-room 'maze' portrayed as a small physical model, and in each room of the model, children have the option of playing several specified games in small groups (two or three children and an undergraduate). The objective is to visit all of the rooms in the maze and play at least ten games at the 'expert' level (there are three difficulty levels for each game); if children accomplish this objective, they can request to be promoted to a 'Wizard's

Assistant' and introduced to even more complex activities. Children keep track of where they are in the Fifth Dimension maze of rooms with small figurines that they move through the model's rooms. On a regular basis, children report to a Wizard through electronic mail about their success and difficulties with different games, and they receive hints from the Wizard that they may communicate to their peers by posting messages on an electronic mail bulletin board.

Nicolopoulou and Cole report that the institutional supports for the Fifth Dimension differed across the two sites and contributed to the emergence of two different 'cultures'. At the library, there was a serious atmosphere in which there were clear institutional rules and regulations. In contrast, at the Boys' and Girls' Club, there was a relaxed, relatively unstructured 'open door policy', and children were permitted to choose activities. Nicolopoulou and Cole examined the consequence of these cultural differences for the play and learning that occurred in the context of 'Mystery House', a software game in which children must use clues to find a murderer and hidden jewels without themselves being killed.

The Mystery House game is complex, requiring investigative activities. Making progress in the game is a long-term affair, and one has to know how to re-establish the prior level reached in the game at each new sitting. Nicolopoulou and Cole see sustained progress in Mystery House only possible through interactions between peers that support the historical development and transmission of knowledge.

To document the effectiveness of interactional processes, Nicolopoulou and Cole assigned progress scores to groups of children who played Mystery House together (using two or three children and an undergraduate), and they found that the pattern of progress in Mystery House differed across the two sites over the course of the year. The average scores were higher at the Library site, and only the Library site showed steady progress over the course of the year. Nicolopoulou and Cole argue that the Library site worked more effectively due to a culture that generated and maintained norms for collaborative learning involving greater commitment to the Fifth Dimension and social cohesion among peers. Indeed, Nicolopoulou and Cole report that at the library, children showed greater rates of problem-solving interaction, their interactions were more coherent and there was greater extent of overlap in individual membership on different teams.

Peer interactions in classrooms

In their classroom-based research and development project in primary school mathematics, Cobb and his associates have also adopted a sociocultural perspective on children's learning. These investigators (Wood 1991; Yackel 1991; Cobb *et al.*, in press a, b; Yackel *et al.*, in press) have worked to create mathematical activities and norms that differ substantially from the traditional mathematics classrooms. Teachers work to establish group norms in which 'children are . . . expected to explain and, if challenged, justify their solutions . . . to try to understand others' explanations and ask questions for clarification'. On the other hand, the 'teacher's role is to question, probe, and make suggestions based on the student's comments, rather than impose predetermined methods' (Wood 1991: 358). Clearly, this normative structure has strong implications for the nature of peer interactions in the classroom, and Cobb *et al.* address their analyses to the way in which these norms are reflected in student mathematical sense-making activities.

In one analysis of peer questioning in their enquiry classrooms, Yackel (1991) provides an illustration of ways in which classroom norms are interwoven with peer interactions. The teacher had presented his second grade class with the challenging problem of $46 + 38 + 54 = \_\_$, and children's ensuing participation led them to evaluate not simply peers' solutions but also the forms of peers' arguments – in this case, an elementary form of proof by contradiction. A girl named Donnelle attempted to explain how she arrived at her correct solution of 138: She first added 40 and 30 to arrive at 70; she then added 70 and 8 to obtain 78; however, she then erred by adding 78 to 50 to arrive at 116. Some of her peers raised their hands, as is customary in the classroom, to ask her questions pertaining to this problematic step in her solution process. Another child, Travonda, tried to explain a contradictory consequence of the incorrect 116 sum, pointing out that Donnelle will not end with her original sum, 138, if the intermediate term is 116, since the remaining numbers added to 116 will not yield 138. While Donnelle does not understand Travonda's argument, Yackel points out that the argument provides the class with the opportunity to reflect upon this complex form of argumentation. Indeed, another child, Jameel, then asks Travonda the source of 116, and the discussion continues about the nature of Donnelle's contradiction, even beyond the efforts of the teacher to curtail the lively and conceptually rich interchange.

In their work, Cobb *et al.* also highlight the critical status of norms for mathematical justification. For instance, in one excerpt (to which we will refer again later), Cobb *et al.* (in press) describe two children, Jack and Anne, working together to find the sum of five twelves. As the excerpt begins, Jack had written five twelves in vertical, column format while Anne had *both* written and completed the problem using the standard addition algorithm, arriving at the correct sum of 60. Anne's explanation to Jack of her correct answer was a repetition of the rules for carrying out the standard algorithm; in Jack's view, however, Anne's solution made no sense, and should have been 610 (the application of the column addition algorithm without carrying), not 60. Jack repeatedly (four times) queried and challenged Anne's justifications, perplexed as to why the sum of the ones column, '10' should be separated into a '0' and a '1'. With each query, Anne cited the standard school algorithmic procedures she used to arrive at her sum, a set of rules that made no mathematical sense to Jack. Cobb *et al.* conclude that for Anne the procedural description served as an appropriate justification, and she concluded that Jack was not listening. For Jack, on the other hand, Anne's procedural description was akin to number magic and made no conceptual sense. As Cobb *et al.* explain, the differences between Jack's and Anne's mathematical understandings resulted in a failure to communicate effectively, pointing to the critical status of norms for what counts as a mathematical justification in peer argumentation.

Implications of Saxe's emergent goals model for recent sociocultural approaches

The sociocultural approaches contribute important perspectives on peer processes in math learning. The illustrative Nicolopoulou and Cole and Cobb *et al.* analyses show peer interactional processes as situated in larger institutional contexts and communities in which norms, values and institutional supports are interwoven with the character of peer interactions.

While the conceptual links made between interactional and sociocultural processes are compelling in the newly emerging sociocultural approaches, to date we do not yet see either systematic ways for analysing peer interactions or ways for co-ordinating these possible analyses with a treatment of cognitive development. Indeed, we can ask of both the Nicolopoulou and Cole study and the Cobb *et al.* studies, what should count as critical data in interactions? What is the import of such data for mathematics learning?

To make progress towards addressing such issues, we need a treatment of cognitive development that is articulated in relation to a treatment of peer interaction. In the next section, we show how Saxe's treatment of emergent goals is co-ordinated with a treatment of cognitive development and transfer. In Saxe's treatment, we find addressed a number of the concerns raised by the sociocultural approaches.

COMPONENTS 2 AND 3

Components 2 and 3 of Saxe's model concern the process of cognitive development and the interplay of cognitive developments across practices. These components shift our focus from questions of how goals emerge in practices (Component 1) to questions of the cognitive developments children structure in their efforts to accomplish emergent goals. As previously noted, we will treat Components 2 and 3 only briefly here.

Component 2: form–function shifts in cognitive development

Saxe presents a treatment of cognitive development in terms of shifting relations between form and function.[1] Cultural forms, which are historically elaborated constructions like number systems, currency systems and social conventions, become cognitive ones as they are acquired and used by individuals in daily life to accomplish various cognitive functions like counting and arithmetic. Saxe argues that there is a dynamic relation between form and function: children appropriate prior forms to accomplish newly emerging cognitive functions and specialize these forms to serve those functions more adequately. The process of appropriation and specialization, in turn, leads to conditions for novel cognitive functions to emerge. For our purposes here, we are concerned with the way children appropriate cognitive forms to serve functions related to peer-influenced emergent goals in practices, and in the interplay between form and function across practices.

To illustrate the form-function model, consider how Jack, one of the two children in Cobb *et al.*'s example (p. 125) inappropriately used the historically elaborated algorithmic form for addition to solve the arithmetical problem of five twelves. We assume that Jack had used the standard addition algorithm successfully to serve arithmetical functions when problems did not require regrouping of tens. Now, to solve the five twelves problem, Jack brings to bear his prior algorithmic form, yielding the incorrect result, 610. The realization that his answer is not appropriate will likely lead Jack to more reflective analyses, and we expect (perhaps with further assistance) that he will construct the mapping between the conceptual operations on quantities entailed in the addition of five twelves and Anne's syntactic manipulations used to carry out the algorithmic solution.

Anne, on the other hand, shows that she applies an appropriate strategic form to serve the arithmetical function, though there is no evidence that she understands the link between her syntactical manipulations and the conceptual operations linked to quantities in her application of the algorithm. Jack's repeated challenges appear to do little to prompt her to try to generate the mapping between her procedural application and the conceptual operations. One might wish that the interaction would have led Anne to bring to bear other forms that could be specialized to serve the arithmetical function of the addition of five twelves, forms like base–10 blocks. A base–10 block procedure (creating five groups of one 10 and two 1 blocks and then re-grouping the 1s into a 10) might help to render the conceptual operations entailed in the use of the algorithmic form more transparent (see Fuson 1990; Fuson and Burghardt 1991). Indeed, the construction of mappings across different forms may in turn create conditions for the construction of new form-function relations. For instance, Anne's creation of the mapping between base–10 block solution and the algorithmic solution in addition may be useful to her as she tries to make sense of regrouping operations in applying the standard subtraction algorithm with borrowing.

Component 3: the interplay between mathematics learning across practices: the problem of transfer

Researchers often treat transfer – the application of learning in one context to solve a problem in another – as a process of generalization of prior learning or of alignment of prior cognitive forms to new problems. In the methods associated with these conceptualizations of transfer, subjects are typically presented with some short-term learning exercises, and then transfer is assessed in terms of pass/fail performances on laboratory tasks that differ from the learning exercises in some principled way. In Saxe's framework, transfer is viewed as a phenomenon that differs substantially from this traditional view of transfer, one in which social and peer processes may be involved in central ways.

In contrast to laboratory tasks, which are brief and in which children are permitted only very limited interaction with an experimenter under controlled conditions, classroom and other daily practices engage children with recurring problems, and there are often social supports for appropriating knowledge constructed in one practice to accomplish emergent goals in another. Although some treatments of transfer point to the importance of integrating analyses of social and cognitive developmental processes in treatments of learning across contexts (Laboratory of Comparative Human Cognition 1983; Saxe 1989), generally absent are investigations of peer processes in cognitive development. In Saxe's model, peers may be instrumental in helping one another bring forward understandings linked to one activity to accomplish current goals. Thus, if we apply this analysis to the interchange between Jack and Anne, we ask questions about the emergent interactions in which transfer may take place: does Jack's repeated questioning eventually lead Anne to recall the base–10 block discussion with the prior class, and to thus generate a mapping from one form, base–10 blocks to another? And, if so, who accomplished the transfer? Clearly, the 'transfer' would have resulted from an interaction intrinsically linked to the constructive activities of the peers in interaction with one another.

SUMMARY REMARKS ON EXISTING RESEARCH

Research on peer processes should be grounded in a general treatment of cognitive development that provides a conceptual basis for understanding how children's activities with peers may be interwoven with children's learning and development. Peer interactions should be conceptualized as emerging in purposeful activities that give interactions form and meaning and that themselves undergo shifts in organization and structure over time. Research on the social context of cognitive development should be guided by systematic treatments of cognitive development and by analyses of peer interaction embedded in systematic treatments of activity. To date, however, these two analytic concerns have not been well represented and co-ordinated in the literatures we reviewed.

In that the co-operative learning research is concerned with identifying contexts that enhance students' motivation to learn, this literature does not contribute directly to analyses of links between peer interaction and the process of conceptual change in children. Nevertheless, we can draw implications from the work that suggest how particular activity structures may support the emergence of particular kinds of goals. Co-operative learning arrangements appear to contribute to the establishment of group norms (through incentives) and social organizational processes that influence the character of interactions. Analyses motivated by a conceptual framework like Saxe's could reveal how the complexities of teacher-organized incentive structures provide a context that facilitates children's construction of new understandings, and the way these processes may interact with knowledge domain and activity setting.

In the collaborative problem-solving research we do find analyses of peer interactions guided in varying degrees by treatments of cognitive development. Piagetian theory has been the dominant perspective, and accordingly researchers have focused on sociocognitive conflict as the context for children's construction of novel cognitive developments. This approach, however, has not included consideration of how variations in activity structures constrain and influence interactional processes and emergent goals. Indeed, the analyses are limited to peer interactions of very limited duration as children engage with laboratory tasks that are often atypical of children's everyday practices.

Research that has adopted a sociocultural perspective does incorporate institutional and sociocultural processes in analyses of peer interactions. We see this as an important development in work in peer interaction. This work is early in its development.

Lacking in this work to date are unifying constructs that integrate the analysis of cognitive developmental with sociocultural processes.

NEW DIRECTIONS

There is a movement in the United States for reform of the traditional mathematics curriculum emphasizing calculation and computation. Documents like the National Council of Teachers of Mathematics' *Curriculum and Evaluation Standards* (1989) have called for new instructional practices that engage students in mathematical activities that are investigative and have meaning to them, and some of these efforts incorporate peer interaction. The Cobb *et al.* project is one that is responsive to this call. In the remainder of this chapter, we describe two of our own projects in which we use the three-component model to guide research and development effort on the social contexts of mathematics learning. Our presentation highlights those aspects of the projects that concern peer interaction.

Treasure Hunt: a classroom practice

On the basis of Saxe's prior work on cultural practices, our Peer Interaction Research group[2] set out to design a classroom practice that could support, through play, the emergence of mathematically rich environments. We developed a classroom game for elementary children called Treasure Hunt, and we are currently studying the way in which children's math learning is interwoven with this classroom practice. We have observed children as they played the game twice weekly over a two-and-a-half-month period for about half an hour per session; we videotaped the first and last session of play for each dyad and the preliminary analyses sketched below are based on these videotape records. Further, we arranged for play of the game so that we could collect videotapes when children were first learning to play and after they had become more expert at play in order to observe general transformations in the organization of play. Finally, we designed our study as a comparison among three groups. Half of the Treasure Hunt dyads were of the same ability and half were of mixed ability; an additional comparison group of non-game players were drawn from the same classrooms and matched for ability with the game playing groups. We administered post-tests to all groups, assessing both base–10 block arithmetic and standard orthographic arithmetic. Consistent with Saxe's model, we targeted children's emergent *mathematical* goals as the focus for analysis and analysed processes of goal formation with reference to the four-parameter model.

Emergent goals in Treasure Hunt (Component 1)

Treasure Hunt is a thematic board game in which children assume the roles of treasure hunters in search of gold doubloons that consist of gold painted base–10 blocks (in denominations of 1, 10, 100 and 1000), and the object of play is to acquire the most gold. In their search to acquire gold, children sail small ships around six islands situated on the board through rolls of a die. Children collect their gold in treasure chests that consist of long rectangular cards organized into thousands, hundreds, tens and ones columns, and they report their quantity of gold on their gold register with the number orthography (see Figure 6.2). Children typically play Treasure Hunt in dyads. In the course of play, children become engaged with various kinds of mathematical problems that are intrinsic to play. For instance, they compare base–10 block representations and standard orthographic representations of quantity as they consider whether to challenge their partner's report of his or her gold; they add, subtract and multiply quantities with base–10 blocks and then translate the results into the standard orthography as they make purchases, collect rent and provide change; and they compare ratios in the course of making best-buy purchases at trading posts.

In Treasure Hunt, the structure of the activity (parameter 1) includes both the rules of the game and children's game-linked motives. In the turn-taking structure, each player must accomplish a number of phases in a turn, including a Challenge, Rent, Purchase, Region and Check Phase (see Figure 6.3). Across phases, children are guided by the motive to acquire more gold, and in each phase children often are making efforts to accomplish emergent mathematical goals linked to particular phases. For instance, in a *Purchase Phase*, players select supplies to buy at island trading posts, often attempting to add supply values and then subtract the sum from their gold, and perhaps even to compare prices. In the *Check Phase*, children compare their gold

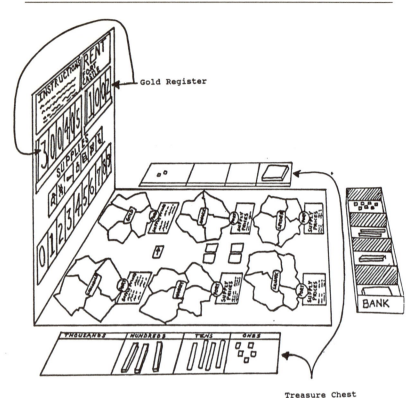

Gold Register

Treasure Chest

Figure 6.2 The Treasure Hunt Game.

and gold registers to make sure that their gold registers adequately represent their quantities of gold.

The particular artifacts and conventions (parameter 2) that are features of play figure prominently in children's mathematical goals. Consider again the Purchase Phase. Motivated by a concern to acquire more gold, players make purchases at the trading post, spending the base–10 block gold doubloons contained in their treasure chests and reported in their gold registers (see Figure 6.3); in their purchases, children's mathematics takes on the form of base–10 block manipulations as contrasted with the standard number orthography. For instance, a child may have one 1000 block, and four 1 blocks of gold in her treasure chest, and want to buy 27 doubloons' worth of supplies. To perform a subtraction of 1004 – 27 requires her to construct subgoals involving equival-

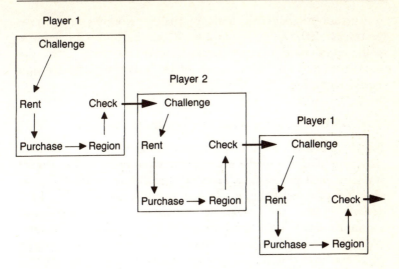

Figure 6.3 The turn-taking structure of Treasure Hunt.

ence trades of larger blocks for smaller blocks in order to accomplish the subtraction; in contrast, with the orthography, she would apply the school-linked column subtraction procedure with borrowing, a solution process in which different subgoals emerge.

The prior understandings (parameter 3) that children bring to the activity also constrain children's construction of mathematical goals in play. For instance, children who do not yet understand the denominational structure of blocks may treat all blocks with a value of unity; others may seek assistance when accomplishing gold problems, relying on their partners to help them structure the sequence of goals that would lead to an adequate exchange. Goals are rooted in children's conceptual constructions, and analyses of processes of goal formation must be grounded in a treatment of children's understandings.

The particular social interactions (parameter 4) that are intrinsic to play occasion the emergence of or modify mathematical goals. For instance, in a player's efforts to pay 27 doubloons for treasure chests and maps from the gold in her own treasure chest currently totalling 1004 (1(1000) 4(1)), she may get stuck, not able to obtain the needed 27 doubloons from either the 1000 block or the four 1s. At this point the opponent may suggest trading the 1000 block for 100s, and the player may use the suggestion as a basis

to structure the goal of the trade, by analogy working out successive trades (100 block for ten 10s, 10 block for ten 1s) leading
to the appropriate denominational form for payment. Here, the
mathematical goals and subgoals of the player emerge through
the interaction.

Examples of ongoing analyses of emergent goals

The application of the four-parameter model to Treasure Hunt is
providing insight into the interplay between social and cognitive
developmental processes as goals emerge during problem formation and problem solution. In our ongoing analyses, we have
devised means of analysing children's construction and
accomplishment of mathematical goals in each phase of each turn.
We expect to find younger children are forming less complex
goals and that children's goals are interwoven with the various
artifacts of the game, like base–10 blocks, price-ratios at trading
posts, and translations between orthographic and base–10 representations of quantity. Further, we expect to find that peers
provide for one another supports for constructing and accomplishing mathematical goals, as when one less competent player counts
base–10 blocks to make a purchase and the opponent provides
change, accomplishing a more complex problem of subtraction.

Our analyses of emergent goals provides a basis to proceed
with the second and third analytic components: the emergence of
novel representational forms for quantity, the use of these forms
to accomplish various game-linked arithmetical functions, and
the transfer between the mathematics of Treasure Hunt and the
mathematics of the standard school classroom.

*Form-function shifts (Component 2) and transfer (Component 3) in
analyses of Treasure Hunt*

We are organizing our analyses of children's mathematics learning
(Component 2) with reference to the form-function model, focusing on the development of arithmetical problem-solving. In one
of our ongoing analyses, we examine a game-linked form – gold
doubloons – and the interplay in development between this form
and emerging cognitive functions. Below, we sketch the direction
of our preliminary efforts.

In the rules of the game, children use gold doubloons as a

medium of exchange. They buy supplies with gold, pay rent with gold, challenge with the aim of acquiring more gold and report their quantity of gold on their register. But children interpret the rules in their own terms, and in this transformation there is a complex developmental process as children strive to make sense of the external structure of the doubloons (e.g. one 1000 piece is equivalent to ten 100 pieces). We have observed differences among children's solutions to doubloon-linked arithmetic problems that reflect this process.

For instance, in a Purchase Phase, a player may need to produce a payment of 14 doubloons. The variety of ways that children attempt to accomplish payments like these display different relations between cognitive forms and functions. Some children are organizing *doubloon-linked strategic forms* to accomplish strictly *enumerative functions*: they might count and pay 14 pieces of any doubloon denomination, while other children respect the denominational structure of the doubloons in their problem solutions, yet will limit themselves to paying only 1s pieces, a specialization of their counting strategy to serve the enumerative function. More specialized game-linked cognitive forms reflect a differentiated treatment of the doubloons that serve a function that is shifting from enumeration to addition: when faced with insufficient 1s pieces, children pay with 'mixed denominations', counting 10s pieces with ten strokes and in this way incorporate both 10s and 1s pieces into their solutions. Here the prior form that served the earlier function of enumeration is appropriated to accomplish the newly emerging game-linked cognitive function of addition. As children's understanding of the denominational structure of doubloons deepens, we see a further development – an abbreviation of the mixed doubloon counting procedure: rather than counting a 10-unit block as ten 1s, children treat a 10 piece as a single term in a composition of multi-denominational terms. Further form-function relations in children's doubloon-linked activities are detailed elsewhere (Saxe, 1991b).

We are also analysing 'transfer' (Component 3) in Treasure Hunt. In one set of analyses, we are focusing on whether and in what way children may use knowledge generated in the play of Treasure Hunt to address arithmetical problems linked to their standard classroom practices. For example, we are studying Treasure Hunters' solution of standard school problems and contrasting these solutions with our comparison group of non-game players.

In another set of analyses, we are studying occasions in which one child serves as a catalyst for the other to apply prior knowledge to the creation and accomplishment of mathematical goals that emerge in play.

Concluding remarks about Treasure Hunt and its relation to Saxe's three-component framework

Guided by the three-component model, we wanted to create a classroom practice that would support children's interactive construction of rich mathematical environments. We took care to create a game in which arithmetical goals would emerge within an activity where children felt some ownership and investment. We made sure that arithmetical problems took form in a medium (base–10 blocks) in which computational procedures provided greater conceptual transparency than the standard orthography-linked algorithms, and we provided contexts in which children would be motivated to map arithmetical transformations from one symbolic medium to transformations in the other. Further, we created other artifacts, like the price ratios for purchases, that supported children's creation of particular kinds of mathematical goals, and ones that could be appropriated and manipulated by children.

In the design of the practice, we also took care to create ways of facilitating the analysis of cognitive development with the three-component approach. We created a game that was amenable to observation. Further, we wanted to capture complete practice-participation with a single video camera in such a way that we could code and analyse children's manipulations of game-linked artifacts. We are currently engaged with the analysis of these videotapes.

Portfolio practice

A second effort linked to the framework is currently in its development phase (Gearhart *et al.* 1991), and we provide a brief sketch here of those aspects of the planned project concerned with peer interaction. Our goal is to use insights gleaned from the framework to create a peer-based fifth grade classroom mathematics practice that integrates instruction and assessment in ways consistent with the reform movement in mathematics education.

Central to the practice is the student portfolio – as we view it, an assembly of a student's work that is a presentation of in-progress investigative activities and the resulting products of those activities. In the portfolio practice we are developing, the portfolio is an evolving artifact that supports teachers' efforts to create a classroom culture (cf. Cobb *et al.*, in press a; Nicolopoulou and Cole, in press) in which students are invested in mathematical work, and purposeful and insightful work is valued by participants. Values include, for example, making sense in mathematical enquiry, valuing multiple strategies in sense-making activities, using multiple means of communicating mathematical information, exploring the uses of different mathematical ideas and applying mathematics to meaningful problems. As students review and organize their portfolio collections, they become engaged in reflection on what they have come to understand and the value of their understandings, and they generate questions that motivate new investigations.

A general schema for our practice is contained in Figure 6.4. During a prototypical math period, the teacher begins with whole class instruction that is based on innovative curricular approaches that emphasize mathematics investigation (e.g. Corwin *et al.* 1990); students then break up in small groups to carry on math activities at centres where peer interaction is valued and encouraged. The teacher circulates to assist as needed, to observe and to engage students in dialogue that could help reveal their understandings as well as to reinforce classroom values about what constitutes good and interesting work. Every two weeks or so, small groups of students are provided time to make selections

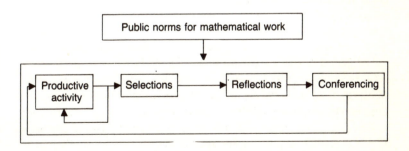

Figure 6.4 The structure of a portfolio practice.

from their work to include in their portfolio according to certain teacher-guided constraints that help students review what they have learned and how they feel about their efforts. These selections are later presented in small teacher-led groups in which peers and the teacher make joint evaluations of one another's work and plans for further work.

We plan to use the three-component approach as a basis for the construction of assessment tools that teachers will incorporate in their instructional practices, and that students will eventually internalize and use in assessing themselves. Among the targeted assessment domains of relevance to the present chapter include the quality and character of peer processes in investigative activities, evaluative activities and conferencing. In these areas, we plan to provide teachers with queries to assist their observations of group processes linked to mathematics learning as well as their guidance of conferencing discussions. Teachers' use of these tools will support public criteria for evaluation of student work and provide teachers with insight into situated processes central to peer-based mathematics learning.

We are developing queries that reflect all components of the model: the evolving norms that peers manifest in discussions of one another's work and their emergence in relation to the structure of the portfolio practice (Component 1, parameter 1); the available artifacts (e.g. software, manipulatives, geoboards) and the way they do or do not create supportive contexts for sustained peer-based investigative activities (Component 1, parameter 2); variations in students' mathematical understandings that constrain the ways they participate with peers in investigative activities (Component 1, parameter 3); the dynamic exchanges between peers that may or may not support the emergence of new mathematical goals (Component 1, parameter 4); construction of processes of peer interaction – the changing strategic forms children are structuring to serve varying mathematical functions in their investigative activities (Component 2); and the way peers may facilitate one another's use of mathematical understandings constructed in prior activities to accomplish new emergent goals in the current activity (transfer, Component 3).

CONCLUDING REMARKS

In his seminal volume, *Thought and Language* (1986), Vygotsky raised critical issues regarding the choice of a unit of analysis to guide conceptual and empirical inquiry in psychological studies. He argued that, rather than breaking down psychological phenomena into their most rudimentary elements as was the goal of the associationism of his day, we need to identify units that have properties of the central phenomena we are trying to explain. To make his point, Vygotsky noted that we do not study the elements of water if we are interested in understanding the properties of water; oxygen and hydrogen both burn, whereas water extinguishes fire. To understand properties of water, we study the water molecule.

While Vygotsky used his unit-of-analysis discussion to motivate his treatment of the interfunctional relations between language and thought, his discussion is just as valuable as an approach to the study of peer interaction and cognitive development. We noted when reviewing prior approaches that peer interactions have often been studied as an isolated element that affects cognitive change. We would argue, with Vygotsky, that just as isolating language and studying its effect upon thought distorts and poorly frames the analysis of thought/language relations, so too does this elementalist methodological approach distort intrinsic relations between peer and cognitive developmental processes. Instead, we need to create appropriate analytic units to capture the complex relations that obtain between children's developing cognitions and forms of social organization, social norms, artifacts and social interactional processes.

We have argued that Saxe's construct of emergent goals offers a critical unit for analysis of relations between peer processes and cognitive development. In Saxe's interpretation of goals, we find a representation of the relations between the constructive activities of the child and the social and cultural processes in which peer processes are embedded and take form. In this chapter, we have endeavoured to use the construct of emergent goals as a basis to review and critique existing approaches to the study of peer interactions and cognitive development. The approach provided a valuable perspective, and we see Saxe's framework as an important new direction that integrates the fruits of prior work and points to new directions for further research and the development of educational practices.

NOTES

The paper was prepared while Geoffrey Saxe was funded by grants from the Spencer Foundation (M890224) and the National Science Foundation (MDR–8855643), Maryl Gearhart was supported by funding from the Advanced Development Group, Apple Computer, Inc., and Mary Note and Pamela Paduano were supported by pre-doctoral traineeships from the National Institutes of Mental Health. The opinions expressed in this chapter are not necessarily those of the funding agencies.

1. The form-function model is an adaptation of that presented in Werner and Kaplan (1962).
2. This group includes Joseph Becker, Teresita Bermudez, Steven Guberman, Marta Laupa, Scott Lewis, David Niemi, Mary Note, Pamela Paduano, Geoffrey Saxe, Rachelle Seelinger and Christine Starczak.

REFERENCES

Ames, G. and Murray, F. (1982) 'When two wrongs make a right: promoting cognitive change by social conflict', *Developmental Psychology*, 18, 894–7.

Aronson, E., Blaney, N., Stephan, C., Sikes, J. and Snapp, M. (1978) *The Jigsaw Classroom*, Beverly Hills, CA, Sage.

Bearison, D. J., Magzamen, S. and Filardo, E. K. (1986) 'Socio-cognitive conflict and cognitive growth in young children', *Merrill-Palmer Quarterly* 32 (1), 51–72.

Behrend, S. D. and Resnick, L. B. (1991) 'Peer collaboration in a causal reasoning task', unpublished manuscript, Pittsburgh, PA, University of Pittsburgh.

Botvin, G. J. and Murray, F. B. (1975) 'The efficacy of peer modeling and social conflict in the acquisition of conservation', *Child Development* 46, 796–9.

California State Department of Education (1990, draft) *Mathematics Framework for California Public Schools: K–12*, Sacramento, CA.

Cobb, P., Wood, T. and Yackel, E. (in press a) 'Characteristics of classroom mathematics traditions: an interactional analysis', in C. Maher and R. Davis (eds) *Relating Schools to Reality in Mathematics Learning*, Englewood Cliffs, NJ, Prentice Hall.

Cobb, P., Wood, T. and Yackel, E. (in press b) 'Interaction and learning in mathematics classroom situations', *Educational Studies in Mathematics*.

Cobb, P., Yackel, E. Wood, T., Wheatley, G. and Merkel, G. (1988) 'Research into practice: creating a problem solving atmosphere', *Arithmetic Teacher* 36 (1), 46–8.

Corwin, R. B., Russell, S. J. and Tierney, C. C. (1990) 'Seeing fractions: representations of wholes and parts. A unit for the upper elementary grades', Technical Education Research Center (TERC), Sacramento, CA, California Department of Education.

Damon, W. (1984) 'Peer education: the untapped potential', *Journal of Applied Developmental Psychology* 5, 331–43.

Dasen, P. R. (1977) 'Are cognitive processes universal? A contribution to cross-cultural Piagetian psychology', in N. Warren (ed.) *Studies in Cross-cultural Psychology*, London, Academic Press.

Doise, W., Mugny, G. and Perret-Clermont, A. N. (1975) 'Social inter-action and the development of cognitive operations', *European Journal of Social Psychology* 5, 367–83.

Doise, W. and Mugny, G. (1984) *The Social Development of the Intellect*, Oxford, Pergamon.

Ellis, S. and Gauvain, M. (in press) 'Social and cultural influences on children's collaborative interactions', in L. T. Winegar and J. Valsiner (eds) *Children's Development Within Social Context*, Hillsdale, NJ, Erlbaum.

Forman, E. and McPhail, J. (1989) 'What have we learned about the cognitive benefits of peer interaction? A Vygotskian critique', paper presented at the Annual meeting of the American Educational Research Association, San Francisco, CA.

Fuson, K. C. (1990) 'Conceptual structures for multiunit numbers: impli-cations for learning and teaching multidigit addition, subtraction, and place-value', *Cognition and Instruction*, 7, 343–404.

Fuson, K. C. and Burghardt, B. (1991) 'Group case studies of second graders inventing multidigit addition procedures for bse-ten blocks and written marks', paper presented at the Fifteenth Psychology of Mathematics Education Conference, Assisi, Italy.

Gearhart, M., Saxe, G. B. and Stipek, D. (1991) 'Portfolios in practice: integrating assessment and instruction in elementary mathematics', proposal submitted to the National Science Foundation, UCLA, Los Angeles, CA.

Glachan, M. and Light, P. (1982) 'Peer interaction and learning: can two wrongs make a right?' pp. 238–62, in G. Butterworth and P. Light (eds) *Social Cognition: Studies of the Development of Understanding*, Chi-cago, University of Chicago Press.

Hatano, G. (1988) 'Social and motivational bases for mathematical under-standing', in G. B. Saxe and M. Gearhart (eds) *Children's Mathematics*, San Francisco, CA, Jossey-Bass.

Johnson, D. W. and Johnson, R. (1975) *Learning Together and Alone: Cooperative, Competitive, and Individualization*, Englewood Cliffs, NJ, Prentice-Hall.

Johnson, D. W. and Johnson, R. (1978) 'Cooperative, competitive, and individualistic learning', *Journal of Research and Development in Edu-cation*, 12, 3–15.

Johnson, D. W. and Johnson, R. (1979) 'Conflict in the classroom: controversy and learning', *Review of Educational Research* 49, 51–70.

Johnson, R. T., Johnson, D. W. and Stanne, M. B. (1985) 'Effects of cooperative, competitive, and individualistic goal structures on com-puter-assisted instruction', *Journal of Educational Psychology* 77, 668–78.

Light, P. and Glachan, M. (1985) 'Facilitation of individual problem solving through peer interaction', *Educational Psychology* 3–4, 217–25.

Miller, S. A. and Brownell, C. A. (1975) 'Peers, persuasion, and Piaget: dyadic interaction between conservers and nonconservers', *Child Development* 46, 992–7.

Mugny, G. and Doise, W. (1978) 'Socio-cognitive conflict and structure of individual and collective performances', *European Journal of Social Psychology* 8, 181–92.

National Council of Teachers of Mathematics (1989) *Curriculum and Evaluation Standards for School Mathematics*, Reston, VA, NCTM.

Nicolopoulou, A. and Cole, M. (in press) 'The fifth dimension, its play-world, and its institutional contexts: the generation and transmission of shared knowledge in the culture of collaborative learning', in N. Minick and E. Forman (eds) *The Institutional and Social Context of Mind: New Directions in Vygotskian Theory and Research*, New York, Oxford University Press.

Noddings, N. (1985) 'Small groups as a setting for research on mathematical problem solving', in E. A. Silver (ed.) *Teaching and Learning Mathematical Problem Solving*, Hillsdale, NJ, Erlbaum.

Perret-Clermont, A. N. (1980) 'Social interaction and cognitive development in children', *European Monographs in Social Psychology* 19, London, Academic Press.

Peterson, P. L. and Swing, S. R. (1985) 'Students' cognitions as mediators of the effectiveness of small-group learning', *Journal of Educational Psychology* 77, 299–312.

Peterson, P. L., Wilkinson, L. C., Spinelli, F. and Swing, S. R. (1984) 'Merging the process-product and the sociolinguistic paradigms: research on small-group processes', pp. 126–52 in P. L. Peterson, L. C. Wilkinson and M. Hallinan (eds) *The Social Context of Instruction*, Orlando, Academic Press.

Piaget, J. (1963) *The Origins of Intelligence in Children*, New York, Norton.

Piaget, J. (1966) 'Need and significance of cross-cultural studies in genetic psychology', *International Journal of Psychology* 1, 3–13.

Piaget, J. (1970) 'Piaget's theory', in P. H. Mussen (ed.) *Carmichael's Manual of Child Psychology* (3rd edition, vol. 1, pp. 703–32), New York, Wiley.

Piaget, J. (1977) *The Development of Thought: Equilibration of Cognitive Structures*, New York, Viking.

Saxe, G. B. (1981) 'Body parts as numerals: a developmental analysis of numeration among a village population in Papua New Guinea', *Child Development* 52, 306–16.

Saxe, G. B. (1982) 'Developing forms of arithmetic operations among the Oksapmin of Papua New Guinea', *Developmental Psychology* 18, (4), 583–94.

Saxe, G. B. (1985) 'The effects of schooling on arithmetical understandings: studies with Oksapmin children in Papua New Guinea', *Journal of Educational Psychology* 77 (5), 503–13.

Saxe, G. B. (1988a) 'Candy selling and math learning', *Educational Researcher* 17 (6), 14–21.

Saxe, G. B. (1988b) 'The mathematics of child street vendors', *Child Development* 59, 1415–25.

Saxe, G. B. (1989) 'Transfer of learning across cultural practices', *Cognition and Instruction* 6 (4), 325–30.

Saxe, G. B. (1990) 'The interplay between children's learning in school and non-school social contexts', in M. Gardner, J. Greeno, F. Reis and A. Schoenfeld (eds) *Toward a Scientific Practice of Science Education*, Hillsdale, NJ, Erlbaum.

Saxe, G. B. (1991a) *Culture and Cognitive Development: Studies in Mathematical Understanding*, Hillsdale, NJ, Lawrence Erlbaum & Associates, Inc.

Saxe, G. B. (1991b) 'From the field to the classroom: studies in children's mathematics', invited address for the Meetings of the National Council for Teachers of Mathematics.

Saxe, G. B. (in press) 'Studying children's learning in context: problems and prospects', *Journal of the Learning Sciences*.

Saxe, G. B. and Gearhart, M. (1990) 'The development of topological concepts in unschooled straw weavers', *British Journal of Developmental Psychology* 8, 251–8.

Saxe, G. B., Guberman, S. R. and Gearhart, M. (1987) 'Social processes in early number development', *Monographs of the Society for Research in Child Development* 52 (2).

Saxe, G. B. and Moylan, T. (1982) 'The development of measurement operations among the Oksapmin of Papua Guinea', *Child Development* 53, 1242–8.

Silverman, I. and Geiringer, E. (1973) 'Dyadic interaction and conservation induction: a test of Piaget's equilibration model', *Child Development* 44, 815–20.

Slavin, R. E. (1977) 'Classroom reward structure: an analytical and practical review', *Review of Educational Research* 47, 633–50.

Slavin, R. E. (1980) 'Cooperative learning', *Review of Educational Research* 50, 315–42.

Slavin, R. E. (1983a) *Cooperative Learning*, New York, Longman.

Slavin, R. E. (1983b) 'When does cooperative learning increase student achievement?' *Psychological Bulletin* 94, 429–45.

Slavin, R. E. (1987) 'Developmental and motivational perspectives on cooperative learning: a reconciliation', *Child Development* 58, 1161–7.

Swing, S. R. and Peterson, P. L. (1982) 'The relationship of student ability and small-group interaction to student achievement', *American Educational Research Journal* 19, 259–74.

Vygotsky, L. S. (1978) *Mind in Society: The Development of Higher Psychological Processes*, edited by M. Cole, V. John-Steiner, S. Scribner and E. Souberman, Cambridge, MA, Harvard University Press.

Vygotsky, L. V. (1986) in A. Kozulin (ed.) *Thought and Language*, Cambridge, MA, MIT Press.

Webb, N. M. (1982a) 'Group composition, group interaction and achievement in cooperative small groups', *Journal of Educational Psychology* 74, 475–84.

Webb, N. M. (1982b) 'Peer interaction and learning in cooperative small groups', *Journal of Educational Psychology* 74, 642–55.

Webb, N. M. (1982c) 'Student interaction and learning in small groups', *Review of Educational Research* 52, 421–45.

Webb, N. M. (1991) 'Task-related verbal interaction and mathematics learning in small groups', unpublished manuscript, UCLA Los Angeles, CA.

Werner, H. and Kaplan, B. (1962) *Symbol Formation*, New York, Wiley.

Wertsch, J. V. (1984) 'The zone of proximal development: some conceptual issues', in B. Rogoff and J. V. Wertsch (eds) *Children's Learning in the Zone of Proximal Development. New Directions for Child Development*, San Francisco, Jossey-Bass.

Wood, T. (1991) 'Learning in an enquiry mathematics classroom', *Proceedings of the Fifteenth Psychology of Mathematics Education Conference*, Assisi, Italy.

Yackel, E. (1991) 'The role of peer questioning during class discussion in second grade mathematics', *Proceedings of the Fifteenth Psychology of Mathematics Education Conference*, Assisi, Italy.

Yackel, E., Cobb, P. and Wood, T. (in press) 'Small group interactions as a source of learning opportunities in second grade mathematics', *Journal for Research in Mathematics Education*.

Chapter 7

The practice of assessment

Ingrid Lunt

INTRODUCTION

The practice of assessment both in psychology and therefore in
education has long been dominated by Western theoretical paradigms derived from a positivist and reductionist tradition, and in
particular the psychometric tradition exemplified by IQ tests. As
developed and practised particularly in the UK and the USA this
psychometric tradition relies on what have been termed 'static'
and norm-based forms of assessment. As will be discussed later
in this chapter, there is an increasing awareness of some of the
problems inherent in traditional static assessment procedures in
terms of their descriptive, predictive and prescriptive functions.
Dynamic assessment, which in its recent developments derives
substantially either explicitly or implicitly from the theoretical
formulations of Vygotsky, offers an alternative approach to the
complex task of assessment which has the potential to overcome
some of the problems inherent in traditional 'static' forms of
assessment. In this chapter I would like to consider some of those
problems and the issues involved in assessment, then to examine
relevant parts of Vygotsky's theory and its significance for assessment practice. Some of the issues will be illustrated by a critical
consideration of some relatively well-known developments in the
field of dynamic assessment. I will then attempt to consider some
implications for future practice.

By way of introduction to Vygotsky's work, it has to be
remembered at the outset that Vygotsky's writing was very much
the product of the intellectual, social, political and cultural climate
in Russia of the 1920s and early 1930s, that his early death at the
age of 38 prevented a fully-worked out formulation of his theory

and therefore that much of his writing consists of notes which
have been selectively and sometimes confusingly translated (many
quite recently) into English. Vygotsky's work drew on and
covered a wide range of disciplines. Although he

> has been presented in the English literature mainly as a theor-
> etician, concerned chiefly with the relationship between speech
> and thinking . . . he was also a defectologist, a skilled clinician,
> a teacher, an innovator in the philosophy and methodology of
> science and a not inconsiderable figure in the development of
> Marxist thought.
>
> (Sutton 1983: 190)

As such, Vygotsky was concerned both at the theoretical and at
a practical and clinical level with questions of human development
in the broadest sense. His writing is very much the product of
the social and political context of the Soviet Union at that time.
Zinchenko and Davydov (1985: vii) suggests that 'his notion of
the semiotic or symbolic nature of higher mental functions and
consciousness is very closely tied to the theory and practice of
Russian symbolism . . . during this period'. Vygotsky's theory
lays an emphasis on the role of the social and of society in
providing a framework for the child's development and a belief
that much of learning is mediated through social interactions both
at an interpersonal level and at a sociocultural level. Cognitive
processes and development are the result of social and cultural
interactions such that all psychological processes are initially social
and only later become individual.

> It is only in recent years that his much more extensive views
> about the relationship between individual development and
> sociohistorical evolution have been appreciated. For (Vygot-
> sky), the child's development depends upon her using, so to
> speak, the tool kit of the culture to express the powers of
> mind.
>
> (Bruner and Haste 1987: 5)

Vygotsky emphasizes the dialectical relationship between the individual and the social and the dependence on this relationship of
the evolution of the culture and the development of the individual.

> From the very first days of the child's development his activi-
> ties acquire a meaning of their own in a system of social

behaviour and, being directed towards a definite purpose, are refracted through the prism of the child's environment. The path from object to child and from child to object passes through another person. This complex human structure is the product of a developmental process deeply rooted in the links between individual and social history.

(Vygotsky 1978: 30)

Vygotsky himself had a very practical interest in the questions raised by the issue of assessment since such questions provided a vehicle for his exploration of the relationship between learning or instruction and development. For Vygotsky, the task of assessment, that is of exploring the processes of a child's learning and understanding, enabled him to develop a theory of development which embraced the dialectical relationship between the individual and the social.

A quiet revolution has taken place in developmental psychology in the last decade. It is not only that we have begun to think again of the child as a social being – one who plays and talks with others, learns through interactions with parents and teachers – but because we have come once more to appreciate that through such social life, the child acquires a framework for interpreting experience and learns how to negotiate meaning in a manner congruent with the requirements of the culture. 'Making sense' is a social process; it is an activity that is always situated in a cultural and historical context.

(Bruner and Haste 1987: 1)

Central to Vygotsky's theorizing on the process of development and the role of adult mediation is the idea of the zone of proximal development, through which the social could become individual. As we will see later, the zone of proximal development provides the foundation and potential for some of the most important recent initiatives in the assessment of individual children.

CRITICISMS OF TRADITIONAL ASSESSMENT PRACTICE

The assessment and testing movement originated formally at the beginning of this century and has, until recently, been dominated by the psychometric tradition particularly of intelligence or IQ tests. As is well known, these tests are standardized and 'static' procedures which seek to evaluate a child's individual performance by reference to a norm or 'average' group and usually by the allocation of an IQ 'score' derived from the child's performance on a range of tasks carried out in a standardized situation. Particularly in Britain and the USA, long and widespread use of intelligence tests, especially in relation to special education, has more recently given way to concerns about their usefulness, appropriateness or indeed validity for either the groups or the purposes for which they have frequently been used (Quicke 1982, 1984; Tomlinson 1982). Amongst professional psychologists in the UK, the Stanford Binet tests, followed by Wechsler tests and, more recently, the British Ability Scales, have traditionally been used both for diagnostic and for predictive purposes to inform educational decision-making. Further, despite more than four decades of documentation, criticism and debate about the shortcomings and limitations of IQ as a measure of 'intelligence' or potential especially among children from non-middle-class and non-Western backgrounds, the notion of IQ is still widely used and accepted in some circles as an indicator of academic potential. Critics of intelligence tests typically state that IQ tests label children inappropriately, that they do not offer information for curriculum planning, that they are culturally biased and that their claims to validity and reliability are not justified (e.g. Gillham 1978; Quicke 1984; Solity and Bull 1987; Feiler 1988). On the other hand, IQ tests have claimed considerable validity and continue to do so, in assigning a measure of mental ability to an individual on the basis of performance in a standard test situation. However sophisticated the model of intelligence on which these tests are based, it assumes the existence of fixed and measurable characteristics within an individual which develop in an orderly (and predictable) fashion. Further, it implies 'a positivist conception of what to expect of children at various ages and stages; that is, a conception that regards it as a relatively uncontroversial matter to assess a child's level, stage, need or skills with respect to emotional or cognitive functioning' (Quicke 1984: 69). Indeed these tests are based on a concept of 'ability' as a stable or static characteristic within the individual which will to a substantial extent determine future learning.

The way educationalists refer to children's 'ability' is a potentially insidious form of discrimination. So, although we may no longer support the use of intelligence tests to ascertain children's ability and learning potential, the language of the intelligence test still abounds. This may in the most negative instances, lead to children being quite arbitrarily identified as lacking in intelligence or ability, with the inevitable consequence that expectations for their future learning are low.

(Solity 1991: 15)

To counter some of the criticisms levelled at intelligence tests, more recently so-called curriculum-based assessment (CBA) or criterion-referenced tests, checklists and procedures have been developed which have theoretical origins in behavioural psychology and seek to evaluate an individual's performance against specific criteria or objectives within a curriculum area. These approaches usually derive from the specification of a sequence of learning objectives and aim to find out what the child has learned in order to plan the next teaching (or learning) step (Faupel 1986; Lister and Cameron 1986; Solity and Bull 1987). The intention here is to use task analysis to break down complex instructional objectives within a curriculum area into component skill elements which can be programmed into manageable incremental steps. 'The model is essentially a test-teach-test model. Once skill development strengths and weaknesses have been assessed, specific instructional objectives are written and particular strategies are used to teach the skill' (Mercer and Ysseldyke 1977). In the UK, CBA has led to a number of so-called curriculum packages (for example SNAP: Ainscow and Muncey 1981; Datapac: Akerman et al. 1983) which aim to develop assessment through teaching and to link the process of assessment with learning outcomes. Recently, however, there has been a growing awareness of some of the limitations of these procedures and in particular reservations both about a somewhat mechanistic and individualistic psychology which forms their theoretical base and about the pedagogical assumptions underlying task analysis. Although it is possible using curriculum-based or criterion-referenced assessment procedures to link teaching to assessment and hence to explore a learner's *level* of attainment, they do not usually provide information either about a learner's learning strategies or about the social and interactional features of the learning situation. Such forms of assessment do not answer the 'how' or 'why' questions in their analysis of children's success or failure in learning. Nor do they provide qualitative information about a learner's future learning potential or pedagogical needs. A growing number of psychologists and educationalists are realizing the importance of context in the assessment of the individual (Reynolds *et al.* 1984; Fredrickson *et al.* 1991). 'An increased focus on the interactive nature of learning and the fact that an examination of what children learn cannot be divorced from considerations of how they are taught and the contexts in which learning takes place' (Solity 1991) has led many professionals to search for more interactive and qualitative forms of assessment. Within this search there has been an interest in the exploration of cognitive and metacognitive strategies, learning style and affective aspects of learning and performance.

The past decade has witnessed a further and specific crisis in the field of assessment. This is particularly severe in relation to a large majority of those children who are presented for assessment: namely all those children whose backgrounds (linguistic, ethnic, class) and life experience are different from a 'norm' and in particular children from ethnic minority backgrounds. For example Cummins's (1984) analysis of referrals and psychological assessments of more than 400 students from minority language backgrounds has pointed both to the inherent limitations of any static 'one-shot' approach to assessing educational potential and to the widespread use of IQ test measures in the assessment of these students. In its most extreme form, this has led to states in the USA and to LEAs within the UK prohibiting the use of IQ tests for minority ethnic group members. For these children, it is said, both the process and the product of assessment are likely to be unfair and potentially discriminatory. As Jones (1988) writes 'A crisis exists in the psychoeducational assessment of minority group children.'

Bransford *et al.* (1987) suggest that dissatisfaction with traditional assessment tools, especially standardized tests of intelligence, is most often grounded in one or more of three basic arguments:

1 Traditional assessments deal only with the products of learning, disregarding learning processes.
2 Traditional assessments do not address the responsiveness of the child to instruction.

3 Traditional assessments do not provide prescriptive information regarding potentially effective intervention techniques.

Both psychometric assessment and curriculum-based assessment are examples of what have become known as 'static' assessment procedures (in contrast to 'dynamic' assessment procedures). The contrast between static and dynamic assessment exists at two levels. The first level refers to the test procedure itself, the static test situation compared with the dynamic test situation; the second level refers to the nature of what is being investigated or measured, that is, the product compared with the process of learning. At the first level, that of the test situation, typically in the static assessment the tester is required to present a number of tasks to the child, observe and record the child's response and performance and score or interpret the result. Interaction between assessor and assessed is not permitted. Indeed the standardization relies on the creation of as near identical (standard) test situations as possible and this by definition rules out anything more than a standard interaction. For IQ tests important questions of standardization, reliability and validity demand standardized and formalized interaction; for curriculum-based assessment the aim is to establish accurately what the child can and cannot do, *on her own*.

> These two views of the assessment process share an important characteristic: both focus on the performance of the child at the individual-developmental or unassisted level. Most often, strict limits are placed on the kinds of assistance the tester may give, and how it 'counts' in arriving at a score. The aim is an objective measure of how much the child can do alone; the examiner-examinee interaction is standardized, controlled, and minimized. Given this goal, to allow unrestricted aid to testees would introduce errors of measurement, make assessment unreliable and norms meaningless.
>
> (Gallimore *et al.* 1989: 56)

The shortcomings of <u>different kinds of 'static' assessment</u> procedures have been well documented by those involved in developing alternative 'dynamic' assessment procedures (Brown and French 1979; Feuerstein 1979; Brown and Campione 1986; Budoff 1987; Campione and Brown 1987; Lidz 1987; Minick 1987; Campione 1989). At the first level of distinction between static and dynamic assessment procedures, there are considerable problems with the 'static' assessment situation. The child is isolated from her context both in terms of place and of time and placed in an unfamiliar and often artificial situation. Her responses, cognitive and metacognitive, affective and attributional, are highly individual and idiosyncratic and depend on her particular range of prior experiences and characteristics, yet they are to be compared to a 'norm' which assumes that a particular individual has had equivalent opportunities to learn the particular skills required by the test or that this issue is of minimum relevance. The responses produced in a single 'one-off' static situation are assumed to be representative of her 'ability' thus equating attainment on a specific task with ability or potential for future learning. Her expectations and perceptions of the test situation and tasks are likely to be different from and unexplored by the tester, yet these may be important factors influencing her performance on the test. At the second level of distinction between static and dynamic assessment, the implied distinction between product and process questions the very nature and purpose of the assessment process. Static assessment techniques focus on what the child already knows and therefore the *product* of learning and on what the child can do *on her own*. The intention of these procedures is to establish levels of competence, which are often subsequently confused with and used as measures of potential. Dynamic assessment procedures, on the other hand, involve a dynamic interactional exploration of a learner's learning and thinking *processes* and aim to investigate a learner's strategies for learning and ways in which these may be extended or enhanced. Since it offers individuals an opportunity to learn, dynamic assessment has the potential to show important information about individual strategies and processes of learning and, therefore, to offer potentially useful suggestions about teaching.

The assumptions of static assessment procedures carry with them considerable problems which may be considered under the headings of descriptive generality, predictive validity and prescriptive validity. There is an assumption that the tasks or items in the test can be considered to be representative of the child's full range of competence, even though only a narrow and standardized sample of the child's cognitive repertoire has been tapped. Since the test situation is highly specific it does not permit a full exploration of an individual child's cognitive functioning and certainly not individual potential. This may particularly be the case for minority groups and groups for whom the tests have not been standardized and whose underachievement has been well documented (for example Tomlinson 1981; Cummins 1984). Static tests claim predictive validity with the result that achievement may become synonymous with potential, yet they offer no information on the child's responsiveness to teaching or potential for learning. In assuming a common set of prior learning experiences, they leave no room for the differential effects of different instructional paradigms and experiences and their influence on future performance. Finally and perhaps most significantly, their focus on the *product* rather than the *process* of learning emphasizes the outcomes rather than the strategies for learning and offers no information on the child's response to teaching, her cognitive and metacognitive strategies, how she made correct or incorrect responses or indeed, in the event of an incorrect response, how the child may be helped to make a correct response. Although some prescriptive use has been made of information from static assessment procedures in planning instructional and remedial programmes, for example in learning profiles, subskills or ability training programmes, these have been criticized by Brown and Campione (1986) as the 'leap to instruction' phenomenon and have often been found to be unsuccessful or inappropriate. Frederickson *et al.* (1991) suggest that

> psychologists need to give greater consideration to 'why' questions (and) ought to be able to provide a comprehensive picture of 'the whole child in context' through generating and testing a broad range of hypotheses, and being able to construe the child's problems from a range of different perspectives.
>
> (Frederickson *et al.* 1991: 21)

Awareness of the complexity of the task of assessing children's learning or potential has, in a sense, never been greater than now. In the UK, the government has set itself the task of developing a national assessment programme in order 'to improve standards'. Although these assessment programmes have as their focus the assessment of the majority rather than a concern with the minority for whom school learning is more difficult, assessment of all children's attainment and potential is now of central political, educational and psychological concern. This concern and focus has excited considerable debate and controversy. Psychometrics is enjoying an unprecedented boom as an industry and new and more sophisticated forms of intelligence tests are being developed both in the UK and the USA. It remains to be seen how far these new developments will be able to address some of the limitations of traditional assessment procedures, in particular in providing useful information on the *processes* of learning and cognitive development. Yet

> since the inception of the testing movement at the turn of the century, the goals of assessment have remained the same. The idea is to develop tests that will generate descriptions of individual learners in terms of their strengths and weaknesses that will (a) predict how well they are likely to do in academic settings and (b) inform the development of instructional programmes that can facilitate the performance of those predicted to experience particular difficulties.
>
> (Campione 1989: 151)

It is suggested here that dynamic assessment procedures offer a powerful perspective on our understanding of children's learning and the role of instruction in facilitating this as well as useful and important information for the achievement of the goals of assessment.

DYNAMIC ASSESSMENT

Partly inspired by the motivation to address some of the problems inherent in static assessment procedures, there has been an increasing interest in the West over the past ten to fifteen years in the development of more 'dynamic' or 'interactive' assessment procedures. Campione *et al.* (1984) have noted that these developments have consistently been motivated by the belief that static approaches to the assessment of learning ability or learning potential have failed to provide the kind of information that educators need in order to facilitate the psychological development and educational progress of children. As Minick writes:

> When faced with a child who performs poorly in school, the educator wants to know whether these difficulties are a function of the child's ultimate potential for learning, the child's current level of readiness as defined by previous learning opportunities, or other factors associated with the social context of schooling . . . he wants a qualitative assessment of the

child's current level of functioning and some indication of the kinds of instruction that might facilitate development.

(Minick 1987: 116)

He suggests further that all those in the dynamic assessment movement recognize the need to develop assessment devices that provide:

a) direct measures of the child's potential for learning and development;
b) information on the processes that lead to the child's success or failure at cognitive tasks; and
c) information on what might be done to facilitate the child's education and development.

(Minick 1987: 117)

Dynamic assessment (or mediated or assisted assessment as it is sometimes named) involves a dynamic interaction between tester and learner (testee) with a focus on the *process* rather than the *product* of learning. Common to all forms of dynamic assessment is a notion of prospective rather than retrospective assessment and an emphasis on an understanding of *how* the child learns rather than on *what* the child has already learned. This focus has its origins in the theorizing of Vygotsky, in particular in his work on the relationship between learning (or instruction) and development, the role of the adult in mediating understanding and the central place of the zone of proximal development in an understanding of an individual child's cognitive development.

VYGOTSKY'S THEORY

For Vygotsky instruction is at the heart of learning and plays a central and leading role in development. In contrast with other psychologists such as Piaget, who would suggest that learning follows development, and Skinner, who equates learning with development, Vygotsky considered that instruction precedes and leads development and wrote that 'the only "good learning" is that which is in advance of development' (Vygotsky 1978: 89). It is this emphasis on the central role of instruction combined with his belief in the social nature of learning which led Vygotsky to explore the extent to which children could go further in their understanding in co-operation with another more knowledgeable person than on their own. Vygotsky suggested that 'instruction is only useful when it moves ahead of development. When it does, it impels or awakens a whole series of functions that are in a state of maturation lying in the zone of proximal development' (Vygotsky 1987: 212). Vygotsky's theory rests on his belief that cognitive processes are the result of social and cultural inter-actions, and that all higher mental functioning in the individual has its origins in the social. His argument that all psychological processes are initially social and shared between people, especially adults and children, led to his general genetic law of cultural development.

> Every function in the cultural development of the child comes on the stage twice, in two respects: first in the social, later in the psychological, first in relations between people as an interpsychological category, afterwards within the child as an intrapsychological category.
>
> (Vygotsky 1978)

Advanced human psychological processes have their origins in collaborative activity which is mediated by verbal interaction. Thus the child is introduced to new concepts through social activity (particularly instructional activity by an adult) and, through a process of internalization, s/he is enabled to learn the new concept and take it on as her own. Vygotsky emphasized the role of semiotic mediation, particularly language, in effecting the internalization of activity. It is through this mediation that a child is able to transform external activity into internal activity and therefore understanding. The child learns and develops concepts through internalization, transferring from the social (inter-actional) plane to the individual (internal) plane. Following his emphasis on the central place of instruction at the heart of cognitive development, Vygotsky emphasizes the central role of the teacher or mediator in 'leading' development.

It is in the zone of proximal development that this 'leading' or 'mediation' is enabled to take place *through collaborative activity*.

> When adults help children to accomplish things that they are unable to achieve alone, they are fostering the development of knowledge and ability . . . From this perspective, which places instruction at the heart of development, a child's potential for

learning is revealed and indeed is often realised in interactions with more knowledgeable others.

(Wood 1988: 24)

For this reason, any assessment which does not explore the zone of proximal development must only be a partial assessment since it takes into account only those functions which have already developed and not those which are in the process of developing and which, by definition, are developing through collaborative activity. Minick (1987) suggests that 'assessment practices that focus entirely on the child's unaided performance fail to tap important differences in mental functioning that can be identified by analysing how the child responds to assistance from adults or more capable peers'. Since the child's emergent abilities are manifest only in collaborative activity and in mediated activity, full assessment needs to incorporate and explore this kind of interaction. The zone of proximal development provides 'an account of how the more competent assist the young and less competent to reach that higher ground, ground from which to reflect more abstractly about the nature of things' (Bruner 1986: 73).

VYGOTSKY'S ZONE OF PROXIMAL DEVELOPMENT

We propose that an essential feature of learning is that it creates the zone of proximal development; that is, learning awakens a variety of internal developmental processes that are able to operate only when the child is interacting with people in his environment and in cooperation with his peers. Once these processes are internalised, they become part of the child's independent developmental achievement.

(Vygotsky 1978: 90)

Here Vygotsky emphasizes the importance of the 'social' in the child's development, though it should also be emphasized that the social relationship implied by Vygotsky is a specific and 'instructional' relationship. In order to facilitate learning and teaching (the word '*obuchenie*' in Russian as in some other languages includes both concepts), the concept of mediated learning implies the bridge across from teaching to learning or, to put it another way, the gradual transfer of the control of thought from the adult to the child in the zone of proximal development. In a now well-known quotation, Vygotsky illustrated the concept as follows:

> Suppose I investigate two children upon entrance into school, both of whom are ten years old chronologically and eight years old in terms of mental development. Can I say that they are the same age mentally? Of course. What does this mean? It means that they can independently deal with tasks up to the degree of difficulty that has been standardised for the eight-year-old level. If I stop at this point, people would imagine that the subsequent course of mental development and school learning for these children will be the same, because it depends on their intellect . . . Now imagine that I do not terminate my study at this point, but only begin it. These children seem to be capable of handling problems up to an eight-year-old's level, but not beyond that. Suppose that I show them various ways of dealing with the problem. Different experimenters might employ different modes of demonstration in different cases: some might run through an entire demonstration and ask the children to repeat it, others might initiate the solution and ask the child to finish it, or offer leading questions. In short, in some way or another I propose that the children solve the problem with my assistance. Under these circumstances it turns out that the first child can deal with problems up to a twelve-year-old's level, the second up to a nine-year-old's. Now, are these children mentally the same?
>
> When it was first shown that the capability of children with equal levels of mental development to learn under a teacher's guidance varied to a high degree, it became apparent that those children were not mentally the same age and that the subsequent course of their learning would obviously be different. This difference between twelve and eight, or between nine and eight, is what we call *the zone of proximal development. It is the distance between the actual developmental level as determined by independent problem-solving and the level of potential development as determined through problem-solving under adult guidance or in collaboration with more capable peers.*

(Vygotsky 1978: 85–6, italics in the original)

The notion of the zone of proximal development (ZPD) allowed Vygotsky to examine the process of and potential for learning in those functions that have not yet matured but are in the process of maturation, functions that will mature tomorrow but are currently in an embryonic state. These functions could be termed the 'buds' or 'flowers' of development rather than the 'fruits' of development. The actual developmental level characterises mental development retrospectively, while the zone of proximal development characterises mental development prospectively.

(Vygotsky 1978: 86–7).

Vygotsky thus distinguished between two aspects or levels of mental functioning, first, those functions which are already mature and second, those functions which are in the process of maturing or about to mature. Since the process of maturing or learning involves initially collaborative activity (or mediated learning), it is essential that this second level of functions be investigated through collaborative activity, i.e. in the zone of proximal development. Vygotsky stated that 'what the child is able to do in collaboration today he will be able to do independently tomorrow' (Vygotsky 1987: 206). Therefore it is through an analysis of the zone of proximal development that we are able to investigate and try to understand 'those psychological functions which are in the process of development and which are likely to be overlooked if the focus is exclusively on the unassisted child's performance' (Kozulin 1990: 170). For Vygotsky, however, it was not sufficient simply to establish that two individuals differed in the amount or extent of their 'zone of proximal development'; it was important to explore the nature of learning potential in the zone and in particular to find out *how* an individual was responding to adult interaction (instruction) and therefore how s/he was developing and thus to understand the dynamics of the zone of proximal development.

Thus, according to Vygotsky, in order to gain a comprehensive assessment of an individual's cognitive functioning, it is necessary to engage in and to explore collaborative activity, in which a more competent other (adult) 'leads' or 'mediates' the development of the learner. The exploration of such collaborative activity (in the zone of proximal development) will shed light on the nature of the learner's cognitive strategies and on those functions which are about to develop (and which may be present in collaborative or assisted activity). It is through the exploration of the adult 'leading' the learner into cognitive activity apparently beyond the level that the learner attains unaided that we are able to begin to understand how a learner is developing and what strategies might be useful in order to facilitate further development.

> If one accepts the importance of 'scientific' concepts in a child's development, the entire system of intelligence testing based on the assessment of a child's spontaneous concepts becomes problematic . . . it is much more appropriate, reasoned Vygotsky, to focus on the collaborative forms of thinking in which the child's everyday concepts come into contact with the 'scientific' concepts introduced by adults.
>
> (Kozulin 1990: 169)

This notion carries with it profound implications for the practice of instruction and of assessment, raising as it does questions both about the role of the teacher in instruction and about the tester in assessment.

IMPLICATIONS OF VYGOTSKY'S THEORY FOR DYNAMIC ASSESSMENT

Vygotsky's zone of proximal development (sometimes also translated as zone of potential development or zone of next or nearest development) forms the basis for subsequent developments of dynamic assessment procedures both in the USSR and in the West. As is apparent above, for Vygotsky, assessment which focuses only on a child's actual level of attainment or development is incomplete and gives only a partial picture. To gain a complete picture or assessment, it is necessary to assess the child at the second level, i.e. the zone of proximal development. Such assessment by definition involves a dynamic interaction and focuses on the child's processes for learning or ability to interact with a more competent adult.

Within the field of dynamic assessment there is a wide range of different practices. However, different forms of dynamic assessment share an emphasis on the investigation and evaluation of the psychological *processes* involved in learning and a focus on the individual's *potential* for change. Approaches which focus predominantly on the *processes* involved in learning seek and yield mainly qualitative information, whereas approaches which focus on *potential* (for change) often seek and yield quantitative information. This difference in focus reflects rather different interpretations of Vygotsky's theory. On the one hand are those concerned with finding out the extent or amount of the zone of proximal development, while on the other hand are those interested in exploring the nature and process of the child's 'next' learning. Campione (1989) has produced a useful taxonomy of different approaches to dynamic assessment. He suggests that although there are common fundamental features, noted above, to dynamic assessment procedures, their differences can be understood in terms of their positions on three dimensions: *focus, interaction, target.*

First, *focus* refers to the different ways in which potential for change is being evaluated: this is either by looking for an improvement in score using a test-teach-retest procedure or by looking at the underlying processes involved in learning or change. This reflects the quantitative/qualitative distinction referred to above. For example, at one end of this continuum, children are tested on a particular test or task, then given some practice or instruction and subsequently tested for improvement or receptivity to instruction (i.e. test-train-retest procedure). Scores indicate measures of improvement or change and could be thought to indicate amount of potential for learning. In theory it is possible to use any test or task in this way. This procedure has been used particularly by Budoff (1987) and by Campione and Brown (1984, quoted in Campione 1989). At the other end of this continuum, children are given a test or task, their performance and strategies are observed, they are then given instruction and assisted activity and again their strategies are observed, with a view to specifying and understanding the processes involved in their learning. A method which lies half-way along this continuum (one end of which produces quantitative data, the other end of which produces qualitative data) has been used by the present author and was also demonstrated to the present author and colleague in a recent visit to Moscow by Professor Rozanova of the Moscow Academy of Sciences Institute of Defectology which was founded by Vygotsky and whose members regard themselves as developing Vygotsky's work. This will be discussed on p. 165.

Second, *interaction* refers to the kind of interaction between the child and the tester. This may be said to lie on a continuum, one end being structured and standardized, the other end being more flexible, unstructured and clinical. At one end, Budoff (1987) and

Campione and Brown (1987) use a standardized interview format with the aim of producing quantitative data which may have some predictive properties. It is intended that such quantitative data will demonstrate the amount or nature of improvement or the amount of help required to master a particular task, or, in the case of Campione and Brown, to succeed in a transfer task. Such quantitative data differentiates between individuals with different 'potential' for learning in a way that would not be possible using 'static' procedures. At the other end is the more clinical interview used by Feuerstein (1981) and by Bransford *et al.* (1987). In this kind of interview, the tester is sensitive to and guided by the learner and the learner's responses, following up errors, exploring learning strategies and investigating strengths and weaknesses. Again this is the kind of interview format which has been used by the present author using a range of tasks including traditional performance subtests from the WISC-R and which has yielded rich diagnostic information.

Third, *target* refers to the kind of skills which are being considered in the assessment. These may be specific skills and processes related to curriculum or domain-specific areas, or more general and global skills or processes. For example, Brown and French (1979) and Ferrara (1987, quoted in Campione 1989) have focused on specific content domains whereas Feuerstein *et al.* (1980) have focused on more general cognitive skills. This issue raises questions about generalizability which will be discussed later.

Therefore within the dynamic assessment movement there are two distinct traditions, one tradition using standardized methods, the other using clinical methods, with other work falling on a continuum between these two. Both traditions clearly have their origins in the zone of proximal development though as Minick (1987) points out, each tradition has interpreted Vygotsky's writing very differently. The first group of assessment techniques (Budoff and Friedman 1964; Budoff and Hamilton 1976; Brown and French 1979; Campione *et al.* 1984; Brown and Ferrara 1985) use a standardized approach and rely on a scripted prompt format and have been designed to provide quantitative measures of a child's learning ability or learning efficiency. The product of the assessment procedure is a quantitative measure of the child's ability to be modified by instruction. A second group of assessment techniques, developed in the work of Feuerstein and his colleagues (Feuerstein 1979; Feuerstein *et al.* 1980) use a clinical approach and rely on a form of mediated learning which is designed to produce qualitative information on the nature of the child's psychological processes and the kind of help she needs to learn further. In comparing the two approaches, Minick (1987) suggests that Feuerstein and colleagues have sacrificed the capacity to produce quantitative measures of learning ability in an effort to gain access to information on the qualitative nature of the child's psychological processes and on the kind of assistance that the child needs to attain more adequate levels of performance; on the other hand, Campione and colleagues have sacrificed sensitivity to these qualitative factors in their effort to obtain valid, reliable and quantifiable measures of learning ability. 'From the educator's perspective, these quantitative and qualitative data complement one another. In designing assessment procedures, however, techniques that maximize access to one type of information often minimize access to the other' (Minick 1987: 118).

Standardized approaches in dynamic assessment

Standarized approaches aim to combine the strengths of a mediated learning situation with the benefits of comparison across individuals. In the Learning Potential and Educability Program Budoff uses a test-train-retest procedure to measure learning potential (Budoff and Friedman 1964; Budoff and Hamilton 1976; Budoff 1987). It reflects a definition of intelligence as the ability to profit from experience. According to Budoff (1987) the learning potential test-train-retest assessment paradigm aims to minimize the artificiality of the test situation by helping the child to become familiar with the test content and with the tester in a context designed to enhance the child's sense of competence. The materials used are IQ-type reasoning tasks such as Ravens Matrices (the Ravens Learning Potential Test RLPT) and Kohs blocks (the Kohs Learning Potential Task KLPT) which are presented with a standard set of prompts to measure a child's ability to profit from learning experiences or their problem-solving capability. Budoff has been concerned to establish the validity and reliability of the concept of learning potential and has maintained norm-referenced criteria. He concludes that

> with low-income and/or non-white or non-English speaking students, a training-based assessment process represents a more

culture-fair means of measuring general ability to reason or intelligence, when it is defined as the ability to learn and profit from experience.

(Budoff 1987: 53)

Budoff and colleagues have used tasks involving what are assumed to be general problem-solving skills. Campione and Brown (1987) have also used general problem-solving tasks in a series of studies using transfer tasks in which they report a demonstration of diagnostic utility and predictive validity. Tasks which involve general reasoning skills may be questioned on the grounds that such skills may not necessarily generalize to or provide a measure of other more specific learning abilities and indeed this has been a criticism of IQ tests themselves. In order to address this issue, Ferrara (1987) used transfer tasks in mathematics to find out how much help learners required to solve transfer problems of a mathematical nature. She used a series of graduated hints of different kinds to explore the amount and kind of help that would benefit different learners. Here too the focus was on quantitative information. The information yielded by quantitative studies such as these appears to hold promise for a more comprehensive approach to diagnosis and identification which may still retain some of the psychometric properties of more traditional and 'static' forms of assessment. However, the use of a standard format and the search for quantitative information with some psychometric predictive properties means that these methods may also have to sacrifice the qualitative information which may be derived through detailed exploration using a dynamically interactive and flexible interview format which by its unpredictability may yield greater depth of understanding of the processes and dynamics of the individual learner and her learning.

Clinical approaches in dynamic assessment

The best-known example of more clinical approaches is the Learning Potential Assessment Device (LPAD) and Instrumental Enrichment (IE) programme of Reuven Feuerstein. Like other forms of dynamic assessment, he also uses a test-train-retest procedure involving tasks which are variants of IQ-type test items and involve general problem-solving skills; however, unlike other

procedures, his assessment and interview format retains a flexi-
bility and responsiveness to the learner. The interaction between
child and tester is therefore unstandardized and clinical and is
designed to maximize the sensitivity and responsiveness of the
tester to the individual child and to the dynamics of the assessment
situation. According to Feuerstein (1979: 167), intelligence is

> the capacity of an individual to use previously acquired experi-
> ences to adjust to new situations. The two factors stressed in
> this definition are the capacity of the individual to be modified
> by learning and the ability of the individual to use whatever
> modification has occurred for future adjustments.

Central to Feuerstein's theory is the idea of 'modifiability' and
the task of assessment is to explore an individual's potential for
being modified by learning, through a process of active involvement and interaction with a more knowledgeable 'other', that is
through mediated learning. Feuerstein suggests that 'mediated
learning is the training given to the human organism by an experienced adult who frames, selects, focuses and feeds back an
environmental experience in such a way as to create appropriate
learning sets' (Feuerstein 1979). In this way, the child learns
through the mediation of a supportive teacher who leads her into
the zone of proximal development where she will be made aware
of the significance of her activities and thence, through internalization, take over the cognitive regulatory functions for herself
that she originally experienced through the mediation of or in
collaboration with an adult. In this form of assessment, the tester
functions as teacher, devising a dynamic and interactive assess-
ment-through-teaching procedure in which the two activities,
assessment and instruction, are inextricably intertwined. It is
through this process of assessment-and-teaching that the tester is
able to be sensitive to the learner's emergent cognitive strategies
and abilities and to 'lead' development at the same time as being
guided by the responses of the learner. Minick (1987) argues that
this approach is closer to the theories of Vygotsky who was
concerned more with the qualitative assessment of psychological
processes and the dynamics of their development rather than with
the quantitative assessment of learning efficiency or potential. It
is this difference in focus between the interaction itself and the
outcome of the interaction which is paralleled by the difference

between qualitative information about the processes of development and quantitative information about the product of the training session that provides a fruitful ground for future developments which might integrate the positive features of standardized and quantitative approaches with the beneficial aspects of clinical and qualitative approaches.

The present author has been involved in the development of an assessment procedure which resembles that demonstrated by Professor Rozanova in Moscow. This involves the use of general problem-solving tasks, in this case two of the performance subtests of the Wechsler Scales (block design and picture arrangement) and two subtests of the British Ability Scales (matrices and rotation of letter-like forms). These tasks have been presented clinically, that is by responding to the learner both by giving feedback and instruction on the tasks and by exploring meaning and understanding and inviting the learner to articulate the problem-solving steps being taken. Learners have been encouraged to verbalize their strategies for solving problems and for seeking solutions. It has been found that these processes of verbalization and feedback have given confidence to the learner and reduced the anxiety caused by a test situation. It is suggested that this may be particularly relevant for children of different and minority backgrounds for whom an assessment situation may be particularly unfamiliar and stressful. Attention has been given to an analysis of a child's incorrect responses both with a view to understanding how the learner is thinking and to giving feedback to the child in order to increase her own understanding of and therefore control over the learning process and the test situation. Preliminary results have yielded rich qualitative information which has provided useful material on which to build both instructional programmes and to enable teachers to understand individual learners more effectively and sympathetically.

However, such individual assessment is both time-consuming and intense in its demands and could be criticized, again, for focusing on general skills rather than specific curriculum domains, and for focusing on processes within the child in interaction with one adult rather than in interaction with the learning situation. Feuerstein (1980) has similarly pointed out some possible limitations in the use of the LPAD. He suggests that the personality characteristics required of the tester (i.e. the ability to be active, encouraging and lively in the dynamic assessment situation) and the time required to administer the LPAD may make this type of assessment of less practical utility for routine assessment of children with learning difficulties. Against this it may be argued that such methods enable an adult to explore an individual learner's cognitive functioning through a dynamic process of interaction and collaboration and that this in itself offers uniquely valuable information to aid both individual and more general pedagogic planning.

CONCLUSIONS

In conclusion it may be said that both standardized and clinical dynamic assessment procedures raise powerful and different issues within the assessment debate and both permit a radical reappraisal of the principles of individual assessment and provide promising pointers for ways forward in the development of more comprehensive, useful and constructive methods of assessment. The current interest in Vygotsky in the UK and the recognition of his contribution as one of the most influential thinkers of the century has meant that assessment approaches drawing on his theoretical formulations, particularly on the role of instruction, have been gaining credibility and popularity. The challenge of the 1990s will be to develop further dynamic assessment procedures which combine the strengths of qualitative descriptions of processes of learning with quantitative information on individual differences and which will yield appropriate and practical information for instructional programmes. In this way it may be possible to develop a theory and practice of assessment which applies ideas derived from Vygotsky's theorizing on the zone of proximal development which makes possible qualitative assessment of psychological processes also useful for instructional planning. Such assessment will need to take into account both the social and contextual factors surrounding individual learning and the interactions involved in instruction and the way that these affect an individual's learning. Finally, words or concepts such as 'intelligence' or 'ability' or 'potential' have been shown to have a new significance when 'mediated' through Vygotsky's zone of proximal development and assessment procedures in the future will need to address the conceptual confusion inherent in the use of these terms. It is suggested that dynamic assessment procedures offer a creative method of exploring an individual's processes of and potential for learning and development and that they provide useful and constructive information for teachers and other professionals.

REFERENCES

Ackerman, T., Cooper, P., Faupel, A., Gillett, D., Kenwood, P., Leadbetter, P., Mason, E., Matthews, C., Mawer, P., Tweddle, D., Williams, H. and Winteringham D. P. (1983) *The Datapac User's Guide*, Birmingham University.

Ainscow, M. and Muncey, J. (1981) *SNAP*, Cardiff, Drake Educational Associates.

Bransford, J. D., Delclos, V. R., Vye, N. J., Burns, M. S. and Hasselbring, T. S. (1987) 'State of the art and future directions', in C. S. Lidz (ed.) *Dynamic Assessment: An Interactional Approach to Evaluating Learning Potential*, London, Guilford Press.

Brown, A. L. and Campione, J. C. (1986) 'Psychological theory and the study of learning disabilities', *American Psychologist* 41, 1059–68.

Brown, A. L. and Ferrara, R. A. (1985) 'Diagnosing zones of proximal development', in J. V. Wertsch (ed.) *Culture, Communication and Cognition: Vygotskian Perspectives*, Cambridge, Cambridge University Press.

Brown, A. L. and French, L. A. (1979) 'The zone of potential development: implications for intelligence testing in the year 2000', *Intelligence* 3, 255–73.

Bruner, J. (1986) *Actual Minds, Possible Worlds*, Cambridge, MA, Harvard University Press.

Bruner, J. and Haste, H. (eds) (1987) *Making Sense: The Child's Construction of the World*, London, Routledge.

Budoff, M. (1987) 'The validity of learning potential', in C. S. Lidz (ed.) *Dynamic Assessment: An Interactional Approach to Evaluating Learning Potential*, New York, Guilford Press.

Budoff, M. and Friedman, M. (1984) ' "Learning potential" as an assessment approach to the adolescent mentally retarded', *Journal of Consulting Psychology*, 28, 434–9.

Budoff, M. and Hamilton, J. L. (1976) 'Optimising test performance of moderately and severely mentally retarded adolescents and adults', *American Journal of Mental Deficiency* 81, 49–57.

Campione, J. C. (1989) 'Assisted assessment: a taxonomy of approaches and an outline of strengths and weaknesses', *Journal of Learning Disabilities* 22 (3), 151–65.

Campione, J. C. and Brown, A. L. (1987) 'Linking dynamic assessment with school achievement', in C. S. Lidz (ed.) *Dynamic Assessment: An Interactional Approach to Evaluating Learning Potential*, New York, Guilford Press.

Campione, J. C., Brown, A. L., Ferrara, R. A. and Bryant, N. R. (1984) 'The zone of proximal development', in B. Rogoff and J.

Wertsch (eds) *Children's Learning in the Zone of Proximal Development*, San Francisco, Jossey-Bass.

Cummins, J. (1984) *Bilingualism and Special Education: Issues in Assessment and Pedagogy*, Clevedon, Multilingual Matters.

Faupel, A. (1986) 'Curriculum management (part 2): teaching curriculum objectives', *Educational Psychology in Practice* 2 (2), 4–16.

Feiler, A. (1988) 'The end of traditional assessment', in G. Thomas and A. Feiler (eds) *Planning for Special Needs: A Whole School Approach*, Oxford, Basil Blackwell.

Ferrara, R. A. (1987) 'Learning mathematics in the zone of proximal development: the importance of flexible use of knowledge', unpublished PhD dissertation, University of Illinois, Champaign.

Feuerstein, R. (1979) *The Dynamic Assessment of Retarded Performers: The Learning Potential Assessment Device, Theory, Instruments and Techniques*, Baltimore, University Park Press.

Feuerstein, R. (1980) *Instrumental Enrichment: An Intervention Programme for Cognitive Modifiability*, Baltimore: University Park Press.

Feuerstein, R., Rand, Y., Hoffman, M. B. and Miller, R. (1980) *Instrumental Enrichment: An Intervention Program for Cognitive Modifiability*, Baltimore, University Park Press.

Frederickson, N., Webster, A. and Wright, A. (1991) 'Psychological assessment: a change of emphasis', *Educational Psychology in Practice* 7 (1), 20–9.

Gallimore, R., Tharp, R. and Rueda, R. (1989) 'The social context of cognitive functioning in the lives of mildly handicapped persons', in D. Sugden (ed.) *Cognitive Approaches in Special Education*, Lewes, Falmer Press.

Gillham, B. (1978) 'The failure of psychometrics', in B. Gilham (ed.) *Reconstructing Educational Psychology*, Beckenham, Croom Helm.

Jones, R. L. (ed.) (1988) *Psychoeducational Assessment of Minority Group Children: A Casebook*, Berkeley, CA, Cobb & Henry.

Kozulin, A. (1990) *Vygotsky's Psychology: A Biography of Ideas*, Hemel Hempstead, Harvester Wheatsheaf.

Lidz, C. S. (ed.) (1987) *Dynamic Assessment: An Interactional Approach to Evaluating Learning Potential*, New York, Guilford Press.

Lister, T. A. J. and Cameron, R. J. (1986) 'Curriculum management (part 1): planning curriculum objectives', *Educational Psychology in Practice* 2 (1), 6–15.

Mercer, J. R. and Ysseldyke, J. (1977) 'Designing diagnostic–intervention programs', in T. Oakland (ed.) *Psychological and Educational Assessment of Minority Children*, New York, Brunner/Mazel.

Minick, N. (1987) 'Implications of Vygotsky's theories for dynamic assessment', in C. S. Lidz (ed.) *Dynamic Assessment: An Interactional Approach to Evaluating Learning Potential*, New York, Guilford Press.

Quicke, J. (1982) *The Cautious Expert*, Milton Keynes, Open University Press.

Quicke, J. (1984) 'The role of the educational psychologist in the post-

Warnock era', in L. Barton and S. Tomlinson (eds) *Special Education and Social Interests*, Beckenham, Croom Helm.

Reynolds, C. R., Gutkin, T. B., Elliott, S. N. and Witt, J. C. (1984) *School Psychology: Essentials of Theory and Practice*, New York, John Wiley & Sons.

Solity, J. E. (1991) 'Special Needs: a discriminatory concept?' *Educational Psychology in Practice* 7 (1), 12–19.

Solity, J. and Bull, S. (1987) *Special Needs: Bridging the Curriculum Gap*, Milton Keynes, Open University Press.

Sutton, A. (1983) 'An introduction to Soviet developmental psychology', in S. Meadows (ed.) *Developing Thinking*, London, Methuen.

Tomlinson, S. (1981) *Educational Subnormality: A Study in Decision-making*, London, Routledge & Kegan Paul.

Tomlinson, S. (1982) *A Sociology of Special Education*, London, Routledge & Kegan Paul.

Vygotsky, L. S. (1978) 'Mind in society: the development of higher psychological processes', in M. Cole, V. John-Steiner, S. Scribner and E. Souberman (eds and trans.) Cambridge, MA, Harvard University Press.

Vygotsky, L. S. (1987) *Thinking and Speech*, in *L. S. Vygotsky, Collected Works* (vol. 1, 39–285), edited by R. Rieber and A. Carton, translated by N. Minick, New York, Plenum.

Wood, D. (1988) *How Children Think and Learn*, Oxford, Basil Blackwell.

Zinchenko, V. P. and Davydov, V. V. (1985) 'Foreword' to J. V. Wertsch *Vygotsky and the Social Formation of Mind*, Cambridge, MA, Harvard University Press.

Chapter 8

Learning in primary schools

Andrew Pollard

This chapter begins by considering the changing influence of Piagetian and Vygotskian ideas regarding primary education. I then draw on some recent ethnographic research to illustrate some possible further applications of Vygotsky's ideas to the study of primary education.

Primary education has, for almost two decades, been strongly influenced by 'child centred' interpretations of psychology deriving from Piaget's work. Of course, Piaget's work was directed, in an overarching sense, towards the study of 'genetic epistemology', but the route towards this analysis was through many detailed studies of children's thinking and behaviour. Careful development and use of the clinical method over many years enabled him to generate a model of learning processes based on the interaction between individuals and their environment and involving development through successive stages of equilibration, each of which was taken to be associated with particular capacities and ways of thinking. This model was powerfully adopted by primary school teachers in the UK in the years following the Plowden Report (CACE 1967) and was used as a professional legitimation for 'progressive' classroom practices which, ostensibly, gave children a large degree of control over their learning.

From the late 1970s on, this Piagetian model, which implicitly conceptualized children as *individual* 'active scientists', began to be superseded by an image of children as *social* beings who construct their understandings (learn) from social interaction within specific sociocultural settings. They are thus seen as intelligent social actors who, although their knowledge base may be limited in absolute terms, are capable in many ways. For instance, processes of 'intellectual search' have been identified in young children (Tizard and Hughes 1984) as have children's capacities to develop sophisticated forms of representation for meaning and understanding. Such findings are being found with younger and younger children as research goes on.

The theoretical basis of such psychological research is strongly influenced by Vygotsky (1962, 1978). Of particular importance is his comparative work on the interrelations of thought, language and culture and, at another level, on the role of adults in scaffolding children's understanding across the 'zone of proximal development' – the extension of understanding which can be attained with appropriate support from others. According to Bruner and Haste (1987), this social constructivist approach has brought about a 'quiet revolution' in developmental psychology in the last decade and this is certainly borne out by the impact in education of work such as that by Donaldson (1978), Hughes (1986), Bruner (1986) and Edwards and Mercer (1987).

A key thrust of such new approaches is to recognize the way in which the social context influences perspectives and behaviour. One particularly interesting way of conceptualizing this has been provided by Helen Haste (1987) in her model of 'intra-individual', 'interpersonal' and 'socio-historical' factors affecting learning.

The intra-individual domain is the province of the cognitive psychologists who have accumulated so many insights into the ways in which individuals assimilate experiences and construct understanding. The interpersonal is the domain of social interaction – the area in which meanings are negotiated and through which cultural norms and social conventions are learned. The socio-historical is the domain of culturally defined and historically accumulated justification and explanation. It is a socio-historical resource for both interpersonal interaction and intra-individual reflection.

Such conceptualization of factors and domains affecting learning begins to make it possible to break out of the individualist assumptions which have been common in child psychology, so that wider social issues can be addressed. Sociologists could have much to offer here for, as Apple (1986) has argued:

> We do not confront abstract 'learners' in schools. Instead, we see specific classed, raced and gendered subjects, people whose biographies are intimately linked to the economic, political and

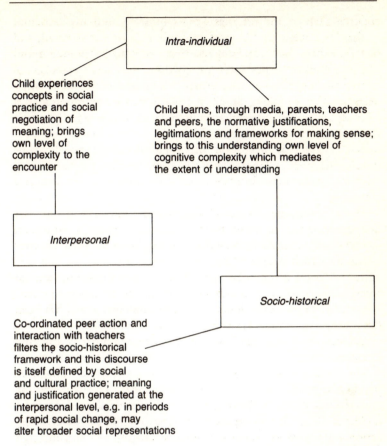

Figure 8.1 The relationship between intra-individual, interpersonal and socio-historical factors in learning (from Haste 1987: 175).

ideological trajectories of their families and communities, to the political economies of their neighbourhoods.

(Apple 1986: 5)

In other words, intra-individual learning cannot really be understood without reference to both interpersonal experiences and socio-historical circumstances.

There is, arguably, some way to go in the development of working relationships and analytical tools before psychologists and sociologists concerned with children's learning are able to take on the full import of Vygotsky's inspiration, as reflected in Haste's framework and Apple's suggestion. However, a growing consensus about the interrelatedness of social and psychological factors *does* seem to be emerging and this is underpinned, not just by theory and empirical research, but also by the common-sense and lived experiences of children, teachers, parents and others. If we are to investigate the issue of learning in valid ways, then our first problem, as social scientists, is really to find ways of bridging artificial disciplinary boundaries which could preclude the realization of Vygotsky's vision.

This chapter is based on the suggestion that one way of developing such collaborative work could be through the linking of social constructivist psychology and symbolic interactionist sociology.

These approaches share a basic assumption that people are active and make decisions on the basis of meanings. However, whilst social constructivist work has begun to identify the processes by which people 'make sense' in social situations, and thus come to 'know', symbolic interactionist studies promise to provide more detailed and incisive accounts of the dynamics and constraints of the contexts in which learning takes place. The two approaches are, arguably, complementary.

Some years ago I began to toy with this potential sociological contribution through the publication of a collection of papers which highlighted the influence of social contexts in schools on children's thinking and learning (Pollard 1987). This collection of case studies includes material from 3–12-year-olds and provides a degree of 'thick description' which invites further theorization regarding the nature of such complementarity – a task which I have begun through work in an ethnography and which is reflected in this chapter.

However, before addressing the study and the theoretical issue directly, it is appropriate to place the topic of 'learning in primary schools' in the context of recent policies in England and Wales and in relation to other approaches to classroom teaching/learning processes. In particular, I will have regard below to the work of Neville Bennett because of the sustained quality and impact of his research into classroom teaching and learning over many years.

POLICY AND SUBSTANTIVE CONTEXTS

In recent years, major thrusts of government policy in England and Wales have been directed towards the streamlining of the

management of schools, increasing the effectiveness and accountability of teachers and restructuring the curriculum (Education
Act 1986, Education Reform Act 1988). We do not yet know
whether such initiatives will achieve their aims in terms of the
delivery of the curriculum. However, irrespective of this, it can
be argued that far too little attention has been paid to the actual
reception of the curriculum by learners. Indeed, by focusing on
the issue of learning, one could claim to be anticipating a policy
debate of the future – a claim based on the proposition that when
the dust of reforms of teacher and curriculum management has
settled and we are still chasing that ever-receding Holy Grail of
'educational standards', more detailed attention to learning and
the learners in schools will be perceived as necessary.

The issue also has implications for teachers in primary schools
in a more general way concerning the theoretical underpinning
of practice. Over the past decade or so, there has been a gradual
erosion of the primacy of the Plowden Report's (CACE 1967)
philosophy of 'child centredness', which underpinned much primary school practice. As Piaget's work has been questioned and
research evidence has accumulated about actual classroom
behaviour, so primary school practice has begun to be seen to
lack a 'theoretical base' (Sylva 1987). I would suggest that Vygotskian ideas, suitably applied, have the potential to offer a new
legitimation – indeed, I think there are many forms of innovative
curriculum practice which, perhaps unwittingly, appear to be
based on such precepts. It is worth considering some of these
curriculum initiatives in a little more detail – particularly to see
what they do, and do not, attempt to do.

Throughout the 1980s there were considerable professional
developments in teaching methods regarding the curriculum subjects which make up the primary school curriculum. In almost
every case the innovations embraced a move far away from indi-
vidualized work towards group work, a concern to make the
active and skilled role of the teacher more explicit and a growing
recognition of the capacity of children to construct their understanding together. The idea of problem-solving in small groups
was widely adopted in subjects such as maths, design/technology
and science. Thus 'starting points' for investigation were offered
with the teacher being on hand to monitor, support and extend
the thinking, experimentation and exploration which followed.
Model processes for teaching/learning episodes also came to be

outlined. For instance, the National Writing Project endorsed 'process writing' in which young children were encouraged to draft, share and discuss, redraft, and eventually 'publish' their stories. In Design Technology a process for producing handmade objects evolved. This incorporated conceptualizing, planning, testing, discussing, revising and, eventually 'realizing'. Such trends in pedagogy and curriculum provision have been powerfully sponsored by subject associations such as the Association for Science Education, the National Association for the Teaching of English and the Maths Association. A new form of 'good professional practice' thus emerged through the 1980s, but in a relatively *ad hoc* way. Many of such ideas were incorporated in the National Curriculum which followed the Education Reform Act of 1988. This was particularly noticeable in the Non-statutory Guidance.

The influence of Vygotsky has rarely been explicit in these curricular and pedagogic developments. Indeed, we seem to have experienced almost two parallel but complementary streams of development. The professional teacher has developed through curricular and pedagogic refinement, whilst academic psychologists have worked away with only a partial realization of the significance of their work for practice in primary schools. Certainly, the immense significance of Vygotskian ideas in providing a new legitimation for modern professional practice has yet to be fully realized.

There are also, of course, some important and influential models of learning which emphasize somewhat different factors. For instance, in the past twenty years a considerable amount of research has been conducted with the aim of identifying factors which enable teachers to be 'effective'. However, as Bennett (1987) has argued, whilst the initial work, emphasizing teaching styles, identified some interesting patterns and descriptions, it lacked explanatory power and made few connections with actual practice. It was superseded in the mid–1970s by an 'opportunities to learn' model in which the teacher was seen as the manager of the attention and time of the pupils. A key indicator became the amount of time which the pupil was 'on task'. More recently the focus has also turned to the analysis of what is termed 'quality' of classroom tasks – defined in terms of the degree of appropriate match with children's capacities (e.g. Bennett *et al.* 1984).

Neville Bennett's work represents a sustained and consistent

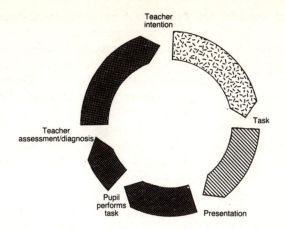

Figure 8.2 A model of classroom task processes (from Bennett and Kell 1989: 27).

attempt to develop and test a model of teaching and learning. His successive studies have focused on different parts of an emerging model and his work continues through his present Leverhulme Project on the quality of teachers' subject knowledge and ability to diagnose learning difficulties. Bennett, and his co-author, Joy Kell, express the model particularly clearly in Figure 8.2.

The very important point which Bennett has empirically documented is that breakdowns can and do occur regularly between each stage in the 'task process cycle' and it is unfortunate that this can sometimes come across as an unappreciative critique of teachers. Rather, I would suggest that it should be seen more constructively, as providing a detailed testimony of just how difficult the job is.

Having said that though, I would also argue, in Vygotskian terms, that such work seriously underplays the importance of the sociocultural situation in which teaching and learning take place and fails to trace the full impact of the subjectivity of the participants. There is no specific emphasis on learners with reference to their responses to the social influences and teaching/learning situations which they experience. The model thus appears as a technical model of teaching – one which is dominated by the teacher, with pupils 'performing' to externally determined tasks.

In terms of the issues raised by Helen Haste, Bennett's analysis is very partial. It is worthwhile and necessary, but it is not sufficient and should be complemented by other work – work which is more informed by sociological perspectives.

Of course, one could level similar criticisms at many of the curricular and pedagogic developments which have evolved over the past decade. Awareness tends to be bounded by the dynamics of groups within the classroom with little explicit consideration of wider social influences on learning. Thus, in terms of Haste's model, one could say that practice is reflecting the intra-individual and inter-individual but is not yet very aware of socio-historical factors affecting the learner. Awareness of socio-historical factors in educational policy-making is another issue altogether!

Among other related educational issues which have emerged regularly in recent research and in HMI surveys has been that of the routine nature of many of the activity structures and class-room tasks in which children engage – particularly in the 'basic' curriculum areas (Alexander 1984). In an attempt to address this issue and to be appreciative to the concerns of teachers, Woods (1990) has drawn on coping strategies theory (e.g. Pollard 1982) to identify problems of the limited 'opportunities to teach' in classrooms. These are constrained by the inadequate resourcing of schools and by the enormous current expectations of teachers.

However, it is also clear that the routinization of tasks and activity structures is not simply the result of a transmission process for which teachers are solely responsible. Indeed, Doyle (1979) has suggested that many pupils seek tasks which are 'low risk' and 'low ambiguity' and both the ORACLE researchers' identification of 'intermittent working' and 'easy riding' (Galton *et al.* 1980) and my own identification of pupil 'drifting' (Pollard and Tann 1987) suggest that pupils' learning stances and strategies could be of considerable significance. Arguably, this is particularly important in the context of the national concern for improvement in the level of learning achievements, given the psychological evidence on the contribution of risk-taking to learning (Claxton 1984) and Dweck's socio-cognitive research on motivation (1986). As Galton's (1987) review of the field in the last twenty years concludes:

> if advances [in our understanding] are to be made, there will [need to] be greater concentration on the social factors affecting pupil learning and [on] the ways in which teachers can create

classroom climates which allow situations of 'high risk' and 'high ambiguity' to be coped with successfully.

(Galton 1987: 44)

This statement underlines a key point in social constructivist models of learning about *control* of the learning process. Since understanding can only be constructed in the mind of the learner, it is essential that learners exercise a significant degree of control of the process – a point to which I will return.

I turn now though, to introduce the empirical study around which my thinking on this topic has developed.

A LONGITUDINAL ETHNOGRAPHY

In 1987 I began a research programme, a longitudinal ethnography, which was designed to explore the potential for applying Vygotskian ideas to the analysis of learning in primary schools. The explicit theoretical strategy for this was to attempt to link social interactionism and social constructivism.

I aimed to monitor the primary school careers of a small cohort of ten children at one primary school by using a variety of qualitative methods and I started from the children's entry to the school at the age of four.

I particularly focused on the social factors which were likely to influence the children's stance, perspectives and strategies regarding learning. Data was thus collected from parents about family life, sibling relationships and the children's emergent identities; from peers and playground contexts concerning peer-group relations; and from teachers with regard to classroom behaviour and academic achievements.

At the heart of the study was regular classroom observation so that the progression of organization, activity structures and routine tasks in each class which the children passed through could be documented – together with the responses of the children to such provision. The main source of data were: field-notes from participant-observation, interviews, teacher records, parent diaries, school documents, photographs, video recordings, sociometry and examples of children's work.

This work built on the sociological studies of teacher/pupil coping strategies in schools which has developed over a number of years (e.g. Woods 1977; Hargreaves 1978; Pollard 1982;

Beynon 1985; Scarth 1987), with its strong influence of symbolic interactionism. Since that work has been generally accepted as a means of conceptualizing and analysing macro-micro linkages as they affect school processes, I judged that it might also prove to be capable of bearing the weight of analysis of socio-historical factors in learning, as raised by Helen Haste (see Figure 8.1.), in addition to the interpersonal factors which are the more obvious provenance of symbolic interactionism.

I also hoped that the study would develop existing work on coping strategies substantively because of the focus on children as pupils developing through schools. This focus was designed to complement the considerable amount of work which is now available on *teacher* strategies and careers (Ball and Goodson 1985; Sikes *et al.* 1985; Nias 1989). Additionally, of course, the study was intended to provide a more explicit focus on learning than is evident in previous sociological work, which, as I argued earlier, has tended to be primarily concerned with differentiation. The main aims of the study were thus:

1 to trace the development of a cohort of young children's stances, perspectives and strategies regarding learning, through consideration of home, playground and classroom settings;
2 to investigate pupil career, in terms of emergent identities and the influences on them, as children move through different teachers and classrooms within their school;
3 to develop the analytic potential of combining social constructivist models of children's learning and symbolic interactionist models of school processes.

In the course of gathering data, I attempted to code and analyse it with the intention of generating grounded theoretical models and concepts (Glaser and Strauss 1967; Hammersley and Atkinson 1983) which could contribute to both professional and academic debate. In keeping with other, earlier work, I do not aspire to 'prove' relationships, believing this to be inappropriate with regard to such subtle issues (or indeed to many aspects of social science more generally). However, through the detailed analysis of the data, I aimed to highlight the most significant issues and patterns in the social relationships which seem to affect pupil learning and career. Others can then relate this analysis to their own circumstances.

This chapter represents an attempt to begin to make sense of the work. It remains tentative in many respects, but certainly indicates the direction in which my thinking is leading.

By the spring of 1990, I had studied nine children (one child had moved schools) over their first three school years with regard to three major social settings (classroom, playground, home). I had collected a large amount of data and faced analytical problems which I aimed to address through the comparison of the nine cases which the children represented.

Before I focus directly on the emerging analysis, an indication of the data is provided below by a brief illustrative account of the educational experiences, over their first two school years, of just two of the children whom I studied.

This is a highly condensed 'account', in almost narrative form, and was written initially for an audience of governors and parents (Pollard 1990). The judgments expressed in it rest on a detailed analysis of data, but the main point which I wish to make requires a holistic understanding, for which narrative documentary is a proven vehicle. I thus hope that the account below serves its purpose in highlighting the importance of contextual factors in learning and in providing a bridge to the theoretical analysis in the final section of this chapter. More complete substantive documentation and analysis will appear in due course.

LEARNING AND DEVELOPING AN IDENTITY

The two children on whom this illustration is based began their school careers together, with twenty-four others, in the same 'reception' class.

The first child, a girl called Sally, was the youngest of the two children of the school caretaker. Her mother also worked in the school as a School Meals Services Assistant and as a cleaner. Her parents had always taken enormous pleasure and pride in Sally's achievements. They celebrated each step as it came but did not seem to overtly press her. Life, for them, seemed very much in perspective. Sally was physically agile and had a good deal of self-confidence. She had known the school and the teaching staff for most of her life. She felt at home. She was very sensitive to 'school rules' and adult concerns and she engaged in each new challenge with zest. Over the years, with her parents' encouragement, she had developed a considerable talent for dancing and had won several competitions. In school she had also taken a

leading role in several class assemblies and had made good progress with her reading and other work. The teachers felt she was
a delightful and rewarding child to teach – convivial and able,
but compliant too. Her friends were mainly girls though she
mixed easily. She was at the centre of a group which was particularly popular in the class and which, over the years since playgroup, had developed strong internal links and friendships
through shared interests, for instance, in 'My Little Pony', playing
at 'mummies and daddies' and reciprocal home visits.

The second child, Daniel, was the fifth and youngest in his
family. His father was an extremely busy business executive and
his mother had devoted the previous sixteen years to caring for
their children, which she saw as a worthwhile but all-absorbing
commitment. She was concerned for Daniel who had had some
difficulties in establishing his identity in the bustle of the family
with four older children. She also felt that he had 'always tended
to worry about things' and was not very confident in himself.
For many years he had tended to play on being the youngest,
the baby of the family, a role which seemed naturally available.
At playgroup he was particularly friendly with a girl, Harriet,
who was later to be in his class at school. However, over their
first year at school, distinct friendships of boys and girls began
to form. It became 'sissy' to play with girls. Daniel, who had
found the transition from the security of home hard to take and
who had to begin to develop a greater self-sufficiency, thus found
the ground-rules of appropriate friendships changing, as the
power of child culture asserted itself. He could not play with
Harriet because she was a girl, but nor was he fully accepted by
the dominant groups of boys.

This insecurity was increased when he moved from the structured and 'motherly' atmosphere of his reception class into the
more volatile environment of his 'middle infant' class. There were
now thirty-one children in his class, most of whom were from
a parallel reception class – within which a group of boys had
developed a reputation for being 'difficult'. The new teacher thus
judged that the class 'needed a firm hand to settle them down
after last year' and, as a caring but experienced infant teacher,
decided to stand no nonsense. It also so happened that this teacher
was somewhat stressed, as a lot of teachers in England and Wales
have been in the late 1980s. She sometimes acted a little harshly
and in other ways which were against her own better judgment.

The environment which Daniel experienced was therefore one which was sometimes a little unpredictable. Whilst he was never one of the ones who 'got into trouble', he was very worried by the possibility that he might 'upset Miss'. Daniel would thus be very careful. He would watch and listen to the teacher, attempting to 'be good' and do exactly what was required. He would check with other children and, on making a first attempt at a task, try to have his efforts approved before proceeding further. Occasionally, at work with a group and with other children also pressing, the teacher might wave Daniel away. He would then drift, unsure, watching to take another opportunity to obtain the reinforcement which he felt he needed. As the year progressed, Daniel became more unhappy and increasingly unwilling to go to school.

Daniel's mother was torn as this situation developed – was the 'problem' caused by Daniel's 'immaturity' or was it because he was frightened of the teacher? She felt it was probably a bit of both but school-gate advice suggested that discussion in school might not go easily. She delayed and the situation worsened, with Daniel making up excuses to avoid school, insisting on returning home for lunch and becoming unwilling to visit the homes of other children. Daniel's mother eventually and tentatively visited the school where the issues were aired.

Over the following weeks the teacher worked hard to support Daniel and to help him settle. Daniel's confidence improved a little, particularly when he found a new friend, a boy, from whom he then became inseparable. Even so, as his mother told me towards the end of the year, 'we are holding on and praying for the end of term'.

These two children attended the same school and were part of the same classes – yet as learners they had quite different characteristics. Whilst Sally was confident, keen to 'have a go' and would take risks, Daniel was insecure, fearful lest he 'got things wrong' in a world in which he felt evaluated and vulnerable. The accident of birth into a small or large family may have been an influence too, with Sally having had the psychological space to flourish and the day-to-day support of both her parents all around her, whilst Daniel had to establish his place in a large family in which both parents faced considerable pressure in their work – be it in an office or domestically. Perhaps too, Daniel's initial solutions to his position, which had served him in good stead in his infancy whilst at home, would simply not transfer into the less bounded environment of school.

TOWARDS AN ANALYTICAL FRAMEWORK

The data which underpins an account such as that reviewed above is highly complex and, in attempting to make sense of it, one can easily lose direction or become distracted. For the purposes of this study, it was crucial to retain the focus on identity and learning whilst also structuring the comparison of cases across settings – with twenty-seven interrelated data sets formed by the nine children and three major settings.

Building on what I take to be key interactionist and constructivist principles, I evolved a simple analytical formula which I found to be powerful and which could be applied to data and cases derived from any setting.

Figure 8.3 Individual, context and learning: an analytic formula.

The relationship between self and others expresses the key symbolic interactionist focus, with its recognition of the importance of social context in the formation of meaning and self. A sense of control in social situations is seen as a product of this. It is an indication of the success, or otherwise, of a child's coping strategies in the politico-cultural context of any particular social setting – home, classroom, playground – and thus reflects the interplay of interests, power, strategies and negotiation. However, it is also a necessary element of the learning process as conceived by social-constructivist psychologists. Only children themselves can 'make sense', understand and learn. They may be supported and instructed by others but, once their understanding has been scaffolded in such ways, it must stand on its own foundations – foundations which can only be secure when the child has been able to control the construction itself.

Teaching and other forms of support by adults are necessary,

Figure 8.4 A social-constructivist model of the teaching/learning process.

but they are not sufficient. Learning also requires conditions which enable each child to control the assembly and construction of *their* understanding.

I have elaborated in Figure 8.4 a model by Rowland (1987) in order to express this point.

It is worth dwelling a little on the importance of the role of an adult as a 'reflective agent' in this model, providing meaningful and appropriate guidance and extension to the cognitive structuring and skill development arising from the child's initial experiences. This, it is suggested, supports the child's attempts to 'make sense' and enables them to cross the zone of proximal development (ZPD). Their thinking is thus *restructured* in the course of further experiences. Of course, the concept of 'reflective agent' is not unrelated to that of 'reflective teaching' (Pollard and Tann 1987), which is becoming a new orthodoxy in terms of course rationales for teacher education in the UK. However, as with sociology of education, present work on reflective teaching is relatively weak on the issue of learning itself. Of great interest too, is the fact that carrying out the role of a reflective agent effectively is dependent on sensitivity *and* accurate knowledge of each child's needs. It thus places a premium on formative, teacher assessment (TGAT 1988) and could be greatly facilitated in England and Wales by the requirements of new legislation – if it is appropriately implemented, a condition which, unfortunately, we cannot take for granted.

To recap – in Figure 8.4 we see the need for appropriate adult support and instruction and its relationship to children's control over their learning. The two are not contradictory. Indeed, I would argue that both are necessary but neither is sufficient for high quality learning. In the cases of Sally and Daniel, Sally was able to negotiate, control and cope with the variety of domestic, classroom and playground settings which she encountered with

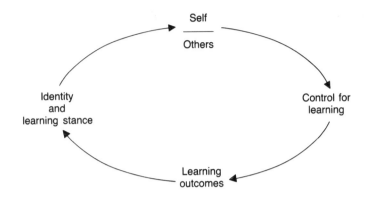

Figure 8.5 A model of learning and identity.

relative ease. She was confident in tackling new learning situations and achieved a great deal. Daniel found things much more difficult in each setting, but particularly in the classroom. He developed two key strategies regarding his learning. First, to watch, check and recheck to make sure that he 'was doing it right' so that he could avoid 'trouble with Miss'. Second, to stay away from school. His learning achievements over the two years were relatively modest.

Of course, the simple formula (Figure 8.3) and the social-constructivist model of interaction in learning (Figure 8.4) express only a small part of the story, and I have developed them further to begin to reflect on the outcomes and consequences of the learning process.

The model in Figure 8.5 expresses the recursive nature of experience. Self-confidence, together with other attributes and other contextual factors (e.g. Bennett *et al.*'s (1984) work on the quality of tasks set), produces particular learning outcomes – successful or otherwise – and with them associated perspectives. These, it is suggested, contribute cumulatively to each child's sense of identity and to their learning stance, and it is with these which, for better or worse, they enter the next setting. Over time, as this cycle moves forward, it tends to develop in patterned ways into what can be identified more clearly as a 'pupil career'.

Thus, in the cases of Sally and Daniel, we might speculate that Sally's pupil career will go from strength to strength, founded on the confidence of her learning stance, whilst Daniel's progress may be more halting. In fact, of course, such speculation is premature. Time will bring new social contexts and experiences and the factor of social class may influence the children's development. This is where the longitudinal design of the study should be significant.

Whatever the empirical outcomes, the nature of the patterns in pupil learning and career is of consequence for both psychologists and sociologists. For psychologists, it highlights processes of learning in context. For sociologists, it begins to relate factors such as social class, gender and race, through the processes of learning and identity formation, and on to long-term social differentiation, career and life chances.

CONCLUSION

In this chapter I have reviewed the growing influence of Vygotsky's ideas on primary education. I have suggested that they are beginning to supplant Piaget's work and that they could provide a new legitimation for effective primary school practice in the 1990s. At the same time, I have argued that what I take to be the full force of the ideas, in linking learning to culture and context, requires much further development. Such possible development has been considered in the context of some of my own ethnographic work, but this is just a small part of a growing field. The influence of Vygotsky is being very widely felt in education and his work is likely to inspire constructive thinking in both professional and academic circles for many years.

NOTE

This chapter is based on an article published in the *British Journal of Sociology of Education* 11 (3), 1990, 'Towards a sociology of learning in primary schools'. I am grateful to the publishers, Carfax, for permission to draw on it here.

REFERENCES

Alexander, R. J. (1984) *Primary Teaching*, London, Cassell.
Apple, M. (1986) *Teachers and Texts*, London, Routledge & Kegan Paul.
Ball, S. and Goodson, I. (1985) *Teachers' Lives and Careers*, London, Falmer.
Bennett, N. (1987) 'The search for the effective primary school teacher', in S. Delamont (ed.) *The Primary School Teacher*, London, Falmer.

Bennett, N., Cockburn, A. and Desforge, C. (1984) *The Quality of Pupil Learning Experiences*, London, Lawrence Erlbaum.

Bennett, N. and Kell, J. (1989) *A Good Start? Four-Year-Olds in Infant Schools*, Oxford, Blackwell.

Beynon, J. (1985) *Initial Encounters in the Secondary School*, London, Falmer.

Bruner, J. (1986) *Actual Minds, Possible Worlds*, London, Harvard.

Bruner, J. and Haste, H. (1987) *Making Sense*, London, Methuen.

CACE (1967) *Children and their Primary Schools* (The Plowden Report), London, HMSO.

Claxton, G. (1984) *Live and Learn*, London, Harper & Row.

Donaldson, M. (1978) *Children's Minds*, London, Fontana.

Doyle, W. (1979) 'Classroom tasks and student abilities', in P. Peterson and H. Walberg (eds) *Research on Teaching*, Berkeley, CA, McCutchan.

Edwards, D. and Mercer, N. (1987) *Common Knowledge*, London, Methuen.

Galton, M. (1987) *Teaching in Primary Schools*, London, David Fulton.

Galton, M., Simon, B. and Croll, P. (1980) *Inside Primary Schools*, London, Routledge & Kegan Paul.

Glaser, B. and Strauss, A. (1967) *The Discovery of Grounded Theory*, Chicago, Aldine.

Hammersley, M. and Atkinson, P. (1983) *Ethnography: Principles into Practice*, London, Tavistock.

Hargreaves, A. (1978) 'The significance of classroom coping strategies', in L. Barton and R. Meighan (eds) *Sociological Interpretations of Schooling and Classrooms*, Driffield, Nafferton.

Hartley, D. (1985) *Understanding Primary Schools*, London, Croom Helm.

Haste, H. (1987) 'Growing into rules', in J. Bruner and H. Haste (eds) *Making Sense*, London, Methuen.

Hughes, M. (1986) *Children and Number*, London, Macmillan.

Nias, J. (1989) *Primary Teachers Talking*, London, Routledge.

Pollard, A. (1982) 'A model of coping strategies', *British Journal of Sociology of Education* 3 (1), 19–37.

Pollard, A. (ed.) (1987) *Children and their Primary Schools, A New Perspective*, London, Falmer.

Pollard, A. (1990) *Learning in Primary Schools*, London, Cassell.

Pollard, A. and Tann, S. (1987) *Reflective Teaching in the Primary School*, London, Cassell.

Rowland, S. (1987) 'Child in control', in A. Pollard (ed.) *Children and their Primary Schools*, London, Falmer.

Scarth, J. (1987) 'Teacher strategies: a review and critique', *British Journal of Sociology of Education* 8 (3), 245–62.

Sikes, P., Measor, L. and Woods, P. (1985) *Teacher Careers: Crises and Continuities*, London, Falmer.

Sylva, K. (1987) 'Plowden: history and prospect-research', *Oxford Review of Education* 14 (1), 3–11.

TGAT (Task Group on Assessment and Testing) (1988) *Report*, London, Department of Education and Science.

Tizard, B. and Hughes, M. (1984) 'The intellectual search of young children', in A. Pollard (ed.) *Children and Their Primary Schools: A New Perspective*, London, Falmer.

Vygotsky, L. S. (1962) *Thought and Language*, New York, Wiley.

Vygotsky, L. S. (1978) *Mind in Society*, London, Harvard.

Woods, P. (1977) 'Teaching for survival', in P. Woods and M. Hammersley (eds) *School Experience*, London, Croom Helm.

Woods, P. (1990) *Teacher Skills and Strategies*, London, Falmer.

Chapter 9

Learning English as an additional language in multilingual classrooms

Josie Levine

OVERVIEW

The basic proposition is straightforward. Multilingual classrooms have obvious potential for the development of English as an additional language. However, the history of trying to turn that potential into reality has been anything but straightforward. It is a history riddled with race, class, cultural and linguistic prejudice, a history of both official and unofficial obstruction to educational development – indeed a classic case of blindness on the part of education to its own provision of *unequal* opportunities. Consequently, theory, practice and principles for the countering of this situation have been initiated and developed from positions of opposition to the educational status quo. Progress has been made, but by no means enough of it for the present situation to be a happy one. Equal opportunities education strives, therefore, to be about the entitlement rhetoric promises, but does not deliver, i.e. about supposed equal rights of access to a meaningful curriculum, to cultural and linguistic respect, to high expectation of achievement and to greater equality of outcomes for all the social groups against which historic prejudices have worked.

Amongst these groups are children of ethnic minority origin who are learning English as an additional language – the majority of whom are also working class. For the majority of them, their education takes place in multilingual classrooms, but unfortunately, very often in an ethos where the rich potential of such classrooms for developing English as an additional language is seriously underdeveloped. However, it is in some of these classrooms that the model for the development of such potential has been shaped.

In the course of this chapter, an emergent good practice is described for a morally responsible, equal opportunities education. Essentially Vygotskian in character, being both interactive and developmental, it is referred to as 'developmental pedagogy'. At the heart of the development of this pedagogy in Britain are a significant minority of teachers in multilingual classrooms.

This developmental pedagogy draws on Vygotskian ideas about:

1 the relationship between cognitive and linguistic development in the 'native language';
2 the role of social and reflective processes in learning development;
3 the relationship between teaching ('instruction') and learning ('development of concepts').

At the heart of this pedagogy is a dialectic comprising:

1 internalization as a result of interaction;
2 conscious awareness resulting from teaching intervention;
3 the learning processes of reflection and analysis.

When multilingual classrooms are actual sites of interactive, analytic, reflective learning, when the learning environment is supportive *and* rigorous, when, through a pedagogically flexible response to cultural and linguistic diversity, wider access to learning is achieved, when bilingual learners are encouraged to use all their linguistic resources in school, then we have an educational and linguistic environment which allows additional language learning to be a 'normal' part of learning. It is this 'normalized' *language* learning, within the freedom and rigour of a broad *curricula* provision, that is essential to the achievement of true educational entitlement for bilingual pupils.

What lies behind this assertion are some obvious, but educationally and linguistically underexploited, contextual truths. Bilingual learners in multilingual classes in Britain are learning to use English as an additional language for central purposes in their lives. They do so in a context where the target language is both the dominant language in society *and* the medium of instruction in school. In other words, they have real purpose for acquiring the target language and they have living access to it. Furthermore, consonant with their age and experience, they already have a more developed use of at least one other language. It makes both human and pedagogic sense to use the natural features of pupils' lives to build an educational context out of what they have natural access to and out of what they already know and can do, rather than to continue with methodologies that deny them these natural learning 'aids.'

In the context of bilingual pupils' learning of English, it is this 'naturalized' orientation for learning *and* for additional language learning and development which I see as a superior basis for formulating a theory and practice for successful additional language learning, and indeed, not only for bilingual pupils.

CONFLICTS AND TENSIONS

When children came to the UK speaking a range of languages other than English, they were not perceived as already experienced users of language, competent communicators about to start a new phase of their lives – a phase in which they would begin to add an *additional* language, English, to their repertoires. Instead, they were regarded as being in linguistic and cultural deficit. Their previous languages and learning experiences were ignored; their cultural backgrounds were seen as irrelevant to English schooling; they found themselves disparagingly dubbed 'non-English speakers', sometimes even, 'children with no language', 'beginner learners' (and not just of English) – and they were regarded as unequipped for participation in 'normal' classrooms. The education system perceived as paramount the need to learn English, and to learn it discretely, separated from their other curricular learning. Once the newcomers had learned English, *then* they would be allowed to learn the 'other' subjects.

So, 'Special English' classes were established and bilingual pupils were then described, not as pupils of English, Maths, Geography or whatever, but as 'learners of English as a second language', E2L kids', terms which, in effect, reflected the linguistic and cultural prejudice of the dominant social group. 'Special English' classes were taught primarily on the basis of withdrawal from the mainstream curriculum. Thus, within the already existing hierarchical organization of British schooling, these children were yet further marginalized. As a result, even the positive functions these 'special' classes performed were soon outweighed by the structural effect such classes inevitably had in compounding the conditions of underachievement already established by the educational system for the majority of working-class pupils.

Recently the term 'bilingual pupils' has begun to be used, and more recently still, the phrase 'pupils acquiring English as an additional language'. The term 'multilingual classrooms' came into use prior to these, as some kind of acknowledgement that it was normal to have many languages represented in one classroom. However, the description does not refer to multilanguage *use* in these classrooms, but to the range of languages spoken by the pupils, not in school, but at home.

These newer terms genuinely offer a more accurate construction of bilingual pupils:

1 as developing learners;
2 to be understood and valued as already competent and knowledgeable;
3 with what they know, including their linguistic prowess productively linked with their present and future learning;
4 with their English language learning enterprise being about developing a linguistic repertoire that *adds to* rather than replaces already known languages.

Nevertheless, even the newer terms are suspect, and the reasons for suspicion are currently not hard to find. With so great a weight being placed on the use of Standard English in the National Curriculum, with bilingualism and the right to use one's first language recognized as a prerogative of Welsh schools only (DES 1989), with so much political emphasis on 'our' national heritage, it would seem that the linguistic communities of Britain's ethnic minorities are likely to continue to experience the downgrading of their languages in relation to English. Consequently, we can also anticipate that schools are likely to continue to underachieve in meeting the intellectual and skill development needs of their bilingual pupils.

Even where there is belated recognition of bilingual pupils – not as deficient, but as pupils developing both their learning and their bilingual proficiency – the issue of ethnic minority pupils' rights to bilingual education remains beyond the pale. Bilingual education would be feasible to develop where one community language dominates, as is the case for Welsh speakers, but there is virtually no support for it via political will or vision within the educational system. The fact of the matter is that even in multicultural and multilingual classrooms our educational culture is such that there are relatively few classrooms where teachers are fully committed to developing the sort of interactive pedagogies that are, I argue, the only honest means of achieving equal opportunities education for pupils suffering the social class, gender, ethnocentric and linguistic discrimination of the British educational system.

In consequence, there is manifest tension between the possible and the actual in multilingual classrooms, which is not eased by the continuing presence of traditional forms of restrictive thinking about language and education. For example:

1 continued questioning of bilingualism set against the goal of learning English as an additional language, *as though one must necessarily exclude or diminish the value of the other*;
2 bilingualism set against the feasibility of successful curriculum learning, *as though it was inconceivable that a pedagogy could be developed which took advantage of linking learning* and *language development*;
3 linguistic and cultural diversity set against 'British culture and language', *as though there was no relationship between such sectionalism and the systematic exclusion from curricular success of British working-class culture, interests and forms of thinking*.

Assuredly, the downgrading of pupils' bilingualism and the constraints of withdrawal classes on pupils' access to the mainstream curriculum contribute to pupils' underachievement in school, and as such, are components of institutionalized racial and class discrimination. This discrimination within the education system constitutes the most successful and longstanding 'con' trick perpetrated by 'education'.

RACE AND CLASS PREJUDICE AND THE EDUCATIONAL OFFER IN MULTILINGUAL CLASSROOMS

Both working-class children and bilingual learners in English schools have had a poor deal. This is because the educational base has always been a diverse, class-ridden system promoting the type of education most accessible to the dominant power group, and in which, broadly speaking, achievement has depended either on pupils originating in the middle classes, or – in keeping with the meritocratic ideal – on being able and willing to espouse its precepts.

Despite the fact that class is a consistently acknowledged factor in success and failure in the school system, the obvious conclusion is equally consistently evaded: that an education system founded and maintained along class dimensions is instrinsically structured against groups with cultural and intellectual traditions different from the hegemonic 'norm'. Failure within the system is seen as residing in those against whom the system is most prejudiced, those at the bottom of the class and culture hierarchy. It is their 'backgrounds' which assign them to educational failure, not the educational system itself.

The different types of schools (public *vs* state; grammar *vs* technical *vs* secondary modern) have functioned historically to separate the different groups in society on grounds of birth, money and parental and/or intended profession. Furthermore, within the hierarchy of the system, streaming had been used across all types of schooling to *further* differentiate, delineate and maintain boundaries between socio-economic groups on the basis of children's 'ability' as measured by the 'norms' of the system. The attempt to rank groups to such a degree of homogeneity invariably led to every school having its 'Remove' classes, its remedial sub-system, for those who could not, or would not, cope.

It was into this educational system that bilingual pupils came. As with working-class children, they were required to acquire along with their English, the linguistic modes and forms of thought which formed the world view characteristic of the dominant class minority within the population. Within the structures and practices of such a 'class-centric' curriculum, a whole range of stratifications, qualitative differences, within the educational offer existed. 'Education' became a successive watering down of the dominant class's curriculum, each successive dilution being the means by which pupils were deemed to be receiving the education 'suited to their age, ability and aptitude'. For example, those who had not passed the old 11+ examination, 80 per cent of the population, had successive stages of 'access' to the least rigorous version of a curriculum which, by virtue of its starting point, met neither their intellectual needs nor acknowledged (let alone ascribed status to) their interests, forms of thinking, or their cultural presence.

Language education played its part in this constructed lack of opportunity for the majority population. Faithful to the elitist tradition outlined above, language education for most pupils was, in effect, about learning 'correct' English. In fact, modern foreign language learning was, for most pupils, conspicuous by its absence in their curriculum. Only the 'clever' kids had access to additional language learning – the cleverest of all, to the elitist prize of Latin and Greek. This elitism must surely be a basic factor in any account of the failure of the British people generally to acquire additional languages.

Provision for bilingual youngsters yet to develop English as an additional language was mapped onto this deeply divisive structure, and with inherent race prejudice mapped onto the legacy of class prejudice. Almost automatically those who could not speak English were ranked at the bottom of the pile, their cultural backgrounds and linguistic abilities not only ignored but regarded as a hindrance to both their progress in English and to their achievement in school.

Given the then existing standard language teaching practices (structural-grammatical; behaviouristic methodology) and the so limited experience of the British people of *natural* second or foreign language learning, inevitably, provision for the newcomers was made on the basis of the simplistic assumptions that pupils would need to know English *before* they could or *should* participate in 'normal' classes. The narrowly defined, 'correct', *linguistic* aspects of the curriculum were seen as both separate from and *prior* to *educational* aspects. Thus did 'Special English' lessons fit into an already existing educational culture of streaming and withdrawal. Notwithstanding the commitment, caring and concern of so many of these 'special English' teachers towards their pupils, the overall system was clearly a disadvantaging one.

Indeed, no better design could have been conceived for denying bilingual learners in English schools the conditions of success. They were deprived by the established structures and practices of schooling of curricular access to precisely those areas of experience and linguistic interaction for which they were so earnestly, but nevertheless inadequately, being prepared in their 'Special English' classes. On top of this, they were separated from use of their mother-tongues by virtue of ethnocentrism, by power-play (how would teachers and other pupils know what their pupils were doing or saying if they did not speak English in class?) and by shiboleths about language learning (mother tongues seen as interfering with learning a new language). Basically, *all* school children were being told that the English language in its standard forms, and English people – particularly those with 'received' accents – were superior to other languages and people.

Antipathetic to the interests of all working-class children and to bilingual learners in particular, these were policies for *mis*-education. Practice and policy acted to structure underachievement; to construct and/or confirm racist attitudes among the school population; and to maintain narrow attitudes to language education in the whole of society. Linguistic imperialism was encouraged; bi- and multi-lingualism discouraged. And in using primarily the methods of teaching English as a *foreign*, rather than as a second language, the isolation of 'Special English' from subject teaching and curriculum learning was preserved and strengthened.

This combination of the establishment of a category of 'Special English' teachers teaching separately from the mainstream curriculum and using the traditions of *foreign* language teaching conspired to delay the development of strategies, techniques and pedagogies designed to meet the mainstream and real language needs of bilingual learners. Separation also seriously delayed the establishment of fruitful links between those 'Special English' teachers who *were* trying to develop more appropriate language teaching strategies and mainstream teachers who were developing mixed ability language across the curriculum padagogies.

This delay has been especially galling when one considers what the two movements hold in common for creating improved teaching methods for *all* children and, therefore, equality of outcome for the working-class majority, black, white, girls and bilingual learners. Both movements have constructed pedagogies stemming from recognition of the generative power of the relationships between language, experience and learning. Both movements seek to positively incorporate, rather than counter-productively deny, the truly intellectually rigorous *social* contexts of learning, the *necessity* of such a context for developing knowledge in depth, skills and understanding. Both movements recognize how disabling it is for learners if the learning environment separates them from what they already know and can already do.

Nevertheless, despite the very considerable structural divisions between these two sets of teachers, partnerships have been instituted amongst teachers who are morally, politically and intellectually committed to rigorous equal opportunities education. Sadly, they still have to work against ignorance of the cognitive links between first and second language development and between these and learning development.

Despite the enormous growth of knowledge about language (about its interactive as well as grammatical structures, about the essential social base of language acquisition and development, about the relationships between thought, language and learning, about its use as a means of individual empowerment, and its function as a tool of control and oppression), it is not this newer, more relevant pedagogic and linguistic knowledge which has *fundamentally* influenced any of the reformist policy proposals contained in the National Curriculum, although ghostly traces of it can be seen there.

No better examples of the maintenance of a narrow view of language, and of the 'ghostliness' of new knowledge within the reforms can be found than in the language model offered by the Committee of Enquiry into the Teaching of the English Language (DES 1988) and in the consequent proposals for English in the National Curriculum for ages 5 to 16 (DES 1989).

Despite the National Curriculum proposing committee's pragmatically finer intentions, basically the National Curriculum for English sings an all too familiar refrain. Dangers lurk within the National Curriculum for all pupils membershipped to multilingual classes. For example, despite the careful statement in the *National Curriculum Proposals* (DES 1989: 4.14) that *all* languages and dialects are rule governed, that their rules differ, and that it is not the case that Standard English possesses rules and the others do not, the effect of the repeated exhortation to teach Standard English is to affirm the historic position of the English establishment that English is superior to other languages and Standard English to other varieties of English. *The National Curriculum Proposals* are also inherently undermining of their own purported support both for a broad approach to languages and for teaching which acknowledges and supports 'a firmly based but flexible and developing linguistic and cultural identity' (DES 1989: 2.12). In section 10.10 the implication is that pupils' mother tongues will function only as a bridge to their competence in English, and, although in section 3.11 we are invited to view bilingual pupils as an 'enormous resource', this turns out to be significant only insofar as their knowledge of languages can inform *other pupils'* knowledge about *English* (DES 1989: 10.12).

Clearly, the past is ever with us, and never more so than in the proposals for assessment in the National Curriculum. No obeisance to the notion of cultural diversity can overcome the downright inequity inherent in such forms of assessment. The fact that the Speaking and Listening Attainment Targets (where bilingual pupils in the process of acquiring English were more likely to have been able to be assessed as achieving more of the aspects of achievement than for the Reading and Writing Attainment Targets) were omitted from the first National Attainment Tests is one more example of structured inequity.

On the other hand, the fact that Speaking and Listening is a focus for attainment along with Reading and Writing in the National Curriculum should mean an increase in teachers' understanding of the importance of *talking to learn*. This has the potential for contributing to the communicative and interactive base essential to naturalizing learning for everyone. However, as the London Association for the Teaching of English notes in its *Responses to English from Ages 11–16* (1989), 'the nuances are wrong'. Whatever good, interactive pedagogy teachers manage to preserve, or even the requirements of the National Curriculum happen to promote, assessment of pupils within a rigid level of attainment – based on assumptions of learning and language development being an organized series of linear progressions – disallows wider acknowledgement of pupils' actual potential. Bilingual pupils inexperienced in using English will be confirmed as low language and learning achievers, and other working–class pupils, their culture and language also highly constrained, will also be so confirmed, with consequent further low expectations virtually assured. Slotting pupils into 'levels' is but a few steps away from the wholesale reconstitution of streaming and to an over-use of 'Special English' withdrawal teaching and of 'Remedial' classes – all of which are intellectually and educationally crude and politically simplistic ways of making provision for pupils' 'differentiated learning needs'.

If fears about the effects of the statutory requirements of the National Curriculum on bilingual pupils in the process of learning English needed confirming, confirmation is found in the timing and the content of the National Curriculum Council's leaflet *Circular Number 11: The Needs of Bilingual Pupils* (NCC 1991). This was published just prior to the onset of the first application of assessment at Key Stage 1, as the anticipated dangers were becoming ever more clearly defined. It urges schools to consider both 'how to ensure full access to the National Curriculum and Assessments for all pupils' and also to value languages other than English spoken by pupils and used in the classroom' (NCC 1991). It emphasizes:

1 that 'language teaching is the professional responsibility of all teachers';
2 that 'the National Curriculum is for all pupils except the few for whom modification and disapplication is appropriate';
3 that 'like all pupils, bilingual pupils should have access to stimulating curriculum which, at the same time, helps their language development';
4 that 'bilingual children are able to understand and develop concepts even when their ability to express them in English is limited [in support of which they quote evidence given to the National Curriculum English Working Group] 'where bilingual children need extra help, this should be given as part of normal lessons' adding that 'withdrawal of bilingual pupils for separate teaching . . . can lead to a narrow, unbalanced curriculum and [to] isolation from pupils with greater experience of English' (NCC 1991).

All of this, the circular stresses, means beginning with present good practice (developed, I remind you, in multilingual classrooms). Some helpful suggestions follow. For example,

> work can be carried out in different language and peer groups to encourage the use of preferred languages, or in multilingual groups to help pupils benefit from the experience of other languages. This would enable the teacher to observe and identify where language support is needed.
>
> (NCC 1991)

I do not draw attention to this leaflet in order to question whether or not these pragmatic hints about good practice are necessary; of course, they are. The question is, rather, whether such hints on their own are sufficient to amount to a *good enough* practice; and, of course, they are not. What is needed is an in-depth practice, one that goes well beyond the hints of the NCC leaflet.

Such in-depth good practice exists. What is needed now is for it to be more widely recognized, more widely practised and further developed.

DEVELOPMENTAL PEDAGOGY: ALTERNATIVE STRATEGY FOR MULTILINGUAL CLASSROOMS

Multilingual classrooms, although not alone in acting as prompts to pedagogic development, have obviously been *the* significant site for the development of an equal opportunities education. Such classrooms were perceived by many teachers as threatening, but for others the existence of such dynamic classrooms provided the creative disruption to the educational status quo which allowed them to take the practical and theoretical steps necessary for establishing egalitarian frames of reference in the support of learning.

These theoretical and practical frames of reference hold that the goal of educational development and achievement is most effectively attained through social and intellectual processes conceived as partnerships between the participants. Such a partnership orientation is one in which successive stages of development are seen as the outcomes of the processes of experimental methodology which, in turn, are open to reflection, analysis and further development by its practitioners. A strong element of teachers' action research is thus an integral component of successful teaching and learning within this practice.

Educational partnerships are conceived as dynamic and dialectical learning relationships. Their aim is the promotion and development of skills, supportiveness, intellectual rigour, meaning and mutuality. Pupils' language and learning repertoires grow by means both of their participation in meaningful interaction with other people, with resources and texts, and by direct instruction.

Organizationally, classroom partnerships tend to fall into three, interrelated categories.

1 *Pupils working and learning in pairs and/or small groups* (often called 'collaborative learning').
2 *Teachers* working with pupils as a whole class group, or with individuals, pairs or small groups in an instructional and/or facilitating role.
3 *Teachers planning and working together to support pupils' learning,*

sometimes planning materials and strategies together prior to lessons, sometimes teaching together (often called 'support teaching', 'co-operative teaching' and most recently 'partnership teaching').

Such partnerships, when taken in conjunction with curriculum content, materials and assignments which attend to the socio-cultural aspects of the development, acquisition and application of knowledge, have the potential for advantaging learning in several crucial ways.

1 Partnerships between pupils and between pupils and teachers, being naturally various, but also appropriately structured, provide many subtly differing language-saturated and, therefore, rich language learning environments.

2 They enable responsibility for the curriculum enterprise to be shared, as appropriate, between the various participants – pupils and teachers alike.

3 Participants' own histories, skills, knowledge, forms of thinking and language enter the classroom, and through that validation, learners' confidence may be founded, maintained and developed.

4 Learning proceeds dialectically. That is, participants' already internalized skills and knowledge, together with those more conscious analytic processes motivated by new experience and challenge, form both the shared learning ground and contribute to each individual's change and growth.

5 Being active settings for gaining knowledge and developing skills, partnerships provide an educational environment akin to the socially interactive context in which participants have experienced their 'natural' learning. Concepts, skills, knowledge, linguistic repertoire, analytic competence, the confidence to be oppositional as well as to build consensus, may all develop in relation to the quality of the social process.

6 Partnerships provide pupils and teachers with a greater variety of roles. In consequence, they are better positioned to understand 'where each is coming from', and to know the steps which will enable each to achieve learning goals. The 'us and them' battle lines of the traditional classroom are diminished and can be replaced by an inclusive social-learning grouping of 'we', which at the same time supports differences of need and of identity.

7 Within the concept of partnership, pupils' school learning *and* the art of teaching may be seen as productively and creatively linked, both subject to the same 'rules' of development in relation to progress and achievement.
8 Both learning and language internalization is facilitated by participation.

DEVELOPMENTAL PEDAGOGY: STARTING POINTS AND DEVELOPMENTAL STEPS

Clearly, such a developmental pedagogy has a Vygotskian ring to it, and yet I have written nothing yet in reference to his thinking about the social origin and nature of learning. Nor yet have I sought to comment on his positioning in *Thought and Language* (1962/1988) of foreign language learning. This is because I have needed to set the context of multilingual classrooms as rich sites for learning and for learning English as an additional language. It is also because without this contextualizing it would be difficult for those who do not have direct experience of partnershipped developmental pedagogy at work to visualize the complex interrelations of factors in such classrooms. For example:

1 the role of *language* in learning,
2 the role of *learning* in language development,
3 the role of *interaction* in the internalization of knowledge and skills – including linguistic skills,
4 the relationship of *learning* to first and second language development,
5 the relationship of first and second language development to *each other*.

But, principally, I have not yet related developmental pedagogy to Vygotsky's theory of learning and development because it is essential to acknowledge the pre-eminent role of teachers in establishing the practice of this interactive pedagogy and also to recognize that pedagogic developments do not arise only out of consciously held theory, in fact, sometimes not at all. The fact is that teachers develop theories as much as theories develop them. Teachers initiate practice on the basis of their own analyses of experience – often against the theories of learning and development with which they came in contact in their training. When they then find an account of learning development which matches closely and *explains* the precepts by which they were already working and which they were working towards, they enter into a dialectic relationship with these theories of learning.

Developmental pedagogy, itself in dialectical relationship to Vygotsky's theories of socially based interactive learning, has come about through a conjunction of significant movements and activities, each of which had separate starting points:

1 teaching and learning activities directed at combating race, class and gender prejudice in educational organization and curricula;
2 that branch of activity within the field of teaching English as a second language in multicultural schools which took its inspiration from generative theories about language (e.g. Chomsky 1965), ideas about linguistic and communicative competence (e.g. Chomsky 1965; Hymes 1971), and the relationship of function and form in language (e.g. Halliday 1969, 1970, 1971), in order to develop practices for the *communicative* teaching of English as a second language;
3 the development of mixed ability teaching.

What teachers of English in the comprehensive school/mixed ability teaching movement found particularly productive in Vygotsky's ideas about linguistic and cognitive development and their relationship to each other were:

1 *the setting of intellectual development in* social *activity* ('In our conception, the true direction of the development of thinking is not from the individual to the socialised, but from the social to the individual' (Vygotsky 1962/1988: 20). 'The child's intellectual growth is contingent on his mastering the social means of thought, that is, language' (1962/1988: 51). 'What the child can do in co-operation today he can do alone tomorrow' (1962/1988: 41).
2 *the centrality given to* meaning and communication *as motivators for learning, thus positioning talk as the most widely accessible starting point for learning* ('The primary function of speech is communication, social intercourse; and 'the development of understanding and communication in childhood . . . has led to the conclusion that *real communication* requires meaning' (1962/1988: 6, my italics)).
3 *the relationship made between* teaching and learning development ('. . . the only good kind of instruction is that which marches

ahead of development and leads it; it must not be aimed so much at the ripe as at the ripening functions'. 'Our investigation demonstrated the social and cultural nature of development of the higher functions during (schooling), i.e. its dependence on co-operation with adults and on instruction' (1962/1988: 104, 105). This is crystallized in Vygotsky's concept of the 'zone of proximal development'. ('. . . the distance between the actual development level as determined by independent problem-solving and the level of potential development as determined through problem-solving under adult guidance or in collaboration with more capable peers' (Vygotsky 1978: 86)).

4 *the highlighting of* conscious reflection *as a generator of development.*

Later, as the practice of developmental pedagogy began to grow, the importance to it of Vygotsky's own methodological approach to the analysis of the relationship between thought and language (analysis of whole units as opposed to analysis of the separate elements of wholes) provided a model for a holistic approach to teaching and learning. ('Unit analysis . . . demonstrates the existence of a dynamic system of meaning in which the affective and the intellectual unite' (Vygotsky 1962/1988: 81).

However, the theory being developed in the early 'Vygotskian' classroom was a theory of development for and in *English as Mother Tongue.* At that point, bilingual learners and additional language learning were not seen as coming within its scope. Of course, bilingual pupils were registered students in these classrooms, but they were metaphorically as well as literally as much out of them as in them, withdrawn from the 'normal' mainstream class to 'Special English.'

At the same time, there were teachers in the 'Special English' service seeking mainstream education for bilingual pupils. They realized that if their charges were ever to learn English well enough to take their rightful places as learners within normal classrooms, they needed not discrete and often 'behaviouristic' language teaching but food for their minds. Later, they also came to realize that the curriculum and bilingualism were, in fact, not divisible.

These teachers began to develop techniques for teaching English which combined curriculum learning and additional language teaching techniques in a linguistically interactive approach to learning influenced by Vygotsky, but by

1 communicative-functional theories of language learning (thinking based on the development of linguistic and communicative competence and on a *functional* approach to understanding language in use, e.g. Chomsky, Hymes, Halliday);
2 ideas about learners' interlanguage in their progress towards facility in a target language (L2, L3, . . .) i.e. that any linguistic state manifested can be analysed as representing an ordered set of 'rules' whereby performance is generated (e.g. Selinker 1972);
3 the concept of Error Analysis (in which learners' errors are viewed as part of the adaptive process towards the target language (Corder 1967, 1971; Richards 1974).

Using this communicative approach to additional language learning, teachers began to note that the stages of development through which pupils passed – including the 'errors' they made – frequently paralleled those of early language development. Supported by the linguistic ideas itemized above, teachers began to follow their professional analytical instincts and to view learners' errors as developmental, rather than failed learning.

It seemed profitable to consider what might be gained from looking at how communicative competence is attained in one's first language and to relate this to promoting competence in a second language. I chose at the time to put it this way (Levine 1972).

> When we learn to use our first language, we do so through exposure to performance of it and in response to the demands and requirements of a variety of situations, roles, relationships and mores in which and according to which we live our lives. In so far as communicative competence equates with having learned language behaviour which is both appropriate and effective for the context of our lives, we all probably learn what we are able to do – no matter how different that is in kind or extent – in much the same way. That is to say, we are, and have been, open to external stimulae and motivation to learn the code and its appropriate use, while at the same time, having the opportunity to exercise an innate drive to learn on the code and on the situations and contexts in which

particular parts of it are used. Among the elements available external to ourselves are:

    (a) situations which 'direct' us towards certain kinds of language behaviour,

    (b) recurring opportunities within situations to hear, imitate, and practise,

    (c) informants who, by their reactions 'tell' us if we have transmitted our intentions,

    (d) informants and contexts which provide models for us,

    (e) informants who teach and correct us.

Among the 'magic' elements which we bring to the situation ourselves are:

    (f) the ability to store chunks of the data of performance for appropriate repetition,

    (g) our own drive to learn, play, practise, imitate,

    (h) the ability to discern underlying systems of rules,

    (i) the ability to organise and categorise the data of performance in such a way that we can (to paraphrase Chomsky (1965) both understand discourse which we have never heard before and also generate entirely novel utterances of our own without having been exposed to all and every utterance in all and every context in which the utterance might occur.

If these observations are applied to the communicative teaching of an additional language, it must surely suggest a more active role for learners in the learning-teaching process, and a more interactive one, allowing development from the data of the environment.

The history of mixed ability teaching in comprehensive schools, and the history of English as a second language meant that interactive teaching and learning practices for English mother tongue pupils in mixed ability mainstream classes *and* the communicative practices for learning English as a second language came to be developed in parallel, but separately from each other. The two movements began to become more integrated within the policy of supporting the learning of English as an additional language within the mainstream (see Bourne 1989; Levine 1990).

As we work to refine the practices of an interactive, socially based, developmental learning theory, it becomes increasingly obvious that such a practice is Vygotskian in character. Instruction aimed at conscious grasp of concepts, knowledge, skills and understanding is in dynamic relationship with, and not in opposition to, natural social and intellectual development. It offers teachers a naturalistic methodology which can put achievement within the reach of many *more* working-class pupils. In this sense, the Vygotskian orientation within pedagogy is not only social, it is socialist.

VYGOTSKY AND THE LEARNING OF ADDITIONAL LANGUAGES

Clearly, I do not consider it useful to think of bilingual pupils in multilingual classrooms as learning or being taught English as if it were a *foreign* language. It is not simply that the foreign languages curriculum has historically been characterized by:

1 subject matter and settings extrinsic to the actual social context of additional language learners;
2 syllabuses based on grammatical 'progressions', arbitrarily chosen;
3 teaching practices based largely on linguistic constructions, rather than primarily on what motivates pupils to learn.

It is, rather and quite fundamentally, that foreign languages are regarded in English culture as 'other' – not being, or needing to be, embedded in the lives of the learners – quite literally 'foreign'.

Of course, people in the UK have learned to use additional languages under this foreign language teaching regime but, as a percentage of our population, these are comparatively very few. Fewer still would claim extensive and flexible use of the language(s) they were taught. In fact, most have been put off learning languages and think of it as a difficult thing to do. How contrary the educational system has been, then, towards the bilingual learners in our schools, for while it is always said that they have a right (more a duty) to become fluent, confident users of English, by and large they have been taught English in the discourse of this historical, 'foreign', (disembedded) practice.

But bilingual pupils are not learning English as a foreign language. They live within the boundaries of the additional language's permeating influence. They have personal access to it. It does not have to be 'given' to them by teachers as their *only* means of contact with it. Pupils have a pressing need to learn it for a wide range of social, educational, pragmatic and heuristic functions. It is the medium of instruction in schools and the dominant language in society. They are going to have to do much more with it than mere translation into it from their first languages. They are going to need to move into the 'deep' language acquisition that the knowing of any language as a genuine 'second' language implies, i.e. they need to go well beyond the stage of translation characteristic of attempts to use a studied, but unfamiliar, foreign language.

Progress has, of course, been made, for example by the development of mainstreaming. But, whilst in theory, mainstreaming is now a widely accepted organizational strategy, in practice the tug of withdrawal for 'Special English' is still strong, and still quite widely used as the major organizational strategy in teaching bilingual learners. The tug is strongest of all where interactive developmental pedagogy in the mainstream is weakest. Problems also arise where false dichotomies are established, as for example, between mainstreaming and withdrawal, where mainstreaming is made to mean that there shall be *no* withdrawal teaching. Yet mainstreaming does not rule out *certain kinds* of withdrawal at certain points. There will still be occasions when teaching groups of bilingual learners together will be appropriate, just as it is appropriate upon occasion to work with other kinds of small groups. However, if the shift towards greater enactment of equal opportunities education is to be more than rhetoric, then what needs to be guarded against are withdrawal practices that overwhelm or marginalize mainstreaming. What is needed is an unequivocal acknowledgement of the learning and using of an additional language in educational social reality, and a commitment to going beyond a brief, early 'pastoral' support for incoming bilingual students to offering an in-depth and continuing developmental pedagogy for mainstream curriculum learning.

We also need to continue to identify the detailed processes of interaction, learning and teaching by which bilingual pupils may most effectively develop their use of English within the curriculum. The simple fact that learners are present in the linguistic context cannot itself ensure success – as the 'osmosis' school of 'thought' might suggest. We do not achieve deep learning of languages just because the range of features of the whole language exist in our environment. Neither the 'osmosis' nor the 'special' add on language teaching 'theory' of putting the second language learning as a *separate* subject on the timetable serves our pupils' true needs and purposes. (Indeed, even contemporary functional-communicative strategies for teaching modern foreign languages do not easily transform into successful second language learning strategies – except when language *and* learning and thinking are *dynamically interrelated.*)

We need to maintain and develop the focus of languages development being an *integral* part of education, achieved *through* it rather than prior to or disembedded from it. And for bilingual learners, the development of additional language learning practices needs to be based upon the fact that we have a situation more akin to the *contextualized and naturalized* ways in which *first* languages are developed.

But what does Vygotsky have to say about this?

In *Thought and Language* (1962/1988) he refers only to learning foreign languages under taught, disembedded conditions. The case he makes for formal learning of foreign languages bears inspection, lest it is employed uncritically to support old-fashioned non-communicative language teaching practice.

In the chapter 'The development of scientific concepts in childhood' in *Thought and Language*, Vygotsky assumes the virtues of learning foreign languages in a disembedded way. Even while he quotes Tolstoy on the uselessness of teachers attempting to transfer concepts directly to their pupils through explanation, he appears to find this method acceptable when employed in foreign language teaching. '[Tolstoy] found that one could not teach children literary language by artificial explanations, compulsive memorising, and repetition *as one does a foreign language*' (Vygotsky 1962/1988: 83, my italics).

In the same chapter, it is possible to interpret another reference to foreign languages as further, serious support for disembedded *learning* of foreign languages. 'The influence of scientific concepts on the mental development of the child is analogous to the effect of learning a foreign language, *a process which is conscious and deliberate from the start*' (Vygotsky 1962/1988: 109, my italics).

He then goes on to describe how in foreign language learning, as is indeed the case, one is aware of phonetic, grammatical and syntactic forms before one develops spontaneous, fluent speech. But Vygotsky then takes for granted that it is through study alone that we attain this fluency.

The child's strong points in a foreign language are his weak points in his native language, and vice versa. In his own language, the child conjugates and declines correctly, but without realising it. He cannot tell the gender, the case, or the tense of a word he is using. In a foreign language he distinguishes between masculine and feminine gender and is conscious of grammatical forms from the beginning. Of phonetics the same is true. Faultlessly articulating his native language, the child is unconscious of the sounds he pronounces, and in learning to spell he has great difficulty in dividing a word into its constituent sounds. In a foreign language he does this easily and his writing does not lag behind his speech. It is the pronunciation, the spontaneous phonetics that he finds harder to master. Easy, spontaneous speech with a quick and sure command of grammatical structures comes to him only as the crowning achievement of *long, arduous study*.

(Vygotsky 1962/1988: 109, my italics)

This suggests a presupposition on Vygotsky's part of a *necessity* to *teach* a foreign language via 'academic' methods, and that it is *because* of these means that access is also gained to those cognitive benefits which are such highly prized outcomes of knowing more than one language, benefits that ensue for learners both in relation to knowledge *of* languages and *about* language.

. . . a foreign language facilitates mastering the higher forms of the native language, [and] the child learns to see his native language as one particular system among many, to view its phenomena under more general categories, and this leads to awareness of his linguistic operations.

(Vygotsky 1962/1988: 110)

These statements would not only seem to make 'success in learning a foreign language . . . contingent on a certain degree of maturity in the native language', but also assume in the learner 'transfer to the new language [of] the system of meanings he already possesses in his own' (Vygotsky 1962/1988: 110).

When taken together, a possible reading of these passages for languages *teaching* is that

1 foreign languages *need* – for the sake of cognitive development – to be taught in a disembedded manner;
2 that the teaching of a foreign language *should* be more con-

cerned with the new language's external manifestations than with semantic aspects – since meaning systems have already been constructed by learners in the acquisition of their first languages;

3 and, remaining with this same point, that children might not be able to learn a foreign language well unless they have what is considered to be a degree of maturity in their first language.

As readers will recognize, such strands of thought are familiar ones within the theories and practices of foreign language teaching. How curiously at variance they are with the deeper meanings that imbue the developmental pedagogy I have outlined in an earlier section, the pedagogy which teachers have constructed (consciously and unconsciously) and which owes so much to Vygotsky's central theory about the relationship between speech and thought and the *social* roots of their development.

It is worth, therefore taking a second look, this time at the positioning of Vygotsky's observations about foreign language learning. After all, in the chapter in which these passages appear, Vygotsky was using the Tolstoy passages to begin to develop his case for a *dialectic* approach to concept development – a dialectic between affect and the inner workings of the mind on the one hand, and learning and instruction on the other. In it, he is working against Tolstoy's apparent determination (on account of his observations about attempting to teach his pupils literary language) to abandon direct teaching. 'What the child needs [wrote Tolstoy] . . . is a chance to acquire new concepts and words from the general linguistic context' (Vygotsky 1962/1988: 83).

In the 1988 edition of *Thought and Language* the Vygotskian text expands on this.

> It is true that concepts and word meanings evolve, and that this is a complex and delicate process. But Tolstoy is wrong when he suggests abandoning any attempt to direct the acquisition of concepts and calls for natural unhindered development. *Suggesting this, he divorces the process of development from that of learning and instruction . . .*
>
> (Vygotsky 1962/1988: 131, my italics)

Now we can see the apparent opposition of first and foreign languages which Vygotsky seems to establish. It is there in that revealing aside in the Tolstoy section and later in the description of the processes of foreign language learning as a school subject. But the opposition is not substantial. It is there by way of demonstrating the genuine need for teaching and learning to be treated as a unitary thing, to be seen as containing developmental pathways that move both in an inward direction *and* outwards; complementary to each other – not in opposition and with development and instruction going hand in hand. 'All our evidence supports the hypothesis that analogous systems develop in reverse directions at the higher and the lower levels, *each system influencing the other and benefitting from the strong points of the other*' (Vygotsky 1962/1988: 110, my italics).

It is this dialectic that is the true legacy of Vygotsky's thinking, along with his methodological analysis and his reconstruction of the integrative relationship between development and instruction. That Vygotsky, in using schooled foreign language learning as an example of conscious learning, left the teaching methodology uninspected is not surprising given the history of pedagogy at that point. But this should not be our position. In multilingual classrooms where pupils are also learning English as an additional language, uninspected pedagogies are dangerous to learning – as are the uninspected pedagogies employed in foreign language classroom teaching. In both contexts, a generative interrelationship between need, experience and instruction needs to be established from the start. The additional language learning, foreign or otherwise, should not be being viewed primarily as based in conscious, academic learning which, when set alongside the so-called unconscious acquisition of first languages is, by inference, open to interpretation as being in opposition to it. Moreover, it is not the case that gaining skill in an additional language is absolutely dependent on prior skill in the first, that concept development is attainable virtually exclusively through one's first language.

We can speculate that had Vygotsky had the benefit of the hindsight granted us by virtue of our working with and building on his interactive, socially based theory of intellectual and skills development, and his illuminating concept of the zone of proximal development, he may well have made problematic, as we do, the disembedded teaching tactics which he seems to take for granted as necessary to higher concept development.

The fact is that the cognitive benefits Vygotsky so rightly

claims for knowing more than one language are not lost when they are communicatively learned; learners remain conscious that they are learning to use a language and they are able to reflect upon that learning. The surface features of the target language (grammar, pronunciation, etc.) are still evident to learners. Communicative language development is not seen as excluding knowledge about language or grammar learning, rather as containing these strategies. Transfer of meaning from first language into second still obtains as a genuine strategy for learners, alongside other strategies. Crucially, the dialectic pathways of development are not lost in developmental pedagogy. Rather, they are enhanced.

Consequently, if multilingual classrooms are to fulfil their enriched potential for the learning of English as an additional language for bilingual pupils, it is essential that teaching practices are framed within Vygotsky's *general* theory of the social basis of learning, and not based upon extracted comments of his that seem to support disembedded, separate development – approaches long associated with classroom foreign language learning, and other unholistic approaches to education.

NOTE

The section in this chapter, 'Race and class prejudice and the educational offer in multilingual classrooms' is based on Levine (1990) 'Bilingual learners in English schools', in *Newsletter* No. 37, Autumn 1990, The British Association of Applied Linguistics.

REFERENCES

Bourne, J. (1989) *Moving into the Mainstream: LEA Provision for Bilingual Pupils*, Windsor, NFER-Nelson.

Chomsky, N. (1965) *Aspects of the Theory of Syntax*, Cambridge, MA, Massachusets Institute of Technology.

Corder, S. P. (1967) 'The significance of learners' errors', *International Review of Applied Linguistics* 5 (5).

Corder, S. P. (1971) 'Idiosyncratic dialects and error analysis', *International Review of Applied Linguistics* 9 (2).

DES (Department of Education and Science) (1988) *Report of the Committee of Enquiry into the Teaching of the English Language* (The Kingman Report), London, HMSO.

DES (Department of Education and Science) (1989) *National Curriculum Proposals for English for Ages 5 to 16* (The Cox Report, Part 2), London, HMSO.

Halliday, M. A. K. (1969) 'Relevant models of language', *Educational Review* 22 (1), University of Birmingham.

Halliday, M. A. K. (1970) 'Language structure and language function', in J. Lyons (ed.) *New Horizons in Linguistics*, Harmondsworth, Penguin.

Halliday, M. A. K. (1971) 'Language in a social perspective', *Educational Review* 23 (3), University of Birmingham.

Hymes, D. (1971) 'On communicative competence', in J. B. Pride and J. Holmes (eds) *Sociolinguistics*, Harmondsworth, Penguin.

Levine, J. (1972) 'Creating environments for developing communicative competence: an approach to making foreign language-learning materials', unpublished dissertation for MA in Linguistics for English Language Teaching, University of Lancaster.

Levine, J. (ed.) (1990) *Bilingual Learners and the Mainstream Curriculum*, London, Falmer.

London Association for the Teaching of English (1989) *Responses to English from Ages 11–16*, London, London Association for the Teaching of English.

NCC (National Curriculum Council) (1991) *Circular Number 11: The Needs of Bilingual Pupils*, London, National Curriculum Council.

Richards, J. (ed.) (1974) *Error Analysis: Perspectives on Second Language Acquisition*, London, Longman.

Selinker, L. (1972) 'Interlanguage', *International Review of Applied Linguistics* 10 (3).

Vygotsky, L. S. (1962/1988) *Thought and Language*, 2nd edn, Cambridge MA, Massachusetts Institute of Technology.

Vygotsky, L. S. (1978) *Mind in Society*, Cambridge, MA, Harvard University Press.

Index

ability testing 148–9
achievement and potential 153, 160–1
action 48, 51–2, 54–5, 70–1, 104, 157
action research by teachers 38, 40, 201
active learning 10
activity 48, 50–1, 54, 99, 103, 104
activity theory xiii, 48–9, 51, 96
age periods 99
agency 70–1
alienation and discourse 82
alterity 73
alternative meanings 9
analytic units *see* objects of study
Anglo-American *see* Western
anti-racist analysis of readings 10
Apple, M. 172–3
artifacts of cultural practices 111, 112, 120
assessment xiv, 35, 60, 145–67, 199, 200
Atkinson, P. 53, 57–8

backgrounds of children 37, 56, 72, 82, 89, 150, 163, 166, 172–3, 190, 193–7
Bakhtin, M. M. 54–5, 69, 73–7, 78, 80, 87, 96, 97
Bearison, D. J. 118, 119
behaviour modification in teaching 42
behaviour, social 46–65

behaviourist approaches to learning 5
Bekhterev, N. 48
Bennett, N. 176–7, 186
Bernstein, B. 40, 47, 57–62, 63, 95, 97
bilingual learners 190–214
body and mind 20
boundaries 54, 61
Bozhovich, L. I. 49
Bransford, J. D. 150–1, 152, 162
Britton, J. N. 2, 5
Brown, A. L. 89, 151, 153, 162, 163
Bruner, J. xii, 12–14, 51, 52, 54, 146, 147, 157, 172
Budoff, M. 151, 161, 162, 163
Bullock Report 2, 5
Burgess, T. 1–29

Campione, J. C. 151, 153, 154, 162, 163
Cassirer, E. 5
categories *see* classification
child-centred approaches 171, 175
Chomsky, N. 204, 206, 207
class *see* socioeconomic
classification 24–5, 26, 56, 60–2, 63
classroom interactions 80–90, 124–5, 130–6, 176–7, 201–3
Cobb, P. 113, 122, 124–6, 130, 137
codes 61, 78
cognitive development *see* development

cognitive form–function shifts 126–7, 134–5
Cole, M. 17, 21, 113, 122–3, 125–6, 137
collaboration: and development 102; and learning 2, 122, 156–7, 159–60, 201; in problem solving 107, 113, 118–21, 175–6
communication: competence of 63–4, 206–7; and interaction 51–2, 59; and learning 204; of meaning 78–80, 204; and signs 40, 54–5, 103; and teaching 42; and words 46, 62, 63
compensatory pedagogy 31–2
conflict 6, 120, 121, 129
consciousness 13, 15, 20–1, 48, 69, 71, 72, 96, 98–9, 103, 104
contextual approaches to sociocultural factors 50–1, 52
contextual constraints on learning 58
contingency of scientific theory 8–9
control 6, 59, 61–2; of learning 179, 185–6
cooperative learning 107, 113, 114–18, 129
coping strategies 178–9, 184–5, 186
cultural bias of tests 148
cultural materialism 5
cultural practices, structure of 111–12, 120
culture: and learning 107, 126–7; politics of 4, 6–7, 10; social construction of 4, 174; transmission of 46, 57–9; see also sociocultural
Cummins, J. 150, 153
curriculum 60, 175, 202; children with learning difficulties 33–41; national 3, 175, 176, 193, 198–9, 200
curriculum-based assessment (CBA) 149, 151

Daniels, H. 40, 46–68
Davydov, V. V. xiii, xiv, xv, 18–21, 32–3, 39, 47, 49, 57, 62–3, 72, 93–106, 146
deaf people 42–3
determinism, social 57
development: and collaboration 102; and education 100–4; and language 191; and learning 102, 155–7; sociocultural influences 18, 20, 25, 46–65, 69–90, 99–100, 104, 108–9, 129–30, 146–7, 172, 204
developmental pedagogy 191, 201–8, 212
dialogicality 73–90, 96; see also discourse
disabled children 41–3
discourse: and alienation 82; inner 72; in schools 64–5, 82–90; and understanding 122; see also dialogicality
disease model of disability 31, 41
Doyle, W. 178
Durkheim, E. 56, 57
dynamic assessment 145, 152, 154–5, 160–7

educational transmission 61
El'konin, D. B. 104
emergent goals 110–40
Emerson, C. 75
English language teaching 2–28, 190–214
equal opportunities education 190–1, 194, 198, 201, 204
equilibration model, Piaget's 118–19
error analysis 206
ethnic minorities 150, 153, 163, 166, 172, 190, 193–201, 204
Evans, P. 30–45
experience 5
experimental psychology 97
explanation and objects of study 19, 47–8

feminist analysis of readings 10
Ferrara, R. A. 162, 163
Feuerstein, R. 151, 162, 164–6
focus of assessment 161

form–function shifts 126–7, 134–5
Foucault, M. 9
framing 61–2, 63
Frederickson, N. 150, 153
French influences on Vygotsky 56–7
functional dualism 77–80, 81–2

Gallimore, R. 82, 89, 151
Galton, M. 178–9
Gearhart, M. 107–40
generalization and learning 38
generic languages 74–90
genetic explanation of development 25, 50, 70–1, 88, 156
German influences on Vygotsky 56–7
goals, learning 38, 109–40
government education policy 174–5
Gramsci, A. 5–6, 7
Griffin, P. 122
groups 51–2, 73, 114–15, 137–8, 175–6, 178, 201

Hall, S. 5
handicapped children 30–43
Haste, H. 146, 147, 172, 173, 177, 180
hegemony 5–6, 10
histories, personal 10
Holquist, M. 73, 75
Holzmann-Hood, L. 51
Humboldt, von 7, 24
Hundeide, K. 56
hypothesis testing teaching 38

identity and learning 181–7
ideology and culture 6
imaginary models of objects 103
implementation of curriculum 35
incentives 114, 116, 117
individual consciousness 69, 72
individual in society xii–xiii, 46–65, 72
individual teaching 37, 38, 82, 201
individuals, children as 4, 171, 173

information transmission 78–80, 81–2, 86–7
initiation-reply-evaluation (I-R-E) 81–2, 88
inner speech/dialogue 3, 72
instruction: and learning 155–7, 160, 165, 167, 191, 204–5; and social context 62–3; and speech 62–3; see also teaching
instrumental acts 48
intelligence 164
interaction: and action 48, 51–2, 54–5; in assessment 161–2; in classroom 124–5, 130–6, 201–3; and communication 51–6, 59, 73–90; and goal formations 113; and internalization 191, 203; and learning 4, 59–60, 184–7, 191, 203; and problem solving 119; systems of 48
interanimation of voices 79–80, 86–90
internalization 38, 53, 55, 71, 99, 102–4, 107–8, 156, 191, 203
interpersonal processes 51–2, 58, 180
interpretation and reading 7–14
interpsychological/ intrapsychological processes 50, 69–90, 102–5, 108–9, 172–4, 178, 204
intersubjectivity 52
interviews in assessment 161–2
introspective psychology 20
IQ tests 31, 145, 147–8, 150–1, 163
Ireson, J. 33, 34, 37
isolating approaches to sociocultural factors 50–1
Ivanov, V. V. 17

Jakobson, R. 54
Jones, R. L. 150
Joravsky, D. 16–17, 23

Kantian thought 4–5
Kell, J. 177
knowledge xiv, 41–2, 118; prior 108, 111, 112–13, 116, 119, 121, 126, 128, 133, 135–6

Kozulin, A. xiii, 14, 21, 47, 48, 49, 55, 57, 159–60

Langer, S. K. 5
language 3, 96; and cognitive development 191; generic 74–90; and interaction 52–6; and internalization 102–3; and learning 199, 203, 204; learning and teaching of 2–28, 190–214; and mediation 70, 77, 156; and mind 3; and semiotics 26–7; social 74–7; and social dialogue 52–6; and thought 2, 4, 22, 23, 26–7, 139, 205
learning: active 10; behaviourist approaches to 5; collaborative 2, 122, 156–7, 159–60, 201; and communication 204; contextual constraints 58; control of 179, 185–6; cooperative 107, 113, 114–18, 129; and culture 107, 126–7; and development 102, 155–7; generalization 38; goals 38, 109–40; and identity 181–7; and instruction 155–7, 160, 165, 167, 191, 204–5; and interaction 4, 59–60, 184–7, 191, 203; internalization 38; and language 199, 203, 204; monitoring of 38, 149–50, 152–4; opportunities for 176; and potential 153, 155, 159, 160–1, 163, 164; in primary schools 171–87; processes of 154–5, 160, 179; risk-taking in 178–9; sociocultural influences 42, 101, 122–6, 172–4, 177–87; teams 114; time for 176; and words 62, 63
Leontiev, A. 48–9, 100, 104
Levine, J. 190–215
literature 8, 16–17
London Association for Teaching of English 199
Lotman, Yu. M. 69, 78–80
Lundt, I. 145–67
Luria, A. R. 14, 15, 70, 104

mainstream teaching of exceptional children 41–3, 209
Marr, N. Ya. 96
Marxism 5–7, 11–13, 15–19; of Vygotsky xiii, 7, 11, 15–18, 24, 57, 97–8
materialism xiii, 5
mathematical understanding 107–40
Mead, G. H. 40, 51, 56, 58
meaning: communication of 78–80, 204; and dialogue 77; generation of 78–80, 81–2, 86–90; and reading 7–14; and self 184; specialization of 63; and texts 78–80; and words 3, 24, 26, 46, 53, 62, 75–7
mediation xiii, 57, 70, 77, 157–9, 164–5; and action 70–1, 104, 157; and language 70, 77, 156; semiotic 6, 25–6, 156; and speech genres 80–90; through signs 62, 102–3
medical model of disability 31, 41
Mehan, H. 81
mentalist/introspective psychology 20
Mercer, J. R. 149
methodology of Vygotsky 7, 20–1, 23, 47–8, 49, 72, 77, 98, 205, 213
Miller, J. 10
mind 3, 5, 20, 25
Minick, N. J. 46, 47, 48, 50–1, 52, 56, 70, 151, 154–5, 157, 162–3, 165
models of objects, imaginary 103
moderate learning difficulties (MLD) 33–41
modes of control 59
modifiability 164
monitoring of learning 38, 149–50, 152–4
multi-voicedness 75, 86–90
multilingual learners 190–214

national curriculum 3, 175, 176, 193, 198–200

Nicolopoulou, A. 113, 122–3, 125–6, 137
norm-based assessment 145, 152, 163
Note, M. 107–40

objective-based curriculum 34–5, 39
objectives of teaching 38–40, 207–8
objects of study 19–21, 24, 47–8, 77, 139, 205
open discussion 87–8
opportunities to learn 176
organizational form 59, 63–5
otherness 73

Paduano, P. 107–40
parody 74
partnership teaching 202–3
pastoral care 37
patterns of significance xii
Pavlov, I. P. 11, 31, 48
pedagogy xiv, 31–2, 61, 64, 104, 191, 201–8, 212
peer interaction 107–40
physiology and psychology 95–6
Piaget, J. 22–3, 58–9, 70, 100–1, 107, 108, 118, 119, 129, 155, 171, 175, 187
Plowden Report 171, 175
politics: of culture 4, 6–7, 10; of psychology 11, 27
Pollard, A. 171–89
portfolio practice 136–8
potential for learning 153, 155, 159, 160–1, 163, 164
power 6, 61–2
primary schools 171–87
prior knowledge 108, 111, 112–13, 116, 119, 121, 126, 128, 133, 135–6
priority of sociality 69, 89–90
problem solving collaboration 107, 113, 118–21, 175–6
psychology: experimental 97; and literature 16–17; Marxist xiii, 7, 11, 15–18, 24, 57, 97–8; and physiology 95–6; in Soviet

Union 11–13, 15–21, 57, 69, 93–7, 146
psychometrics 145, 147–54, 164

qualitative/quantitative assessment 160, 162–3, 164, 165, 166
Quicke, J. 148

Radzikhovskii, L. A. 18–21, 47, 54, 72
reading 1–29
reality, social construction of 52–9, 100
Redmond, P. 33, 34
reflection 185, 191, 205
risk-taking in learning 178–9
Robertshaw, M. 34, 38
Rorty, R. 9
Rowland, S. 185
Rozanova, Professor 161, 165

Sapir, E. 7
Saxe, G. B. 107–40
schools 59–65, 82–90
scientific theory, contingency of 8–9
self 16–17, 71, 184
semiotic mediation 6, 25–6, 48–9, 51, 156
semiotics xiii, 26–7, 47, 65
sensation and thought 25, 26
Shatskii, S. T. 101
Shibutani, T. 56
Shotter, J. 41–2, 54
Shpet, G. G. 96
signs 18, 40, 54–5, 62, 70, 102–3
Skilbeck, M. 34
Skinner, B. F. 155
Slavin, R. E. 113, 114, 115
small groups 51–2, 73, 114–15, 137–8, 175–6, 178, 201
social, meaning of 51–2
social behaviour 46–65
social construction: of culture 4, 174; of reality 52–9, 100
social determinism 57
social dialogue and language 52–6
social interaction see interaction
social knowledge xiv

social language 74–7
social organization of schools 59–65
sociocultural influences: on development 18, 20, 25, 46–65, 69–90, 99–100, 104, 108–9, 129–30, 146–7, 172, 204; on learning and teaching 42, 62–3, 101, 122–6, 172–4, 177–87
socioeconomic background of pupils 72, 82, 89, 150, 163, 166, 172–3, 190, 193–7
sociolinguistics 3
sociology of schools 59–65
Solity, J. E. 148, 149, 150
Solka, A. L. B. 69–92
Soviet psychology xiii, 11–13, 15–21, 57, 69, 93–7, 146
special education 30–43
specialization of tasks 114, 116–17
speech 3, 53, 62–3
speech genres 74–90
Stam, R. 55
static forms of assessment 145, 147–54, 164
Stern, L. 22
Stipek, D. 136
streaming 195, 196, 199
structuralism 47, 58–9
structure: of cultural practices 111–12; of learning environment 37, 59–60, 62–3
Sutton, A. 146
Svertsev, A. N. 95
symbolic interactionism 47, 51–2, 56, 58, 174, 180, 184
symbols 4–5
systemic analysis of consciousness 98–9
systems of interaction 48

Tann, T. 52, 178, 185
targets of assessment 162
tasks: analysis 149, 176–7; specialization 114, 116–17
teachers: action research by 38, 40, 201; training and development 35–7
teaching: behaviour modification in 42; and communication 42; hypothesis testing 38; individual 37, 38, 82, 201; objectives 38–40, 207–8; partnerships 202–3; primary schools 175–8; sociocultural influences 42, 62–3, 101, 122–6, 172–4, 177–87; technical models of 177; whole class 201; see also instruction
teaching-learning process 37, 59
teaching materials: and children with MLD 33–41
team learning 114
testing see assessment
texts 1–29, 77–80, 81–2
Tharp, R. G. 82, 89
thought: and dialogue 78–80, 81–2, 86–90; and language 2, 4, 22, 23, 26–7, 139, 206; and sensation 25; and words 22, 24–5, 26
time for learning 176
tools: signs as 18, 22, 39, 103; speech as 53
Toulmin, S. 98
training and development of teachers 35–7
training-based assessment 163
transfer tasks 110, 128, 135–6, 162, 163
transmission: cultural 57–9; educational 61; of information 78–80, 81–2, 86–7; of knowledge xiv
Tulviste, P. 52, 71, 104
typology see classification

Ukhtomskii 95
understanding 73–4, 79, 122
units of analysis see objects of study
univocal functions of text 78–80, 81–2, 86–8
utterances 73–90

Vagner, V. A. 95
Valsiner, J. 52, 56–7
ventriloquation 75
voices 74, 77–90

Voloshinov, V. N. 54, 55, 69, 73, 74, 79, 87
Vygotsky, L. S.: life of 14–15, 93–6, 105; *Historical Meaning of the Crisis in Psychology* 15, 18, 19, 97; *Mind in Society* 15, 17, 18, 147, 155–6, 157–9; *Pedagogical Psychology* 14; *Psychology of Art* 14, 17; *Thinking and Speech* 47, 62, 156; *Thought and Language* 12, 15, 18, 21–8, 139, 203, 204–5, 210–13

Warnock Report 31
Webb, N. M. 115
Wertsch, J. V. 14, 15, 17, 21, 25–6, 42, 47, 50, 52, 53, 54, 56, 69–92, 110
Western psychology 15–19, 72, 98, 104–5
whole class teaching 201
whole school approach 34
Williams, R. 5, 10

withdrawal teaching 196–7, 199, 200, 205, 209
Wood, D. 156
Wood, T. 113, 122, 124
Woods, P. 178, 179
words 6–7, 23, 26, 96; and classification 24–5, 26; and communication 46, 62, 63; and counter words 74, 79; and learning 62, 63; and meaning 3, 24, 26, 46, 53, 62, 75–7; and thought 22, 24–5, 26

Yackel, E. 113, 122, 124
Yaroshevsky, M. xiii
Ysseldyke, J. 149

Zaporozhets, A. V. 104
Zinchenko, V. P. 32–3, 39, 62–3, 93–106, 146
zone of proximal development (ZPD) 13, 52, 102, 104, 110, 147, 156–67, 185, 205; children with learning difficulties 32–3, 37–8